THE MADWOMAN AND THE BLINDMAN

Jane Eyre, Discourse, Disability

EDITED BY

DAVID BOLT

JULIA MIELE RODAS

ELIZABETH J. DONALDSON

WITH A FOREWORD BY

LENNARD J. DAVIS

 THE OHIO STATE UNIVERSITY PRESS | COLUMBUS

Library of Congress Cataloging-in-Publication Data

The madwoman and the blindman : Jane Eyre, discourse, disability / Edited by David Bolt,
    Julia Miele Rodas, and Elizabeth J. Donaldson ; with a foreword by Lennard J. Davis.
    p. cm.
Includes bibliographical references and index.
ISBN 978-0-8142-1196-0 (cloth : alk. paper)—ISBN 978-0-8142-9297-6 (cd)
1. Brontë, Charlotte, 1816–1855. Jane Eyre—Criticism, Textual. 2. People with disabilities
    in literature. I. Bolt, David, 1966– II. Rodas, Julia Miele, 1965– III. Donaldson, Eliza-
    beth J., 1965–
PR4169.M23 2012
823'.8—dc23
                                    2012027263

Cover design by James A. Baumann
Text design by Juliet Williams
Type set in Adobe Sabon and ITC Galliard
Printed by Sheridan Books, Inc.

9   8   7   6   5   4   3   2   1

Contents

vi

Illustrations

SEEING THE OBJECT AS IN ITSELF IT REALLY IS

Beyond the Metaphor of Disability

LENNARD J. DAVIS

THIS BOOK marks a moment in disability studies that is unique, as far as I can tell. This is the first time a volume on disability examines only one work, in this case, *Jane Eyre*. Many other books and special issues have looked at a variety of artists, filmmakers, novelists, poets, and so on, often under a uniting theme. But the idea of choosing only one literary work as an object of focus from a disability perspective means something quite significant—it means we believe that disability studies has become so capacious, so much of a multidisciplinary and interdisciplinary discourse, that it does not have to multiply its objects to bring along enough variety to sustain a single volume. Indeed, this is a coming of age moment for the study of disability.

To the average reader, the role of disability does not seem particularly obvious in Brontë's novel. Yes, Rochester goes blind and is maimed, but that comes at the end of the novel. The bulk of the story is about a young woman's coming of age and her impassioned and frustrated love affair with her employer. Bertha is seen as a crazed monster, rarely as a woman with affective and cognitive disabilities. It would seem to most people that one could safely get through the issue of disability in *Jane Eyre* in a few short pages and then you would have done with it. As Dr. Johnson once famously remarked about a dog walking on its hind legs, "It is not done well; but you are surprised to find it done at all." So too scholars might not care about the quality of a disability analysis; rather they might be surprised that it was done at all.

So this experiment conducted by David Bolt, Julia Rodas, and Elizabeth Donaldson, with the aid of all the authors in this volume, to see if *Jane Eyre* can sustain this multiple set of readings comes as a surprise but not in the way others might have predicted. In fact, the surprise one registers after reading all the chapters comes from wondering how it has been possible to read *Jane Eyre* without a serious consideration of disability. As the authors point out, while the feminist, colonialist, Freudian, and other dominant readings are more than valid, the point is that they all are largely ignorant of the basic facts about disability. For the most part even the best of these readings simply metaphorize disability. Given the former absence of disability studies in the humanities, there was no real way to talk about disability as disability. We saw this same problem in the case of race in literature, when early analyses of Conrad's *Heart of Darkness,* for example, focused on "man's existential quest for meaning" or the "soul's attempt to find enlightenment"—all the while completely ignoring the issue of race. As Freud once said in regard to his ideas of the phallic symbol, "Sometimes a cigar is just a cigar." Likewise, sometimes disability is just disability.

What does it mean to metaphorize disability? The process of metaphorization is a substitutive one in which you say something is something else. A woman is a rose; a scythe is death. Whether you substitute entire objects for others or you use parts for the whole, the effect is to distract, to disengage from the initial object. When we say a woman is a rose, we are looking away from the woman toward the rose. We are saying that roses smell sweet, look beautiful, and are fecund. Then we turn back to the woman and say "You, too, are all those things."

The problem with metaphor and disability is that disability already involves looking away. As the normate regards the person with a physical disability, the normate both wants to stare and to look away—both actions have the same ends, which are to objectivize and stigmatize by an interrelated process of fascination and rejection (the latter in either or both the forms of disgust and dismissal). So disability has a special relationship to the process of metaphorization that other identities might share or might not. In any case, the idea that in *Jane Eyre* blindness is a metaphor for castration, for example, might work very well in a Freudian or a feminist analysis, but nevertheless such an approach fails to look directly at blindness, as does David Bolt's chapter, as a thing in itself, as an experience and an embodiment that does not have to steal its terms and borrow its existence through the process of metaphorization. Likewise, Bertha's madness is rarely addressed directly as it is in Chris Gabbard's chapter in this collection, and the implications of metaphorizing madness have not been clearly identified as they are in Elizabeth Donaldson's contribution. Instead of the more informed and nuanced readings in this volume, Bertha's madness is generally seen in the line of postcolonial and feminist readings that might include other works like *The Yellow Wallpaper* and *Wide Sargasso Sea*. The chapters in this volume show us that before we can leap to the metaphor, we need to know the object. Before we can interpret the semiotics of disability, we need to understand the subjectivity of being disabled.

I want to make clear that I am not denigrating these identity-based readings, but I think they need to succeed, not precede, disability studies readings. Theoretically those identity-based readings have put the cart before the horse, which means the horse has to do a lot more pushing and the way is not very clear. If we can have a firm understanding and foundation in seeing disabilities as they really are in themselves, as Matthew Arnold may have put it somewhat sightedly, then we might logically move to a more metaphorical and metacritical reading. But historically disability studies has been invisible in its nascence until fairly recently, so we cannot expect feminists or postcolonialists to have access to the increasingly larger and deeper pool of research in disability studies. The reason for this virtual ignoring of the disability studies archive is that disability is, as I have said elsewhere, the most discriminated category of oppression, at least from the point of view of academic recognition, if not in society in general.

I also do not want to imply that we can actually see disability as it is. Obviously we exist now in a postmodern era of analysis, and the idea that something simply *is* no longer works. What I am saying, however, is that we need to begin with disability in all its complexity as a socially constructed entity that exists, too, in an embodied form. Disability is not in fact an object but a way of knowing, a way of being known, and a modality for corporeality. We can put that consideration first before we then use it in a meta-analysis of race, class, gender, sexual orientation, and so on.

Perhaps the largest lesson of this volume is that the very best feminist or postcolonial criticism is only as good as its knowledge base. And, for example, the classic feminist works on *Jane Eyre* have had a pitifully small base on which to make large claims. As a result, the very best feminist works on *Jane Eyre* have had to take a common sense, which is to say ableist, perspective on disability. Thus, it seems logical, if you are not blind, to think of blindness as a form of castration. (If you are blind, you might laugh at this statement, even as you engage in completely uncastrated sex.) It is likewise logical, if you are not a single amputee, to see an amputated arm as an object of horror and of course—inevitably—as a symbol of castration. (If you are a person who is missing an arm, you might laugh at this assumption as you attach your prosthesis so you can be the best of cyborgian lovers.) I have made this point in a somewhat lighthearted manner, but the reality is that these statements only reveal how any reading of *Jane Eyre* that fell back on the received "wisdom" of an ableist culture would be sadly impoverished and diminished. Even ballpark assessments of, say, biblical references to disability can be quite wrong, as Essaka Joshua points out in her chapter in this work. Likewise, from-the-hip assessments of the role of illness can be equally incorrect, as Susannah Mintz helpfully notes. Received wisdom is, in the end, a congealed form of the same ideology that plunged people with disabilities into unemployment, discrimination, segregation, stigma, and even annihilation and death. I do not want to exaggerate or be overly histrionic, but just as statements about the laziness of blacks, the avarice of Jews, the insensitivity of Asians, or the blood-thirstiness of Arabs or Native Americans fall back on stereotypes and local wisdom, so too do classic works such as *The Mad Woman in the Attic* objectivize and stereotype people with disabilities.

One of our aims in reading a novel is to identify with and understand the characters in the work. Despite all our intellectualizing, a novel will never work if we do not make some kind of connection with the main character. How readers have over time come to understand Jane, Rochester, and Bertha tells us a lot about how much ideology and the ideological underpinnings of medical knowledge and psychological knowledge play a part in those acts of understanding and identification. As this volume shows us, the place of disability, illness, madness, and behavior will condition a response in the very-directly-addressed "Reader" of *Jane Eyre*. So even a conventional analysis of this novel will have to grapple with character types available to the culture at a given time. As Julia Rodas points out, the autistic-acting nature of the character of Jane would send different signals of embodiment and psychological existence to various groups of readers. And as Martha Stoddard Holmes indicates, these signals will reverberate through any filmic variation of the text. Margaret Rose Torrell too gives us an opportunity to understand in depth how embodiment will be part of this reception process. In short, the biocultural nature of being is surely vastly significant in any understanding of Brontë's text. Without that perspective, this text and what one can claim to understand about it is so much diminished.

We can say, with the publication of this book, that no one can claim to write knowledgably on *Jane Eyre* without taking into consideration the issue of disability. And if one does, then one may well be continuing the legacy of ableism that, Reader, we can now see has haunted this work from its inception.

Acknowledgments

A BOOK OF THIS SORT is as much the outgrowth of community as it is the product of individual effort. Without the larger discourses of disability studies, literary studies, and Victorian studies, such a book would simply have been unimaginable. In recognition of this fact, we, the editors, acknowledge an extraordinary debt to the communities that have nourished, supported, and inspired our contributions to this project: all our colleagues on the editorial board of the *Journal of Literary & Cultural Disability Studies;* the International Network of Literary & Cultural Disability Scholars (especially Tom Coogan and Irene Rose); the thoughtful and opinionated scholars who comprise the membership of the DS-Hum listserv (especially tireless moderator, Mike Gill); the organizers and attendees of the Victorian Seminar at the Graduate Center of the City University of New York (CUNY); Joseph Straus of the CUNY Graduate Center and William Ebenstein of CUNY's School of Professional Studies (SPS), who recently organized and hosted an open disability studies lecture series; three important groups promoting disability studies thinking at Columbia University (the members of the Future of Disability Studies working group at the Center for the Critical Analysis of Social Difference, the participants in the Seminar on Disability Studies associated with Teachers College, and the organizers of and presenters at the Narrative Medicine Rounds); Marisa Parham and John Drabinski of Amherst College and the SAWG writers; Stuart Murray and the Leeds Centre for Medical Humanities; and Dan Goodley and the Research Institute for Health and Social Change at Manchester Metropolitan University. The work of these and other such groups and the coming together of scholars—in both actual and virtual environments—to question, challenge, and support one another is vital to the scholarly innovation that we hope is represented by this volume.

Many thanks are due, of course, to Heather Cunningham, Ria Cheyne, and the rest of our colleagues in the Centre for Culture & Disability Studies at Liverpool Hope University (especially Claire Penketh, Laura Waite, and Alan Hodkinson), and in the English departments at New York Institute of Technology and CUNY's Bronx Community College.

More immediately, we are grateful for the intelligence, dedication, patience, and fine writing of Chris Gabbard, Essaka Joshua, Susannah Mintz, Martha Stoddard Holmes, and Margaret Rose Torrell, whose contributions, without question, provide the main strengths of this book.

To Lennard J. Davis, who contributed the foreword and has so energetically forwarded the ideas and values of disability studies, we are also greatly indebted.

In addition, thanks are due to the editors and publishers of *Textual Practice, NWSA Journal,* and *Nineteenth-Century Gender Studies* for permission to include revised versions of previously published articles—"The Blindman in the Classic: Feminisms, Ocularcentrism and Charlotte Brontë's *Jane Eyre*" (*Textual Practice* 22.2 [2008]); "The Corpus of the Madwoman: Toward a Feminist Disability Studies Theory of Embodiment and Mental Illness" (*NWSA Journal* 14.3 [2002]); and "'On the Spectrum': Rereading Contact and Affect in *Jane Eyre*" (*Nineteenth-Century Gender Studies* 4.2 [2008]).

We are grateful, as well, to the effort and generosity of the anonymous readers who read our typescript with such critical acumen and to all those involved at The Ohio State University Press, especially our editor and advocate, Sandy Crooms.

Finally, to our family and friends beyond the web of academic life, those who sometimes listened to and helped us argue through the details of our work, who sometimes left us to write and to edit in peace, and who sometimes hounded us out of our solitude for much-needed time at the beach, the pub, or the playground, thank you. Without your measure of wisdom, this book could not have become a reality.

THE MADWOMAN
AND THE BLINDMAN

JULIA MIELE RODAS

ELIZABETH J. DONALDSON

DAVID BOLT

AS ONE OF THE most widely read and widely written about novels in the English language, Charlotte Brontë's *Jane Eyre* (1847) holds an undisputed place in the Western canon and has been subject to critical and theoretical examinations from innumerable ideological, cultural, and literary perspectives. Despite extensive exegesis, however, the pervasive role of disability in the novel has yet to be fully recognized and articulated. While the reintroduction of Edward Fairfax Rochester at the close of the novel as a blind amputee compels one inescapable confrontation with significant physical and sensory impairment, readers too often experience this as the only encounter with disability. In fact, the presence of disability is by no means limited to this single representation. Bertha Mason Rochester, the infamous "madwoman" of the Thornfield attic, can also clearly be understood as a disabled character, one whose vocal, social, cognitive, or psychiatric impairment is exacerbated by mistreatment and neglect. In addition to the impairments of these two major characters, the novel also presents us with a range of other disabled subjects, including a collection of cousins who have singular psychic and social identities: the obsessive-compulsive Eliza Reed who shuns social intercourse and has each moment of her day scheduled "with

1

rigid regularity" (207; ch. 21);1 the bilious John Reed, without apparent familial affection, a possible gambling addict who eventually commits suicide; the ascetic St. John who denies his fleshly appetites to the extent that he deliberately and contentedly invites his own death. Bertha's family, an implicit spectral presence, is replete with disability, her brother Richard with "his feeble mind," another brother "a complete dumb idiot," and her mother "shut up in a lunatic asylum" (269; ch. 27). The life and philosophy of Jane's closest childhood friend, Helen Burns, is thoroughly informed by her chronic degenerative illness. Even Jane herself is characterized in large part by her fundamental social anomaly, by a sense of distance and difference that shapes both her identity and her personal narrative.

Despite the abundance of disability, however, this aspect of the novel has remained strangely disguised in the interpretive writing that surrounds it; the extraordinary presence of disability is typically figured in alternative terms, as a tool for articulating spiritual values, as an expression of sexist oppression or imperialist complicity, or as a symbol of divine punishment. In this interpretive process, embodied experiences of impairment and disability are erased. Conventional interpretive practices, constructing disability as literary device rather than presence, have thus made it difficult for many readers to engage with, or even to recognize, the profusion of impairment and disability in the novel.

Manifestations of disability in *Jane Eyre* have traditionally been understood in almost purely symbolic terms. The blinding and maiming of Rochester, the amputation of his hand, and the "madness" of Bertha have generally been read as deliberately dramatic emblems of other problems within the novel, especially Rochester's hubris and Jane's powerlessness. Rather than occupying its own complex identity position, disability appears, for many readers, to exist as a kind of overlay, a caution against losing control or against defying social convention. Among the interpretive acts that read disability in these stereotypical terms, perhaps none has gained greater currency than Richard Chase's analysis of Rochester's blindness as a symbolic castration, an interpretive gesture so widely disseminated and consumed that it has come to represent the foundational meaning of blindness in *Jane Eyre,* despite the apparent contradiction of Rochester's happy and fruitful marriage. This influential interpretation asserts a common literary and cultural convention, the "blindman"—a figure that serves as a conveniently reductive substitute for the real complexities of a visually impaired,

---

1. The version of the primary text referred to in this introduction is Charlotte Brontë, *Jane Eyre,* ed. Richard J. Dunn, 2nd ed. (New York and London: Norton, 1987).

male identity. This blindman figure presents a feminized rendition of Rochester, depleted and diminished, the loss of his left hand even suggesting phallic amputation.

The "madness" of Bertha, likewise, has most frequently been seen as standing in for some other veiled or unspeakable condition. Bertha is regarded, alternately, as an evocation of Jane's tightly constrained interiority or as the "maddened double" of Brontë herself (Gilbert and Gubar, xi). Adrienne Rich sees the "madwoman" as a caution to the "powerless woman in the England of the 1840s," Jane's "opposite, her image horribly distorted in a warped mirror" ("Jane Eyre," 469). Gayatri Spivak reads Bertha as a different sort of reflection: she is the colonial "Other," a "figure produced by the axiomatics of imperialism" ("Three Women's Texts," 247). Her madness, for Spivak, represents the human/animal frontier that is central to the imperialist project of humanizing the Third World Other. Even fictional interpretations of the novel, like Jean Rhys's groundbreaking *Wide Sargasso Sea,* seem to see Bertha's disability as representing something else; in this instance, her "madness" is reconstructed as the strangulating mask of sexist and imperialist power imposed by an insecure and jealous husband, rather than as an intrinsic quality of Bertha's embodied experience.

While acknowledging the massive debt owed to the community of scholars with whom we have shared *Jane Eyre,* this volume sets out not only to expand upon but also to depart from these long-standing interpretations, offering more nuanced readings of disability presence and asking vital questions about traditions of embodiment, representation, social intercourse, and identity. Customarily, impairment in *Jane Eyre* has been read unproblematically as loss, an undesired deviance from a condition of regularity vital to stable closure of the marriage plot. But the work of disability scholars informs and complicates our understanding of impairment and disability in Brontë's text. For example, Lennard J. Davis has argued that the idea of disability emerges out of a Victorian context, citing the increasing use of statistics during this period, dating the first appearance of the word "normal" to 1840, and pointing to the "coming into consciousness" of the idea of the "norm" in the early years of the Victorian era (*Enforcing Normalcy,* 24). *Jane Eyre's* representations of physiognomy and disability, likewise, participate in an emerging modern medical discourse, a discourse that leads, as Rosemarie Garland-Thomson notes, to eugenics and the "ascending scientific discourse of pathology" at the end of the nineteenth century (*Extraordinary Bodies,* 74). Published in 1847, *Jane Eyre* predates many of the major discoveries in Victorian medicine, such as pasteurization and the germ theory of disease, yet the novel is contemporary with the early use of anesthesia (other than alcohol and opiates) during surgery. Also contemporary with the publication of the novel is the opening of the Earlswood Asylum in 1847, which, in the wake of the Lunatics Act of 1845, signaled the beginning of a significant increase in the institutionalization of people with mental disabilities in large residential hospitals (Wright). *Jane Eyre* is, therefore, historically positioned at a time of radical transformation in the way Victorian bodies and minds were conceptualized, contained, and manipulated.

The legacy of this transformation has been crucial to disability activism and theory, and to disability studies more generally, for in many ways we exist in the context of an increasing medicalization of bodies and minds. Critiques of the "medical model" of disability have been foundational in disability rights activism. As Paul Longmore states, this model posits disability as "a defect located in individuals" and "thereby individualizes and privatizes what is in fundamental ways a social and political problem" (*Why I Burned My Book,* 4). In contrast, Longmore and others argue that disability should be theoretically repositioned as a primarily social, political, legal, and cultural phenomenon. In keeping with the practice of disability studies scholarship, this book builds on an ongoing critique of the medical model and reveals the social and historical context of disability as it is represented in *Jane Eyre,* including an investigation of contemporary medical knowledge and practice. As a canonical text in English literature and culture, published on the cusp of the development of conceptions of normalcy and of modern medicine as we know it, *Jane Eyre* is ripe for such critical engagement. Drawing on the work of disability theorists, as well as scholarship in women's studies, deconstruction, autism studies, masculinity studies, caregiving, theology, psychoanalysis, and film studies, respectively, the contributors to this volume suggest that disability may have both a more pervasive and a more subtle and textured place in Brontë's novel than has hitherto been acknowledged, guiding us to an enriched understanding both of *Jane Eyre* and of the meanings and functions of disability.

In the opening chapter, "The Corpus of the Madwoman: Toward a Feminist Disability Studies Theory of Embodiment and Mental Illness," Elizabeth J. Donaldson builds on the tradition of previous feminist interpretations of the madwoman, proposing a disability studies reading attuned to the connections between physiognomy and madness in *Jane Eyre.* Donaldson argues that Bertha and Rochester reflect iconic contemporary images of raving and melancholy madness, a dyad famously depicted by Cauis Gabriel Cibber's sculptures at the gates of Bethlem "Bedlam" Hospital. A close reading of *Jane Eyre,* furthermore, reveals how the novel's logic of physiognomy and phrenology establishes a clear link between physical impairment and mental illness: Bertha's madness is both chronic and congenital, grounded in a family history of mental illness, while Rochester's is acute and accidental, caused in part by physical trauma. Positioned in the context of Gilbert and Gubar's quintessential reading of Bertha as Jane's "maddened double" (xi), Donaldson departs from the established madness-as-rebellion narrative and rejects the legacy of antipsychiatric readings of the text in order to open a new theoretical space for the analysis of embodiment and mental illness. Using feminist science studies and theories of the body along with insights gained from disability scholarship, she calls for alternate feminist readings of madness that take into account the lived, corporeal experience of mental illness and impairments.

In keeping with the feminist interpretations that have become an essential part of *Jane Eyre*'s theoretical and critical history, the second chapter is informed by a blend of recent and classic works of feminism. Indeed, as is suggested in the title, "The Blindman in the Classic: Feminisms, Ocularcentrism, and *Jane Eyre*," David Bolt frequently points to Gilbert and Gubar's influential study. In his deconstructive reading, however, some feminisms become troubled by the exposure of the normative nature of literary sightedness. After all, the term *ocularcentrism* denotes a perspective and, by extension, a subject position that is dominated by vision. The contention is that, grounded in ocularcentric epistemology and thus instrumental in shoring up what Garland-Thomson calls the "normate's boundries," the trope of the blindman is both ableist and patriarchal (*Extraordinary Bodies*, 8). That is to say, Bolt teases out the inherent bias in Brontë's depiction of the blind Rochester, arguing that such a representation is incompatible with established feminist commendations of the novel. This problem is illustrated in a comparison between *Jane Eyre* and a selection of overtly ocularcentric constructs perpetuated by Rudyard Kipling, Sigmund Freud, and John Milton. Bolt's central concern is not that a female character's empowerment is emphasized by a male counterpart's disempowerment but that male disempowerment is here engendered by a patriarchal mythos of blindness.

The third chapter turns away from Bertha and Rochester, the characters who more evidently embody disability in *Jane Eyre*, to suggest that the novel's heroine may herself be understood in terms of disability identity. "'On the Spectrum': Rereading Contact and Affect in *Jane Eyre*" engages the early writing of autism pioneers Leo Kanner and Hans Asperger and considers Jane's unusual affect and sociality within the context of medical, theoretical, and autobiographical writing on autism, ultimately suggesting that Jane occupies a place on the autistic spectrum. Julia Miele Rodas argues that readers tend to contextualize Jane's emotional experience, the interiority of her passionate emotional life, her reduced affect, and the concealing of her deeply rooted feelings in terms of cultural history, understanding her extreme self-control and apparent poise as fitting with historically appropriate social conventions. Rodas points out, however, that because readers experience this self-control from the inside, Jane's passions are highly visible and her most obvious autistic characteristics—her silence, flattened affect and remoteness—have rarely been noticed or questioned beyond a feminist context. This chapter claims that Jane's aloofness and social idiosyncrasy do not represent a tacit acceptance—as some have argued—of the exploitation and oppression of subject peoples but point rather to the political significance of solitude. Thus, Jane achieves new political stature, becoming a model for effective resistance to social control, her "private fecundity seeding possibilities for oppressed and marginalized peoples, especially autistic persons," who reject the punishing demands of "compulsory sociality."

Margaret Rose Torrell's "'From India-Rubber Back to Flesh': A Reevaluation of Male Embodiment in *Jane Eyre*" explores how Brontë's display of male bodies performs interventions into cultural attitudes about gender and ability and gestures toward a nonhegemonic model of masculinity, which is complemented (rather than conflicted) by physical disability. The chapter examines how embodied status has been used as a dividing line between genders in Euro-American culture, creating a double binary of gender and embodiment, which links masculinity to disembodiment and femininity to embodiment and its counterpart, disability. But while the novel may be said to uphold ableist conceptions in its reconfigurations of gender hierarchies, Torrell argues that there are also moments in which both the gender and ability binaries become unmoored. One such moment is located in the final portrayal of Rochester. According to Torrell, Brontë's representation of Rochester's embodied masculinity, coupled with Jane's embodied femininity, facilitates a reevaluation of both gender and ability hierarchies. For Torrell, then, Rochester achieves a fairly progressive integration of disability and masculinity that anticipates the type of nonoppressive, embodied masculinity discussed by contemporary disability scholars and theorists of masculinity: "just as the India-rubber stretches into flesh, so too does the model of masculinity stretch to encompass new, more inclusive possibilities for male embodiment."

D. Christopher Gabbard's "From Custodial Care to Caring Labor: The Discourse of Who Cares in *Jane Eyre*" situates the novel vis-à-vis 1840s public policy reforms aimed at improving the treatment of mentally ill and disabled people. Gabbard observes that in narrating her story during the decade's latter half, Jane reenacts in miniature the spirit of the national reforms. The chapter presents two cycles of caregiving and disability—Rochester and Bertha in the 1820s and 1830s followed by Jane and Rochester in the 1830s and 1840s—with the two cycles manifesting a paradigm shift in philosophies of caregiving. Gabbard argues that Jane's discovery of the difference between Rochester's "custodial care" and the Rivers' "caring labor" is brought about by her contact with Bertha and the protagonist's subsequent wandering on the heath and convalescence at Moor House. By recourse to Ato Quayson's "implied interlocutor," Gabbard refreshes our understanding of *Jane Eyre* as *bildungsroman*, inferring that Jane develops morally through contact with Bertha, growing in her understanding and ethical consideration of divergent abilities. The reform Jane implements in the treatment of disability is seen in the way she interacts with Rochester at the end, bringing to the fore one of the novel's major themes: the responsibility of the individual charged with caring for another who is unable to live independently. Gabbard argues that the novel privileges the caregiving approaches exemplified by Maria Temple and the Rivers family and implicitly censures those of Rochester, Mrs. Reed, and Mr. Brocklehurst.

Essaka Joshua's "'I Began to See': Biblical Models of Disability in *Jane Eyre*" brings a theological perspective to the project. As Joshua notes, Brontë was "an adept commentator, absorber and interpreter of biblical material, and it is no surprise, given the extent of biblical allusion in *Jane Eyre*, that her biblical intertexts engage with disability." This chapter establishes an important context for reading biblical references within the novel, pointing out that Judeo-Christian scripture itself deploys several models of disability, some negative (e.g., the associations with sin and punishment) and some positive (e.g., the associations with discipleship and spiritual worth). Joshua argues that the novel centers discussion of biblical disability on the spiritual role of sight and blindness and on the physical body's relationship to the spiritual body, and that the allusions to biblical disability in *Jane Eyre* emphasize positive, spiritual gains. In fact, it appears that through her choice of biblical texts, "Brontë dissociates stigma and disability," reinforcing the idea "that disability is a symbol of being saved or chosen, and that it is a route to salvation." Reading the novel with attention to its use of biblical references to disability, Joshua provides a more progressive understanding of the novel's account of disability than is often suggested. The chapter concludes that, if we read in the light of Brontë's consistently redemptionist agenda, Rochester's disability may be understood not as a punishment but rather as an indication of his spiritual well-being.

Susannah Mintz's "Illness, Disability, Recognition in *Jane Eyre*" proposes that the novel reveals the cost of denying or suppressing difference

Introduction

and longs for an alternative form of engagement with embodiment. Making use of the psychoanalytic theory of recognition, this chapter contends that Brontë records the possibility of a form of interaction that acknowledges and accepts the frailties of the body. Recognition insists that true acknowledgement of another's subjectivity is possible—indeed, that it is the basis of political and cultural understanding. Brontë's novel, fascinated as it is by bodies, bodily shape, facial features, extremities of sickness and injury, renders these as axes of heightened intersubjective possibility where subjects are tested for their capacity to tolerate and respect. Representations of disease, disability, or atypical bodies complicate the idea that these are inevitably problematical conditions rather than incidental to problems of social arrangement. In its emphasis on intersubjective regard as a means of disrupting hierarchical binaries of dis/ability, the novel reminds readers of the need for less restrictive or determinative ways of thinking about bodies, selves, illness, and relationships. Mintz juxtaposes the text's unsurprising participation in the structures of normalcy against its depiction of what might obtain between people in a world where "irregularity"—a word that recurs frequently in reference to the shape and symmetry of people's bodies—does not need to be repaired. *Jane Eyre* openly displays troubled bodies, not to make them the fascinating or pitiable spectacles of the readerly stare but rather to return, time and again, to the scene of potential recognition.

In our closing chapter, Martha Stoddard Holmes brings film studies and disability studies together to examine how the novel's descriptions of disability have been portrayed in five key film adaptations ranging from 1944 to 2006. Even though for some readers Rochester's injured body facilitates Jane's desire for him, his disabled body simultaneously presents a series of representational challenges for twentieth- and twenty-first century screen versions of the novel. This chapter, "Visions of Rochester: Screening Desire and Disability in *Jane Eyre*," shows that while Brontë is direct and concrete in her descriptions of Rochester's injuries—he has lost an eye and a hand—and their appearance, film versions vary considerably in organizing special effects makeup, costume, and *mise-en-scène* to depict these impairments. While most versions render Rochester's blindness visible through makeup and props, many counter the film adaptation's need for compression by supplementing the dialogue in which Jane and Rochester work through the meaning of his disability—including its supposed implications for sexuality and marriage. Several add dialogue that frames blindness with angry assumptions of pity, culminating in a rebuff of Jane that does not align with the text of the novel. Further, only one version renders visible Rochester's amputation. Taken in the aggregate, Holmes observes, while film versions of *Jane Eyre* do articulate desire in the context of blindness, anger and pity are presented as obligatory gatekeepers to the happy ending.

These chapters are connected not simply by their engagement with *Jane Eyre* and disability in general but also by their engagement with other more specific themes and critical traditions. The chapters speak to, with, and sometimes against each other. While both Donaldson and Gabbard begin with a reconsideration of Bertha's mental illness, each has a different critical focus: Donaldson, the embodiment of mental illness; Gabbard, the act of caregiving. Bolt brings the process of deconstruction to the figure of the blindman and its ocularcentric premise, both in the novel itself and in the feminist literary criticism that follows. Though working within a similar framework, Torrell deconstructs binaries of male disembodiment and female embodiment. Joshua seeks to recuperate blindness in *Jane Eyre* in the critical context of biblical studies, which contrasts somewhat with Holmes's work on the proliferation of modern film versions. Finally, Rodas positions Jane on the autism spectrum, giving her intense interior life and solitude a positive valence, yet Mintz stresses the close connection between Jane and Rochester and the "heightened intersubjective" relationship that their marriage reveals.

Collectively, these chapters argue that disability is crucial to a critically engaged reading of *Jane Eyre*. The madwoman and the blindman of our title call attention to the central critique of this book, that the massive tradition of scholarship around Brontë's famous novel has largely been content to read the disability of Rochester and Bertha (and other representations of disability in *Jane Eyre*) as static symbol rather than as complex embodiment with meaning, context, and potential beyond that ascribed to the blindman or madwoman tropes. *The Madwoman and the Blindman,* then, marks just one moment in an ongoing conversation about *Jane Eyre*, about the value of disability, and about the importance of disability theory.

THE CORPUS OF
THE MADWOMAN

Toward a Feminist
Disability Studies Theory of
Embodiment and Mental Illness

ELIZABETH J. DONALDSON

OVER THIRTY YEARS AGO, Sandra Gilbert and Susan Gubar published *The Madwoman in the Attic,* a now classic text of early feminist literary criticism. Basing their title on the character of Bertha Mason, a madwoman secretly imprisoned in her husband's attic, Gilbert and Gubar argued that the "maddened doubles" in texts by women writers of the nineteenth and twentieth centuries "function as social surrogates," projecting women writers' anxiety of authorship in a male-dominated literary tradition (xi). Much like the determined women who fueled feminism in the 1960s and 70s, these madwomen rebel against the strictures of patriarchal authority. Since then, the figure of the madwoman as feminist rebel has had a sustained cultural currency. As Elaine Showalter notes, "To contemporary feminist critics, Bertha Mason has become a paradigmatic figure" (68). Furthermore, as Showalter also notes, feminist critics have a sympathy for Bertha Mason that, ironically, Charlotte Brontë does not seem to share (68–69).

Many factors, not the least of which is the proliferation of feminist criticism and reading practices, have contributed to Bertha Mason's paradigmatic status and to contemporary readers' newfound sympathy. Perhaps most notably, Jean Rhys's *Wide Sargasso Sea* (1966), a prequel to *Jane*

Eyre, has influenced a generation of readers' responses to Brontë's character. Rhys's novel tells the story of Bertha "Antoinette" Mason's life in Jamaica before she marries Rochester and moves to England.[1] Rhys gives voice to the previously silent madwoman and depicts what some might consider the causes of her madness—a difficult childhood, a dangerous social climate, and her husband's ultimate betrayal. In her depiction of the events that precede Antoinette's imprisonment in the attic, Rhys departs in important ways from *Jane Eyre*'s configuration of madness, which I discuss in greater detail below. By stressing the causal factors that contribute to Antoinette's emotional state, Rhys also makes it easier for readers to understand and to identify with the originally enigmatic and inarticulate character.

Another factor significantly affecting contemporary readers' sympathy for Bertha Mason is the changing cultural thinking about psychiatry, mental illness, and the asylum from the late 1960s to the present. Psychiatry, feminist critics pointed out, unfairly pathologizes women.[2] Mental illness, according to the antipsychiatry movement, is a myth.[3] The asylum, Foucault explained, is primarily a form of institutional control (*Madness and Civilization*).[4] The reception of Rhys's reevaluation of Bertha Antoinette Mason is in part a product of this particular historical moment in England and in the United States. In this context, Bertha Mason, and the figure of the madwoman in general, became a compelling metaphor for women's rebellion.

Yet this metaphor for rebellion has problematic implications. Although Gilbert and Gubar warn readers against romanticizing madness, the figure of Bertha Mason as a rebellious woman subverting the patriarchal order by burning down her husband's estate has a certain irresistible appeal. Gilbert and Gubar's text and Rhys's novel are, of course, not the only texts that

---

1. In *Jane Eyre*, the madwoman's maiden name is Bertha Antoinette Mason. In Rhys's novel, the parallel character's maiden name is Antoinette Mason, née Cosway; the name *Bertha* is an invention of her husband Edward Rochester, and this renaming emphasizes the formative role he has in forging her mad identity in Rhys's text. I use *Bertha* to refer to Brontë's character, and *Antoinette* to distinguish Rhys's character, although, for those who have read both texts, a hybrid of the two—Bertha Antoinette Cosway Mason Rochester—might best describe the composite character who emerges.

2. Key texts from this period of second-wave feminism include Showalter's *The Female Malady,* which details the gendered nature of ideas about insanity, and Chesler's *Women and Madness* and Ehrenreich and English's *The Sexual Politics of Sickness,* which describe similar phenomena. For data on the predominance of women patients in the mental health care system from this period, see Guttentag, Salasin, and Belle; Howell and Bayes.

3. For very explicit statements of this position, see Szaz, who was in turn influenced by the work of Laing.

4. For American versions of this form of institutional critique, see Goffman, Rothman, and Grob.

figure madness as rebellion. In *Women and Madness,* Phyllis Chesler views women's madness as a journey of mythic proportions: "women have already been bitterly and totally repressed sexually; many may be reacting to or trying to escape from just such repression, and the powerlessness it signifies, by 'going mad'" (37). In the face of such repression, "going mad" might be considered the only sane response to an insane world (see, for example, Deleuze and Guattari). The ability to "go mad" also functions as a class marker of a higher sensibility: this sort of psychological depth has "the glow of transgressive glamour" (Pfister, 176). For example, in *Mockingbird Years,* Emily Fox Gordon describes her stay at a mental hospital as "the fulfillment of an adolescent fantasy":

> The status of mental patient would invest me with significance. [. . .] We had seen the movie *David and Lisa* [1962], a tearjerker about a love affair between two adolescent mental patients, and we were smitten with the romance of madness. I think we believed that if we cultivated dissociation we would become as beautiful as Lisa: our complexions would turn luminous, our faces grow expressive hollows, our hair lie flat and glossy. We spent our days edging cautiously around the grounds, taking drags on shared cigarettes and muttering "a touch can kill," hoping to be noticed by the patients, drawn into their glamorous orbit by the magic of proximity. (5)

Oprah Winfrey's remake of *David and Lisa,* more than thirty years after the original, illustrates the enduring romantic appeal of madness (Winfrey and Kramer).[5] And even more recently, in a film version of Susanna Kaysen's memoir, *Girl, Interrupted,* Angelina Jolie's portrayal of a mental patient reinforces this linkage of mental illness and transgressive glamour for a new generation of young women. Similarly, in *Gothika,* a film that shares the sensibilities of *Wide Sargasso Sea*'s version of the post-Brontë madwoman tale, Halle Berry plays Dr. Miranda Grey, a former psychiatrist turned mental patient who is incarcerated after murdering her husband, a psychiatrist who conceals his madwomen victims in a barn basement rather than an

5. The previous film *David and Lisa* (Perry and Heller 1962) is based on the study by Rubin (1961). See Kesey's novel *One Flew over The Cuckoo's Nest* (1962) and Forman and Douglas's subsequent film (1975) for the masculinized counterpart of the glamorization of madness, which ironically also trivializes and denigrates the experience of people with mental illness. In *Cuckoo's Nest,* the patients fall into two categories: those in therapy appear to suffer from socially produced ailments and are distinguished from the *chronic* (real?) patients, who seem to fall outside the realm of discourse, sympathy, and redemption. This is a point that Mitchell and Snyder also discuss (*Narrative Prosthesis,* 173–74), and that I explore in greater detail in another essay, "The Psychiatric Gaze."

attic. In keeping with the contemporary madwoman tradition in fiction, Dr. Grey's madness is not actually mental illness: her body is possessed by the angry spirit of a woman her husband had abused.

However it is romanticized, madness itself offers women little possibility for true resistance or productive rebellion. As Marta Caminero-Santangelo argues in her aptly titled, *The Madwoman Can't Speak: Or, Why Insanity Is Not Subversive*, Bertha Mason's madness only "offers the illusion of power" (3). Using both fictional madwomen and women's biographical accounts of asylum experiences, Caminero-Santangelo reveals the limited political efficacy of the mad subject. Similarly, Shoshana Felman writes:

> Depressed and terrified women are not about to seize the means of production and reproduction: quite the opposite of rebellion, madness is the impasse confronting those whom cultural conditioning has deprived of the very means of protest or self-affirmation. Far from being a form of contestation, "mental illness" is a request for help, a manifestation both of cultural impotence and of political castration. (8)

Furthermore, and this is a crucial point for my argument here, using madness to represent women's rebellion has undesirable effects due primarily to the inevitable, as the previous quotation illustrates, slippage between "madness" and "mental illness." While Gilbert and Gubar make it clear that their discussion concerns madness as a metaphor, not mental illness in the clinical sense, this distinction proves impossible to maintain. Fictional representations of madness have a way of influencing clinical discourses of mental illness and vice versa. As Showalter has demonstrated, the figure of Bertha Mason circulated in precisely this way during Brontë's time: "Bertha's violence, dangerousness and rage, her regression to an inhuman condition and her sequestration became such a powerful model for Victorian readers, including psychiatrists, that it influenced even medical accounts of female insanity" (68).

Why is the association between women's rebellion/madness and mental illness undesirable? In some ways it is not. Beginning in part with this insight, feminist critiques of psychiatry and psychology have provided us with necessary and important analyses of the gendered politics of psychiatric diagnoses: it is certainly true that women have been disproportionately and in some cases even falsely diagnosed as mentally ill. And it is certainly true that psychiatry and psychiatric hospitals were in dire need of outside critics in the early days before deinstitutionalization and the patient rights movement transformed the mental health care system. However, at this particular historical moment, one in which disability studies is coming of age, I believe that the madness/rebellion configuration subtly reinforces what has become an almost monolithic way of reading mental illness within feminist literary criticism and perhaps in the larger culture of women's studies scholarship.[6] This is undesirable, I would argue, because this configuration of madness, if it remains widely accepted and uncontested, may limit our inquiry into madness/mental illness.

Indeed, one could argue, when madness is used as a metaphor for feminist rebellion, mental illness itself is erased. In *Illness as Metaphor,* Susan Sontag describes "the punitive or sentimental fantasies concocted" about tuberculosis and cancer and attempts to counteract stereotyped conceptions of these diseases (3). In comparison, the madness-as-feminist-rebellion metaphor might at first seem like a positive strategy for combating the stigma traditionally associated with mental illness. However, this metaphor indirectly diminishes the lived experience of many people disabled by mental illness, just as the metaphoric use of terms like *lame, blind,* and *deaf* can misrepresent, in ways that have ultimately harmful political effects, the experience of living with those physical conditions. As someone who often acts as an advocate for family members disabled by severe mental illness, I approach this subject with a certain sense of political urgency. In my experience, theories that pay attention exclusively to the social causes and construction of mad identity while overlooking the material conditions of the body, and the body as a material condition, have a limited political scope.[7] A feminist disability studies theory of mental illness that includes the body, one which theorizes bodies as a "material-semiotic generative nodes" and mental illnesses as physical impairments, would be a timely and productive way of developing the discussion of madness/mental illness within women's studies scholarship (Haraway, "The Biopolitics," 208).[8] Perhaps the most appropri-

6. The impressive body of work by feminist historian Nancy Tomes and recent books by Jonathan Metzl are notable exceptions here. Tomes was an early critic of female malady interpretations of insanity and of the madness-as-feminist-rebellion configuration. Metzl offers nuanced examinations of gender, race, and the historical and cultural contexts of mental illness while still affirming the material reality of mental illness as disease.

7. My mother has schizophrenia. Her emotional distress, paranoid delusions, and hallucinations were formative parts of my childhood, and these untreated symptoms continue to shape our lives. A younger brother of mine also has schizophrenia. After several arrests, periods of homelessness, and forced hospitalizations, he is currently a client of a forensic assertive community treatment team, which provides him with outpatient medical care and the much-needed help of overworked and underpaid social workers. My thinking about mental illness reflects this ongoing personal history.

8. In the time since this essay was originally researched and published (2001), other scholars have made similar remarks. On the subject of mental illness and disability studies

ate and useful way to begin thinking through a theory of embodiment and mental illness is with the paradigmatic figure of women's madness, *Jane Eyre*'s Bertha Mason.

REREADING *THE MADWOMAN IN THE ATTIC*

A feminist disability studies reading that stresses the connections between madness and physiognomy, between the mind and body, provides us with an alternate way of conceptualizing madness in *Jane Eyre*. In this reading, Bertha Mason's madness is a sociomedical condition, a secret family history of mental illness. This family history precedes and supersedes Bertha Mason's marriage. *Jane Eyre*'s plot rests on a structure not exactly of mad doubles but of juxtapositions between normative and non-normative bodies, between the accidental and the congenital, between masculine rationality and feminine embodiment, and between melancholy and raving madness. Reading the body is a central practice in *Jane Eyre*: madness gets its meaning from the novel's underlying logic of physiognomy.

While the novel to a certain extent deconstructs ideals of beauty and the perfect body, it simultaneously is heavily invested in the notion of physiognomy, of reading moral character through facial features.[9] Jane Eyre's rival for Rochester's affection, the "beautiful Miss Ingram," for example, is described as "moulded like a Diana. [. . .] The noble bust, the sloping shoulders, the graceful neck, the dark eyes and black ringlets were all there" (161; ch. 17).[10] Rochester describes his supposed rival for Jane's affection, St. John, as "a graceful Apollo [. . .] tall, fair, blue-eyed, and with a Grecian profile" (422; ch. 37). Yet these classically beautiful bodies enclose flawed

---

theories, Mollow writes, "analyses that privilege disability over impairment deflect attention from the political nature of impairment itself" (288). She also notes that framing disability primarily in terms of social oppression may "sacrifice [. . .] a way of thinking in political terms about the suffering some impairments cause" (287). Nicki also stresses a movement away from an exclusively social model of psychiatric disability: "In order for mental illnesses to be conceived as real illnesses and those afflicted to be treated appropriately, mental illnesses must not be seen purely in terms of their cultural and social components" (83). She notes that "a social constructionist approach to mental illness [. . .] may be used to undermine mental illness as a legitimate illness and disability," which may in turn harm women disabled by psychiatric illnesses (84).

   9. Davis's *Bending over Backwards* observes that Jane's unconventional plainness marks her as an abnormal heroine for a novel (96). Kaplan also notes how "Jane's constellation of defects [. . .] works as a defensive counterdiscourse" ("Afterword," 309).

   10. The version of the primary text referred to in this chapter is Charlotte Brontë, *Jane Eyre* (New York: Bantam, 1981).

characters who are not successful in their matches. St. John rejects the perfect beauty of Rosamond and is in turn rejected by "plain" Jane. Blanche
Ingram's face and her facial expressions contradict her perfect form: "but
her face? Her face was like her mother's; a youthful unfurrowed likeness:
the same low brow, the same high features, the same pride. [. . .] [H]er
laugh was satirical, and so was the habitual expression of her arched and
haughty lip" (161; ch. 17). Beauty may be skin deep, but expression and
gesture are visually evident on and through the surface of the body and,
if read correctly, are accurate manifestations of inner moral character and
identity.

The narrator herself cannot escape becoming the object of the structur-
ing narrative of physiognomy. As Miss Ingram's mother remarks: "I am a
judge of physiognomy, and in hers [Jane's] I see all the faults of her class"
(166; ch. 17). Rochester, a much more sensitive reader than the Ingrams,
also reads Jane's body, more precisely her head and face. Borrowing from
the terms of phrenology, the study of character based on the shape of the
head, Rochester at one point describes Jane as having "a good deal of the
organ of Adhesiveness" (236; ch. 23: see figure 1).

According to phrenology, inner organs of the brain are associated with
specific personality traits and cognitive skills. The over- or underdevelop-
ment of these inner organs can be read through the external shape of the
skull and its protrusions and recesses (Davies, 4). Adhesiveness, sometimes
depicted as two sisters embracing (see figure 2), signifies social bonds and
friendship.[11]

The offhand reference to "the organ of Adhesiveness" is never explained
in *Jane Eyre*, which seems to suggest the audience's familiarity with this
term. In keeping with this emphasis on the continuity between the external
head and the internal mind, Rochester, while posing as a gypsy fortune teller,
quickly throws aside the pretense of reading Jane's palm in favor of reading
her countenance: "what is in a palm? Destiny is not written there. [. . .]
[I]t is in the face: on the forehead, about the eyes, and in the eyes themselves,
in the lines of the mouth" (185–86; ch. 19).[12] Jane, previously skeptical of
the gypsy's powers, then states, "Ah! now you are coming to reality [. . .]

11. Whitman was particularly proud of the development of his organ of adhesiveness.
See Whitman's phrenological chart in the second edition of *Leaves of Grass,* which was published by the American phrenologists Fowler and Wells (reprinted in Madeleine Stern, 76–77).
The image of the two sisters embracing recalls Brontë's relationship to her sisters as well as
the many references in *Jane Eyre* to the likeness between Jane and Rochester, "familiar to me
as my own face in a glass" (190; ch. 19).

12. Although palmistry as a science is discounted in this scene, the gesture of hands is
quite significant in *Jane Eyre,* a point that I discuss in greater detail later.

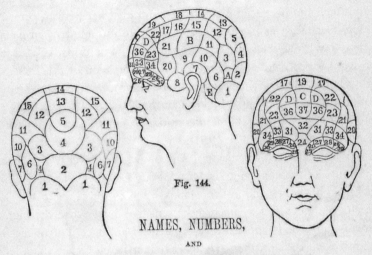

Fig. 144.

NAMES, NUMBERS,

AND

LOCATION OF THE ORGANS.

1. AMATIVENESS.
A. CONJUGAL LOVE.
2. PARENTAL LOVE.
3. FRIENDSHIP.
4. INHABITIVENESS.
5. CONTINUITY.
E. VITATIVENESS.
6. COMBATIVENESS.
7. DESTRUCTIVENESS.
8. ALIMENTIVENESS.
9. ACQUISITIVENESS.
10. SECRETIVENESS.
11. CAUTIOUSNESS.
12. APPROBATIVENESS.

13. SELF-ESTEEM.
14. FIRMNESS.
15. CONSCIENTIOUSNESS.
16. HOPE.
17. SPIRITUALITY.
18. VENERATION.
19. BENEVOLENCE.
20. CONSTRUCTIVENESS.
21. IDEALITY.
B. SUBLIMITY.
22. IMITATION.
23. MIRTH.
24. INDIVIDUALITY
25. FORM.

26. SIZE.
27. WEIGHT.
28. COLOR.
29. ORDER.
30. CALCULATION.
31. LOCALITY.
32. EVENTUALITY.
33. TIME.
34. TUNE.
35. LANGUAGE.
36. CAUSALITY.
37. COMPARISON.
C. HUMAN NATURE.
D. SUAVITY.

In addition to these diagrams, the student of Phrenology should have at hand a PHRENOLOGICAL BUST, somewhere near the size of life, showing the exact location of each organ. Then, by comparing living heads one with another, the differences would appear most palpable. Extend your observations, and compare the well-known characters of those having long and narrow heads with those of persons who have short and broad heads; or compare the high heads with the low, and however skeptical you may be, you will be compelled to accept the general principles of Phrenology.

FIGURE 1. Numbered and listed phrenological organs. From Samuel R. Wells's *New Physiognomy* (1871). Courtesy of the Library Company of Philadelphia.

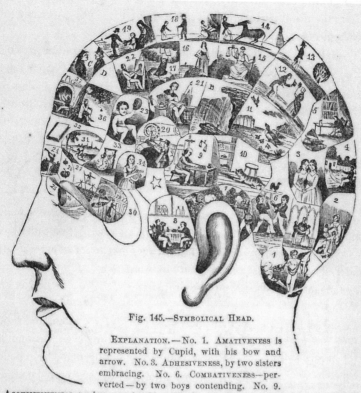

Fig. 145.—Symbolical Head.

Explanation. — No. 1. Amativeness is represented by Cupid, with his bow and arrow. No. 3. Adhesiveness, by two sisters embracing. No. 6. Combativeness—perverted — by two boys contending. No. 9. Acquisitiveness, a miser counting his gold. No. 10. Secretiveness, by a cat watching for a mouse. B. Sublimity, Niagara Falls. 24. Individuality, a boy with a telescope. 31. Locality, by a traveler consulting a guide-board. 36. Causality, Newton studying the laws of gravity by the falling of an apple. 18. Veneration, devotion, and deference, respect, and prayer. 19. Benevolence, the Good Samaritan bestowing charity. No. 17. Spirituality, Moses, on Mount Sinai, receiving the tables from Heaven on which were engraved the Ten Commandments. 16. Hope, the anchor, and a ship at sea. 15. Conscientiousness, Justice, with the scales in one hand and the sword in the other, and so forth. Each organ is represented by a symbol, which in some cases may show the appropriate, and in others the perverted action. The latter is shown in case of the miser, the gluttons, and the fighting boys. It is used as a means of indicating both the location of the organs and to show their natural action as frequently exhibited in life.

Note.—The reader will observe here the natural grouping of the organs. Consider, for instance, the relations so admirably indicated in the arrangement in contiguity of Amativeness, Parental Love, Friendship, and Inhabitiveness; or of Alimentiveness, Acquisitiveness, Secretiveness, Destructiveness, and Combativeness. So Individuality, Form, Size, Weight, Color, Order, and the rest of the Perceptive organs, indicate by their locations their common matter-of-fact tendencies.

FIGURE 2. Illustrated phrenological organs. From Samuel R. Wells's *New Physiognomy* (1871). Courtesy of the Library Company of Philadelphia.

I shall begin to put some faith in you presently" (186; ch. 19). Both Jane and *Jane Eyre* the novel partake in a deep abiding faith in the discerning powers of physiognomy.

Physiognomy was also used to discern madness and idiocy, two mental states that were commonly discussed in tandem. John Caspar Lavater's *Essays on Physiognomy* (1789) introduced to many English readers a connection between facial expressions and insanity. By the time Brontë was writing *Jane Eyre*, Alexander Morison's depictions of madness in texts like *The Physiognomy of Mental Disease* (1840) were familiar and "greatly influential" (Gilman, 100).[13] When Jane first sees Richard Mason, the madwoman's brother, she notes:

> [H]e was a fine-looking man, at first sight especially. On closer examination, you detected something in his face that displeased; or rather, that failed to please. His features were regular, but too relaxed: his eye was large and well cut, but the life looking out of it was a tame, vacant life—at least so I thought. (178; ch. 18)

On second sight, Jane, who fittingly has a distinctive talent for sketching revealing portraits, remarks, "I liked his physiognomy even less than before [. . .]. For a handsome and not unamiable-looking man, he repelled me exceedingly" (178–79; ch. 18). Immediately juxtaposed with Jane's examination, the Ingrams' perceptions of Richard's features differ significantly: "a beautiful man," "a pretty little mouth," "what a sweet-tempered forehead," "such a placid eye and smile!" (179; ch. 18). The Ingrams, of course, are not good judges of character. Jane's more accurate evaluation of Richard's physiognomy is verified later when we learn about Richard's congenital legacy. Richard is Bertha's brother, a Mason, and as such is more than likely destined to hereditary madness or idiocy according to Rochester: "he has some grains of affection in his feeble mind [. . . but he] will probably be in the same state [as his siblings] one day" (291; ch. 27).

The novel's assumptions about biological destiny are also explicitly reinforced in the discussions about Rochester's ward Adèle, "the illegitimate offspring of a French opera-girl [Céline]" (135; ch. 15). Once Rochester discovers that his mistress Céline is having an affair, Adèle's paternity is cast forever in doubt: "the Varens, six months before, had given me this fillette Adèle, who she affirmed, was my daughter; and perhaps she may

---

13. Gilman has compiled an extensive collection of the icons of madness, including Lavater's and Morison's illustrations. My discussion here owes much to Gilman's work. Also see Hartley for a history of physiognomical thinking in the nineteenth century.

be, though I see no proofs of such grim paternity written in her countenance: Pilot [my dog] is more like me than she" (135; ch. 15). Though Jane searches Adèle's face for a resemblance to Mr. Rochester, she "found none; no trait, no turn of expression announced relationship" (136; ch. 15). In the absence of a confirmed, legitimated paternity, Adèle is defined by her matrilineal origins—and she is indelibly, innately French. Jane sees in Adèle "a superficiality of character, inherited probably from her mother, hardly congenial to an English mind" (136; ch. 15); "there was something ludicrous as well as painful in the little Parisienne's earnest and innate devotion to dress" (160; ch. 17). Rochester explains, "I am not her father; but hearing that she was quite destitute, I e'en took the poor thing out of the slime and mud of Paris, and transplanted it here, to grow up clean in the wholesome soil of an English country garden" (135; ch. 15). Adèle's French nature is checked by her English nurture: "As she grew up, a sound English education corrected in a great measure her French defects" (431; ch. 38). For Adèle, female is to male as nature is to nation. And the nation is always England.[14] Embodiment and the imperatives of the physical are a matrilineal legacy. Enculturation and Englishness become patrilineal prerogatives. That Adèle is somehow tainted by her mother is in keeping with the novel's anxious relationship to female and to disabled bodies.

The madness of Bertha Mason, "the true daughter of an infamous mother," is similarly congenital (291; ch. 27). Grounded in her body, her madness is contextualized as a matrilineal legacy of national, ethnic identity and physical disorder: "Bertha Mason is mad; and she came of a mad family; idiots and maniacs through three generations! Her mother, the Creole, was both a madwoman and a drunkard!—as I found out after I had wed the daughter: for they were silent on family secrets before" (277; ch. 26). Yet at the same time, the gestation of her madness is specifically linked to her drinking and to her sexual appetites—failures of the will, not the body, in Rochester's opinion. Therefore, despite Bertha Mason's fated madness, Rochester still holds her morally accountable for her illness. For example, at one point Jane upbraids Rochester for speaking of his wife with contempt, "Sir [. . .] you are inexorable for that unfortunate lady: you speak of her with hate—with vindictive antipathy. It is cruel—she cannot help being

---

14. Female bodies are often identified in tellingly reductive ways in *Jane Eyre*. Blanche Ingram, whose body is said to resemble Bertha Mason's, is "dark as a Spaniard" (162), and Bertha Mason's mother is simply "the Creole" (277). After Bertha Mason's madness manifests itself, Rochester embarks on a geographic search "for the antipodes of the Creole" and chooses an international menu of mistresses—an Italian, a German, and finally the Frenchwoman who is Adèle's mother (296). See also Spivak ("Three Women's Texts").

mad" (286; ch. 27). However, according to Rochester, Bertha Mason can help being mad, although to a limited extent: "her excesses had prematurely developed the germs of insanity" (292; ch. 27). Rochester also, for what it is worth, distinguishes the source of his hatred: he claims to hate her not for being mad but for having those excesses.

Bertha Mason would be recognizable to Victorian readers as an exemplar of "raving madness," depicted by Cauis Gabriel Cibber's well-known sculpted figure over the gates of Bethlem "Bedlam" Hospital (Gilman, 17–19; see figure 3, p. 24, right). Cibber's figure is restrained by chains, a common image in connection with raving madness or mania. Rochester himself mimes key features of this image in a game of charades earlier in the novel: "Amidst this sordid scene, sat a man with his clenched hands resting on his knees, and his eyes bent on the ground. [. . .] As he moved, a chain clanked; to his wrists were attached fetters. 'Bridewell!' exclaimed Colonel Dent, and the charade was solved" (172–73; ch. 18). Bridewell refers simultaneously to the infamous prison and to the secretly imprisoned bride Bertha, as well as to Rochester who is bound to her by marriage. Paraphernalia of the prison, the fetters and chains were all-too-common paraphernalia of the asylum, despite the attempts of reformers. For example, Edward Wakefield's influential 1815 broadside publicized the case of William Norris, who had been fastened to a short, foot-long chain by the neck and warehoused in Bethlem Hospital for over ten years (Gilman, 153–55). However, by the time *Jane Eyre* was published in 1847, only a handful of English asylums had discontinued the practice of mechanically restraining patients (Shortt, 128).[15] In the novel, restraint and isolation are presented as necessary conditions of raving madness. Once Bertha is declared mad, she, "of course," must be sequestered: "since the medical men had pronounced her mad, she had, of course, been shut up" (292; ch. 27). When Rochester publicly reveals Bertha's existence, he restrains her while Jane and others watch: "he mastered her arms; Grace Poole gave him a cord, and he pinioned them behind her: with more rope, which was at hand, he bound her to a chair" (279; ch. 26). Even if Jane Eyre should happen to go mad, she will not escape the requirements of restraint, as Rochester explains:

> Your mind is my treasure, and if it were broken, it would be my treasure
> still: if you raved, my arms should confine you, and not a strait waistcoat—
> your grasp, even in fury would have a charm for me: if you flew at me as

15. In addition to Shortt, other helpful histories of asylum life and mental illness in nineteenth century England and America include Scull, Tomes (*The Art of Asylum Keeping*), Dwyer, and Wright.

wildly as that woman did this morning, I should receive you in an embrace, at least as fond as it would be restrictive. (286; ch. 27)

Whether confined by a straitjacket, also known as an "English camisole," or by Rochester's fond embrace, the mad and manic body appears to warrant physical restraint (Gilman, 153).

Above the gates of Bedlam, Cibber's sculpture of raving madness faced its counterpart, melancholy madness (see figure 3, p. 24, left). Similarly, once Bertha dies in the fire that she begins, Rochester becomes her would-be mirror image, the second half of Cibber's mad dyad. After the fire, Rochester is "blind, and a cripple": he is missing one eye, has limited sight in the remaining eye, and has had one hand amputated (410; ch. 36). Though Rochester's blindness and missing hand might have seemingly little to do with Bertha's madness, these physical alterations mark him as an icon of melancholy madness.[16] In Cibber's sculpture, the clenched hands and chained wrists of the raving madness figure are juxtaposed with the melancholic's hidden hands, which almost seem to disappear at the wrist. In *Seeing the Insane*, Sander Gilman identifies hidden or obscured hands as a conventional element in the iconography of melancholia. Symbolizing "the melancholic's ineffectuality," the hidden hands are also a common gesture of grieving (Gilman, 14). When Rochester shows Jane his amputation, his missing hand alludes to this tradition of images: "'On this arm I have neither hand nor nails,' he said, drawing the mutilated limb from his breast, and showing it to me" (417; ch. 37). Not only is the hand missing, permanently obscured, but the blinded Rochester also draws his hand from his breast. The gesture of hiding this absence further marks him as melancholic. Jane recognizes this quickly, "I will be [. . .] eyes and hands to you. Cease to look so melancholy" (416; ch. 37).

At her death, Bertha's disabling mental illness is transferred to the body of her husband as physical impairment and blindness, which, in turn, are deployed by Brontë to depict melancholy madness. Paradoxically, Rochester's blindness helps to make madness visible. Rochester, because of his blindness, invokes a notion of the inescapable predominance of interior

16. Admittedly, when Jane learns that Rochester is blind, she thinks to herself, "I had dreaded worse. I had dreaded he was mad" (410; ch. 36). While this statement makes a clear distinction between blindness and madness, I would argue that the madness that Brontë is distinguishing from blindness here is raving madness, not melancholy. Jane's fear or dread of raving madness is evident from her previous reactions to Bertha and to Rochester's earlier threat to "try violence," which she prevents in part by repositioning his hand: "I took hold of his clenched hand, loosened the contorted fingers" (287–86; ch. 27). In *Jane Eyre*, though Bertha's raving madness is certainly "worse" than Rochester's blind melancholy, they share a symbiotic relationship.

FIGURE 3. Cauis Gabriel Cibber's sculpted figures of *right*, "raving madness," and *left*, "melancholy madness" over the gates of Bethlem "Bedlam" Hospital, London. Courtesy of the Harvey Cushing-John Jay Whitney Medical Library at Yale University.

vision, an interiority that threatens to separate the self from the exterior world, just as a severe mental illness might. After his impairment, Rochester retreats to the desolate Ferndean manor-house, and his self-imposed exile there parallels the seclusion of Bertha Mason:

> [O]ne saw that all to him was void darkness. He stretched his right hand (the left arm, the mutilated one, he kept hidden in his bosom): he seemed to wish by touch to gain an idea of what lay around him: he met but vacancy still [. . .]. He relinquished the endeavor, folded his arms, and stood quiet and mute in the rain. (413; ch. 37)

Like an inmate in an asylum yard, Rochester's folded arms, his mute gestures, and his inability to seek cover from the rain illustrate the self-neglect and social isolation associated with melancholy madness.

In a text so occupied with looking and with the way faces look, Rochester's blindness and his "cicatrized visage" threaten to place him outside of the novel's prevailing visual economy (417; ch. 37). Yet the vision of Jane keeps him firmly placed within this purview. After the fire, Rochester becomes a safely specular object, and the invisible Jane can now gaze at Rochester whenever she wishes: "in his countenance I saw a change [. . .] that looked desperate and brooding" (412; ch. 37). Jane's narrative encourages readers not to stare but to gaze with pity upon Rochester's newly disabled body: "It is a pity to see it; and a pity to see your eyes—and the scar of fire on your forehead: and the worst of it is, one is in danger of loving you too well for all this; and making too much of you" (417; ch. 37).[17]

Despite the continuity between Bertha's raving madness and Rochester's melancholy, Rochester's impairments differ in significant ways. While Bertha's madness is congenital and chronic, Rochester's is coincidental and curable. In addition to the associations with melancholy, Jane also compares Rochester's impairments to Nebuchadnezzar's temporary madness:

> It is time some one undertook to rehumanize you [. . .] for I see that you are being metamorphosed into a lion, or something of that sort. You have a *faux air* of Nebuchadnezzar in the fields about you, that is certain: your hair reminds me of eagle's feathers; whether your nails are grown like bird's claws or not, I have not yet noticed. (417)

17. See Garland-Thomson for the distinction between the gaze and the stare—"the gaze intensified" that frames the body as "an icon of deviance" (*Extraordinary Bodies*, 26). See also Shapiro's *No Pity* for a critique of the politics of pity regarding the disabled body.

After Nebuchadnezzar has a prophetic dream of a blasted tree and the dissolution of his kingdom, he undergoes a brief period of madness that transforms him into an animal-like, subhuman figure: "he was driven from men, and did eat grass as oxen, and his [. . .] hairs were grown like eagles' feathers, and his nails like bird claws" (Daniel 4:33).[18] Later, Nebuchadnezzar's reason returns to him. Similarly, Rochester's first marriage proposal to Jane is followed by a lightning blast that destroys a tree, foreshadowing Rochester's future punishment and paralleling Nebuchadnezzar's dream. Just as Nebuchadnezzar returns to reason, Rochester wakes from the dream of blindness and of disability. The closed eyes of the sleeping dreamer seem temporarily blinded. Imprisoning and isolating the dreamer, the dream state represents the threat of inescapable interiority, or madness. Rochester wakes—regains his sight—in time to see his newborn son and more importantly, his resemblance in his son's eyes: "When his first-born was put into his arms, he could see that the boy had inherited his own eyes, as they once were—large, brilliant, and black" (432; ch. 38). Rochester can therefore verify his son's paternity by sight, in direct contrast to the inscrutable paternity of Adèle. His son's eyes reinforce the logic of physiognomy and disability in *Jane Eyre:* a legitimate patrilineal succession corrects the female-based legacy of disability. Rochester's restored vision and the exchanged gaze between Rochester and his son confirm the primacy of hereditary traits and are presented as Rochester's triumph over madness, disability, and the disabling female body. "Normalcy," Lennard Davis notes, "has to protect itself by looking into the maw of disability and then recovering from that glance" ("Constructing Normalcy," 26).[19]

TOWARD A FEMINIST DISABILITY STUDIES THEORY OF EMBODIMENT AND MENTAL ILLNESS

Jane Eyre's Bertha Rochester is mental illness incarnate; however, the very embodied nature of Bertha's madness and the novel's insistent physiognomy

18. Although both Rochester's and Bertha's madness are presented as animal-like states, Rochester's madness is nevertheless nobler. Bertha crouches on all fours like a "clothed hyena" (279; ch. 26). Rochester resembles "some wronged and fettered wild beast or bird, dangerous to approach in his sullen woe. The caged eagle, whose gold-ringed eyes cruelty has extinguished, might look as looked that sightless Samson" (412; ch. 37).

19. See also Mitchell and Snyder on narrative prosthesis: a narrative's "need to restore a disabled body to some semblance of an originary wholeness" (*Narrative Prosthesis,* 6). The birth of Rochester's son at the conclusion of *Jane Eyre* and this resemblance in and of Rochester's eyes is in keeping with Mitchell and Snyder's notion of prosthetic intervention (*Narrative Prosthesis*).

often fail to register in a critical climate occupied with the notions of mental illness as primarily socially-produced and of madness as feminist rebellion. A disability studies reading, in contrast, demands closer attention to physical bodies and to the theories of embodiment that structure the novel. Moreover, the field of disability studies may provide the framework for new and alternate ways of theorizing about mental illness from a feminist perspective.

Victorian notions of physiognomy and madness might seem far removed from the neuroscience and psychopharmacology that compose scientific thinking about mental illness today. Yet all share a basic understanding of the brain as a territory to be mapped. Phrenologists drew comparisons between the occurrence of mental disease and the development of organs of the brain. Today magnetic resonance imaging (MRI) scans depict the enlarged brain ventricles of people diagnosed with schizophrenia, positron emission tomography (PET) scans show increased glucose metabolism in people diagnosed with obsessive compulsive disorder, and on the cellular level neuropharmacology targets dopamine receptors between nerve cells to alleviate the symptoms of severe mental illness. Although there is a certain continuity between the medical imaging processes of phrenology and modern neuroscience, there are also crucial differences, and the types of pharmaceutical interventions that psychiatry practices today are a marked departure from the moral treatment advocated in the nineteenth century. Nevertheless, I do want to suggest that the enduring importance of medical imaging and madness might be productively linked to what Donna Haraway would call the "tropic" nature of corporealization: "bodies are perfectly 'real,' and nothing about corporealization is 'merely' fiction. But corporealization is tropic and historically specific at every layer of its tissues" (*Modest Witness*, 142).[20] Though Bertha Rochester is merely fiction, the system of phrenology and physiognomy in which *Jane Eyre* participates is part of the corporealization of mad bodies in the nineteenth century. One of the goals of a feminist disability studies theory of mental illness should be to examine these scientific tropes of the mad body. Furthermore, as Haraway suggests, it is possible to accept the "tropic and historically specific" nature of corporealization (and of medical language) while simultaneously thinking of bodies (and of mental illness) as "real." Haraway's corporealization conceives of bodies as "material-semiotic" nodes, and while Haraway warns against mistaking the tropic for the nontropic (which she refers to as "corporeal fetish-

---

20. Similarly Wilson and Lewiecki-Wilson have also previously noted the potential contributions that corporeal feminism might make to rhetorical studies of disability ("Disability, Rhetoric, and the Body," 3).

ism"), it is equally important, I would argue, not to forget that the material, the nontropic, the thing-in-itself, does still exist in this model (*Modest Witness,* 141–48). Critical approaches which view mental illness as symbolic or as primarily socially constructed often seem to deny the material conditions of the body. Corporealization recognizes a more complex, tangled relationship between the somatic and the semiotic.

Beginning to think through mental illness using this notion of corporealization will necessitate a pivotal shift from the model of madness-as-rebellion currently circulating within some women's studies scholarship, and it will require a more detailed analysis of some of the central terms and concepts of disability studies. More specifically, a theory of the corporealization of mental illness demands a closer examination of the relationship between "impairment" and "disability." The distinction between impairment and disability, the material body and the socially constructed body, has been a crucial one within disability studies. As Davis explains: "An impairment involves a loss [. . .] of sight, hearing, mobility, mental ability, and so on. But an impairment only becomes a disability when the ambient society creates environments with barriers—affective, sensory, cognitive, or architectural" ("Constructing Normalcy," 506–7). What Davis describes here may be termed the impairment-disability system. Like Gayle Rubin's configuration of the sex-gender system—the process by which biological sex is transformed into cultural gender—the impairment-disability system is the process by which biological impairment is transformed into cultural disability. This configuration of the impairment-disability system has been particularly useful for people in the disability rights movement, who combat stigma and who protect the civil rights of people with disabilities: by shifting attention away from the biological (impairment) to the social (disability), one can effectively identify and address discrimination.

However, while the politically strategic distinction between impairment and disability has been particularly useful, it also has its limits. On one level the impairment-disability system enacts a separation between an accidental, physical body (impairment) and a transcendent, social identity (disability). The subsequent focus on the social realm privileges a transcendent civil identity and obscures or represses physical impairment. If impairment occurs in the body and disability occurs in society, then this posits an ideal, disembodied social subject who seems to remain intact, unaltered, even "normal," despite impairment. The language of the Americans with Disabilities Act evokes this ideal: the subject (American) is the stable core that exists independently from the accidental body (with Disability). However, the impairments of severe mental illness challenge the normalizing logic of this model. Using a wheelchair does not disrupt the notion of "American" quite so much as being delusional does. For example, although the physical barriers that exist for wheelchair users are very real and pervasive, they are quite different in nature from mental competency requirements that restrict the abstract right to vote or to refuse medication. The barriers confronting people with severe mental illnesses and cognitive disabilities are more complicated because they involve the concept of the self that is the very foundation of our political system. As Susan Squier writes, "Not only does the discourse of the democratic citizen privilege the intact and autonomous self, but the discourse of medicine figures mental illness as an irreparable, symbolically freighted breach in self-determination" (40).

Theorizing about mental illness from a feminist disability studies perspective, I argue, demands a different focus on impairment. This repositioning, because it requires a shift toward medical models of illness, is not without its risks. As Simi Linton correctly points out, medical definitions of disability in the past have functioned to keep disability "within the purview of the medical establishment, to keep it a personal matter and 'treat' the condition and the person with the condition rather than 'treating' the social processes and policies that constrict disabled people's lives" (11). Borrowing a term from Eve Sedgwick's *Epistemology of the Closet*, Rosemarie Garland-Thomson also points out that medical definitions of impairments have fostered a "minoritizing" view of disability as private tragedy rather than positioning disability as a universal problem affecting everyone ("Feminist Theory," 282).

Adopting a medical model also poses other risks. Thinking about physical impairment, in particular congenital physical impairment, is often characterized by concomitant reductive assumptions about biological bodies. This is the case, for example, with Bertha Mason's madness in *Jane Eyre* and with the definitive powers attributed to pathological genes today. In order to steer clear of the pitfalls of essentialism and biological determinism when conceptualizing mental illness as physical impairment, it is useful to begin with the understanding that bodies are not simply born, but made. As Haraway explains, "bodies as subjects of knowledge are material-semiotic generative nodes. Their boundaries materialize in social interactions; 'objects' like bodies do not preexist as such" ("The Biopolitics," 208). Feminist science studies and feminist examinations of the body can offer us the conceptual modes and the critical language to begin a rigorous denaturalization of impairment within disability studies. In *Bodies That Matter*, Judith Butler revised how we think of the sex-gender system—arguing in part that "sex" is not the static, natural category out of which the social construction of gender emerges. Similarly, reexamining the impairment-disability system, and moreover repositioning mental illness as a physical impairment, seems appropriate and particularly necessary when we speak of severe and chronic mental illnesses within the disability studies rubric.

It is possible, in other words, to begin with the premise that mental illness is a neurobiological disorder and still remain committed to a feminist and a disability studies agenda, and it is important that feminists and disability theorists begin to think about mental illness in these terms.[21] The elision of the physical component of Bertha Rochester's madness in contemporary criticism is not coincidental but is symptomatic of a larger, cultural anxiety surrounding mental illness. This anxiety, I suspect, emerges from the impossible task of reconciling medical discourses of mental illness, which describe the symbolic failure of the self-determined individual, and the competing discourses of democratic citizenship, which imagine will and self as inviolable—a tension that lies at the heart of both liberal individualism and the impairment-disability system. "Democracy," Davis writes, "needs the illusion of equality, and equality needs the fiction of the equal or average citizen" (*Bending over Backwards*, 110). In *Frontiers of Justice*, Martha Nussbaum begins her examination of John Rawls's social contract theory, which is based on the assumption that citizens are "free, equal, and independent," with a similar insight: "We cannot extend the core idea of inviolability and the related idea of reciprocity to people with severe physical and mental impairments without calling these features into question, thus severing ties with the classical social contract tradition" (119). Of course, if one insists that mental illness is a myth, that mental illness does not exist as a material, physical impairment, then one avoids such thorny problems. In this sense, antipsychiatry and conceptions of madness as feminist rebellion are essentially conservative: they do not require a radical rethinking of our central political principles. Tempting though it may be to fall back on

---

21. For many reasons, this is a difficult but necessary statement to make. In a poignant essay about a close friend who has schizophrenia, Prendergast characterizes this dilemma well when she writes, "For an academic like myself with generally poststructuralist leanings, to think of schizophrenia as a 'disease' makes me sound at best conservative and at worst theoretically unsound. I am therefore left wandering far from my usual terrain to find language with which I can address the dilemmas and gaps in understanding that mental illness presents" (190). As Prendergast's essay ultimately illustrates, to conceive of schizophrenia as a "disease," or of severe mental illness as a physically based impairment, does not necessarily result in a conservative, biologically reductive theory of mental illness. On the contrary, to be unable to theorize mental illness as a disease unduly limits our strategies of political and philosophical engagement. Just as Butler has complicated the notion of sex in the sex-gender system, so too can we conceive of a more complex, nuanced, and politically effective notion of mental illness within the impairment-disability system.

concepts that imagine mental illness as purely socially produced, the true radical challenge that Bertha Rochester represents is far more complex. Ideally, this is a challenge that a next wave of madwoman theory, one based on the insights of both feminism and disability studies theory, will begin to address.

THE BLINDMAN IN
THE CLASSIC

Feminisms, Ocularcentrism,
and *Jane Eyre*

DAVID BOLT

THE IDEOLOGICAL BASES of *Jane Eyre* and Rudyard Kipling's *The Light That Failed* (1891) are, according to a number of classic expositions, diametrically opposed. Sandra Gilbert and Susan Gubar commend *Jane Eyre,* for instance, as a work of "rebellious feminism" (338), while George Holbrook Jackson asserts that the "keynote" of *The Light That Failed* is "the love of the masculine life" (234). Indeed, far from being commended as a belief in the equality of the sexes, Kipling's "pugnacious philosophy," with its "insistence upon clean health and a courageous and dangerous life," is said to make "men more like men and women more like women" (Holbrook Jackson, 234). In this chapter I probe the received ideological contrast between the two classic novels, emphasizing an alliance that becomes manifest in the characterization of the blindman. The contention is that many feminist commendations of *Jane Eyre* are underpinned by patriarchal attitudes toward visual impairment that are also found in *The Light That Failed.* What is more, though explicit in *Jane Eyre* and implicit in *The Light That Failed,* both are grounded in the same epistemology as John Milton's *Samson Agonistes* (1671). This intertextuality is notable because, notwithstanding the fact that Milton wrote his greatest works subsequent to the onset of his own visual impairment, *Samson Agonistes* is ocularcentric in the extreme; it is indicative of a dominant visual discourse, claiming that light, the "prime work" of God, "so necessary is to life" that the existence of those without access constitutes a "living death" (lines 70–100).[1]

The functionality of these depictions may be explained in accordance with the Derridean perspective on disability suggested by Mairian Corker and Tom Shakespeare, that although normativism and disability are antagonistic in relation to each other, the definition of the former is dependent on that of the latter: "a person without an impairment can define him/herself as "normal" only in opposition to that which s/he is not—a person with an impairment" (*Disability/Postmodernity: Embodying Disability Theory,* 7). In these terms, alterity is fundamental to the construction of the Self because, as Jacques Derrida puts it in *Of Grammatology,* without the non-presence of the other that is inscribed in the meaning of the present, familiarity would not appear. Thus, following Corker's and Shakespeare's reading of disability as a construct that is not excluded from normativism but integral to its very assertion, I argue that the blindman in the classic is fundamental to the characterization of his sighted counterparts. After all, notwithstanding Rey Chow's assertion that "In terms of plot structure, the fire removes the impediment, the mad woman" (145), the simultaneity of Bertha's suicide and Rochester's blindness is read by Julia Miele Rodas as a migration of one identity into another ("Brontë's *Jane Eyre*"). The suggestion is that the blindman becomes for Jane what the madwoman has been for Rochester, a disabled Other in relation to which the normative Self can emerge.

Binary oppositions are famously criticized in Derrida's *Of Grammatology* because of the way in which one term is privileged over the other, the second term being typically thought of as derivative, inferior, and even parasitic, meaning that the first term, the one more associated with the phallus and the logos, is rendered original and superior. As well as to binary oppositions such as man and woman, male and female, speech and writing, identity and difference, fullness and emptiness, mastery and submission, life and death, the criticism is applicable to normativism and disability—and, more specifically, for the purpose of this chapter, to the sighted and the blind. On the basis of the assertion that deconstruction is an openness toward the other (Derrida, "Deconstruction and the Other," 124), I venture a deconstructive reading insofar as I invert these and a number of related binary oppositions, focusing on secondary constructs in order to reveal their functionality in relation to primary counterparts. Rather than being ignored, incidental

---

1. Milton (1608–74) lost his sight at the age of forty-four (c. 1652). He published *Paradise Lost* in 1667 and *Paradise Regained* and *Samson Agonistes* in 1671.

features such as those that describe Brontë's Rochester (423–24; ch. 36)[2] and Kipling's Dick Heldar (155; ch. 16) as "stone blind" are exposed as a basis for a link between sight and vitality. I should stress that my criticism here is of the ocularcentric subject position and not necessarily of people who have unimpaired vision, for the sighted are a construct just like the blind.

Mapping the quasi lifespan of the blindman, the first section of the chapter focuses on alterity, the second on castration, and the third on melancholia, revealing ocularcentric assumptions about beauty, sexuality, and happiness, respectively. In the first stage of this tragic development, the blindman is differentiated and diminished in grotesque portrayals of haptic perception, the implication being that beauty is naturally—if not solely—perceived by visual means. This virtual castration becomes more Freudian in the second stage, for the blindman's disempowerment creates a spectacle that not only empowers but also arouses the unseen spectator. The resonance with Freudian theory deepens still further in the third stage, as the loss of the capacity for love develops into the various mental features of mourning and indeed melancholia. It is as though the blindman comes to internalize various ocularcentric beliefs, the result being an existential emptiness in relation to which the lives of the sighted characters appear full. Put briefly, interpreting stone blindness as a preliminary of sighted vitality, I subvert the hierarchies of attractiveness over unattractiveness, sexuality over asexuality, spectator over spectacle, happiness over misery, light over darkness, and life over death.

First, though, I must acknowledge that several binary oppositions are subverted within *Jane Eyre,* as plainness triumphs over beauty, poverty over wealth, submission over mastery, and, insofar as the female protagonist narrates her own story rather than being secondary in relation to a male narrator, woman over man. Accordingly, the text has come to be "considered one of the first major examples of a woman overcoming patriarchal and class domination in modern times" (Chow, 144). Nevertheless, criticized by Toril Moi for leaving patriarchal aesthetics intact, Gilbert and Gubar's classic feminist commendation of the novel is problematized by Dale Spender's point about epistemology:

> [F]eminist knowledge is based on the premise that the experience of all human beings is valid and must not be excluded from our understandings, whereas patriarchal knowledge is based on the premise that the experience

---

2. The version of the primary text referred to in this chapter is Charlotte Brontë, *Jane Eyre* (London: Penguin Popular Classics, 1994).

of only half the human population needs to be taken into account and the resulting version can be imposed on the other half. (5)

The problem on which I focus is that Brontë's portrayals of alterity, castration, and melancholia are patriarchal insofar as they are based on ocularcentric epistemology and thus unappreciative of the experience of people who have visual impairments. Male and female roles may well be inverted in the novel, but the underpinning hierarchies of normativism over disability and "the sighted" over "the blind" remain intact. The sustainment of this state of affairs in some feminist expositions is indicative of the fact that writings of the most eminent scholars may prove deficient in relation to disability, that as Rosemarie Garland-Thomson puts it, feminists, like everyone else, including disabled people, have been acculturated to stigmatize those of us whose bodies are deemed aberrant ("Feminist Theory," 286). That is not to say that I impose ideology on the text, a criticism aimed at some feminist and postcolonial readings (Beaty, 184). Instead, informed by the assertion that Gilbert and Gubar's reading of *Jane Eyre* "would be more formidable if it did not implicitly (and unnecessarily) claim that it is a reading of Brontë's 'intention'" (Beaty, 150), the focus is on intertextuality and character functionality.

BEAUTY AND THE HAND OF THE BEHOLDER

Though the maxim that beauty is in the eye of the beholder pertains primarily to the debate about what constitutes attractiveness, it also reduces the likelihood of cultural associations with those of us who have visual impairments. Vision is supposed to be a necessary condition of beauty in *The Light That Failed* when the sightless protagonist Dick Heldar responds to Bessie's advice about his appearance by saying, "Good gracious, child, do you imagine that I think of what becomes me these days?" (173–78; ch. 14). In writings from as far back as Plato the "straight profile of the Greek statue was usually assumed to be the ideal human face. One of its many assets was that it did not resemble the faces of rabbits, goats, apes, frogs, or any other ignoble animals" (Etcoff, 42). If beauty means not looking like a beast, Kipling's protagonist is extricated when he is said to have "hit his shins against the stove, and this suggested to him that it would be better to crawl on all-fours, one hand in front of him" (139; ch. 11). He is described by Torpenhow as being "like a dog" (139; ch. 11), by Bessie as a "beast" (130; ch. 10, and 133; ch. 11), and by the narrator as a "stub-bearded, bowed creature"

(173; ch. 14). Brontë's notion of visual impairment is similarly animalistic, because alluding to the way in which Samson is likened to an eagle (*SA*, line 1695), Jane thinks of Rochester as a "caged eagle, whose gold-ringed eyes cruelty has extinguished'; she is reminded of "some wronged and fettered wild beast or bird, dangerous to approach in his sullen woe" (426; ch. 37). The animalism is sublimated in a general appearance of unkemptness when, with allusion to the way in which the "redundant locks" of Samson are depicted "clustring down" (*SA*, lines 568–69), the "thick and long uncut locks" of Rochester suggest that he is "being metamorphosed into a lion, or something of that sort" and his hair is likened to "eagles' feathers" (431; ch. 37). Identified elsewhere as a problem with Brontë's portrayal of ethnicity (e.g., Spivak, "Three Women's Texts and a Critique of Imperialism"), the blurring of the boundary between the human and the animal invokes the notion of a lower evolutionary status; it implies a sense of animalistic alterity around the blindman and thereby defines the legitimate subject position in relation to the sense of sight.

The five senses are sometimes categorized in relation to a binary opposition between distance and contact. The distance senses of sight and hearing have objects that are spatially separate from the perceiver, while the contact senses of smell, taste, and touch have objects that impinge on the body before perception. The significant point that Jonathan Rée raises about the Aristotelian division is that, "epistemologically and ethically more respectable," the distance senses are "nobler, purer, more detached, and perhaps—by some standards—more masculine than the contact senses" (34). In accordance with this line of thinking, vision might be conceived as a necessary condition of not only the possession but also the perception of beauty. The logical outcome is embodied in the sightless-unsightly pair, a trope that, while not exemplified, is implicit in both *The Light That Failed* and *Jane Eyre:* much as Dick's loss of vision is followed by his union with Bessie Broke, the "wrong woman" (184; ch. 14), who is described as "singularly dull" (130; ch. 10) and a "little fiend" (136; ch. 11), and who is associated with "hussies, trollops; and the like" (176; ch. 14), Rochester's loss of vision is followed by his union with the original plain Jane. The tenor of such a union is that one partner's lack in conventional outward beauty is not an issue when the other lacks the sense by which it is perceived. In *Jane Eyre,* according to Gilbert and Gubar, the scenario offers an "optimistic portrait of an egalitarian relationship" because, "now that they are equals, they can (though one is blind) see and speak even beyond the medium of the flesh" (368–69). Kate Flint departs only slightly from the classic feminist reading by claiming that visual impairment is portrayed as a "form of punishment" that ultimately proves to be a means of illuminating the "inward eye" (*The Victorians and the Visual Imagination,* 80), but the problem is in the very premise that conventional outward beauty cannot be appreciated by those of us who have visual impairments. After all, putting aside the fact that most people who have visual impairments are able to perceive visually, that according to Allan Dodds, only five or ten percent of the legally blind are "unable to make out anything more than changes in light levels" (1), the notion that outward beauty cannot be appreciated via haptic means is patently erroneous. This idea of beauty is highly contentious, but people are frequently considered attractive due to the "curve of their lips or the slimness of their waists" (Etcoff, 71), qualities that, like the Grecian neck and bust of Brontë's Blanche Ingram, may be perceived by touch as well as sight. This form of beauty is no less in the hand than in the eye of the beholder.

While those of us who have visual impairments may simply perceive beauty by haptic rather than visual means, a sense of alterity is evoked by the motif of the groping blindman, which refers to acts of searching, walking, and lecherousness. This motif is applied in *The Light That Failed* to portray the way in which Dick locates a lost item as well as the way in which he walks. He is said not only to have "groped among his canvases" (161; ch. 13) but also to have "groped back to his chair" (159; ch. 13) and to "grope along the corridors" (167; ch. 14). Insofar as walking is displaced in favor of groping, Kipling and Brontë unify in their application of the motif: akin to Kipling's protagonist, Brontë's Rochester is said to have "groped his way back to the house" (427; ch. 37). It is a sense of lecherousness, however, that underpins the moment when Rochester is said to have "groped" until Jane "arrested his wandering hand" (428; ch. 37). This intransitive use of the verb *groped* indicates that Rochester is searching "blindly," but connotations of the more colloquial meaning are sustained by the reference to his wandering hand. Thus, although ignored as a means of perceiving beauty, the sense of touch is exaggerated to the point of grotesqueness as a signifier of alterity.

The lecherous aspect of the groping blindman is of concern because, more than evoking a sense of unattractiveness, it perpetuates the idea of a blind Other who is out to impregnate the sighted Self. Illustrating Terry Eagleton's assertion that for Brontë "almost all human relationships are power-struggles" (*Myths of Power,* 30), the grope becomes a lecherous grip and results in a personification of contagiousness when Jane refers to Rochester by saying, "The muscular hand broke from my custody; my arm was seized, my shoulder, neck, waist—I was entwined and gathered to him" (428; ch. 37). The implicit warning against the dishonorable intentions of the Other illustrates three elements of personified contagiousness: first, irregularity is evoked by the way in which Rochester's hand is objectified almost to the point of disembodiment, as if somehow able to reach further than those of a sighted man; second, strength is denoted by the adjective *muscular*; and third, aggression is conveyed by the fact that Jane is the object of Rochester's desire and therefore rendered sexually vulnerable in his grasp, as well as by the verb *seized*. This personification of contagiousness corresponds with a passage in *The Light That Failed:*

> [Dick] was beginning to learn, not for the first time in his experience, that kissing is a cumulative poison. The more you get of it, the more you want. Bessie gave the kiss promptly, whispering, as she did so, "I was so angry I rubbed out that picture with the turpentine. You aren't angry, are you?"
>
> "What? Say that again." The man's hand had closed on her wrist.
>
> "I rubbed it out with turps and the knife," faltered Bessie. "I thought you'd only have to do it over again. You did do it over again, didn't you? Oh, let go of my wrist; you're hurting me. [. . .] I only meant to do it in fun. You aren't going to hit me?"
>
> "Hit you! No! Let's think."
>
> He did not relax his hold upon her wrist but stood staring at the carpet. (182; ch. 14)

First, irregularity is implicit when Dick is referred to as the man with a hold that he chooses not to relax but that closes on Bessie's wrist automatically, the man who cannot see and yet stands staring at the carpet. Second, Dick's physical strength is apparent in Bessie's assertion that he is hurting her. Third, reminiscent of not only *Jane Eyre* but also the way in which Samson feels a "sudden rage to tear" Dalila "joint by joint" (*SA*, line 953), Kipling invokes the threat of sexual assault by linking the cumulative poison of desire with anger, force, and violence. Dick's exclamation indicates that striking Bessie is not his intention, but the sexual aspect of rape being secondary to the violent, the point to note is that she is not released from his grip while the alternatives are considered. Put briefly, when portrayed as a characteristic of the blindman, touch becomes a grope and ultimately a lecherous grip.

The important detail to note about grotesque depictions of haptic perception is that they are not sexual but hypersexual, which is why Samson, the forebear of both Rochester and Dick, is described by Derrida as "a bit like all the blind, like all one-eyed men or cyclopes," as a "sort of phalloid image, an unveiled sex from head to toe, vaguely obscene and disturbing" (*Memoirs of the Blind,* 106). The hypersexuality is predicated on the notion that the "hand of the blind ventures forth alone or disconnected," that "it feels its way, it gropes," "as if a lidless eye had opened at the tip of the fingers, as if one eye too many had just grown right next to the nail, a single eye, the eye of a cyclops" (*Memoirs of the Blind,* 3). Because the hand of the blindman is animalistic, verging on the monstrous, and therefore classically adverse to beauty, it signifies alterity in relation to which vision appears antithetical and thus normative as a means of perceiving beauty. Hence, according to Freudian theory, the blinding of Oedipus is equivalent to castration, constituting the loss of the sense in which beauty resides and through which desire is excited. Grounded in such ocularcentric epistemology, as is demonstrable when Derrida adds that Samson is a "figure of castration, a castration-figure" (*Memoirs of the Blind,* 106), the sexuality of the blindman appears distinct from that of his sighted counterparts. In effect, then, the grotesque depiction of haptic perception is a preliminary for the symbolic castrations by which the blindman is defined.

COMPLEX CASTRATION

Bearing in mind that in *The Light That Failed,* although "the blindness has made him rather muscular" (144; ch. 12), Dick pictures Maisie "being won by another man, stronger than himself" (140; ch. 11), it is notable that one of Charles Rycroft's various definitions of the word *castration* pertains to "demoralization" in respect of the masculine role (15). The applicability of this definition to *Jane Eyre* is evident in Georgina Kleege's description of Rochester as a "mighty man" who is "brought low': "Once allpowerful, and rather arrogant about it, he is left feeble" (70). Donald Kirtley goes so far as to assert that the castration theme is pronounced, that "until his sight returns, Rochester's masculine vigor is largely held in abeyance, after the fashion of the defeated Samson, with whom Jane identifies her sightless lover" (66). These references to being brought low and held in obeisance may be said to incriminate Rochester's sighted counterparts, thereby revealing a conceptual link with Jeremy Bentham's Panopticon (Bozovic), the essence of the idea being that control can be affected by the very notion of an unseen seer.

That the controlling figure of the Panopticon is not only housed but also represented by a phallic inspection tower invokes another aspect of second-wave feminism from which this chapter departs. I do not deny that the power relationship raises an instructive parallel with Laura Mulvey's concern in "Visual Pleasure and Narrative Cinema" about phallocentrism, that it is paradoxically dependent on the image of the castrated woman, for the political power of ocularcentrism depends on the symbolic castration of the blind. But the dynamic is more complex in *Jane Eyre* and *The Light That Failed,* where it is the blindman's lack that produces vision as a symbolic presence. Indeed, because ocularcentrism is advantageous to the sighted female characters, yet dependent on the castration of the blindman for order and meaning, the very application of Mulvey's feminist theory creates something of a paradox.

The fact that Jane associates Rochester with Samson, a man whose downfall is brought about by a woman, foreshadows the most patriarchal of all psychoanalytic notions, for in "the first instance" the term *castrating* applies to "women who suffer from PENIS-ENVY and therefore disparage or compete with men" (Rycroft, 15). Bearing in mind the claim that it is Jane's aim "simply to strengthen herself, to make herself an equal of the world Rochester represents" (Gilbert and Gubar, 368), we might be tempted to respond to any suggestion of a castrating figure by pointing out that the diminishment of vision is linked with that of strength by male and female characters alike: the Innkeeper tells Jane that Rochester is "helpless, indeed—blind" (424; ch. 36); Jane says, "[T]he powerlessness of the strong man touched my heart to the quick" (434; ch. 37); and Rochester confronts Jane by saying, "You know I was proud of my strength: but what is it now, when I must give it over to foreign guidance, as a child does its weakness?" (441; ch. 37). The point to remember about these and other such assertions of weakness, however, is that all appear within Jane's narrative. This scenario resonates with *The Light That Failed* insofar as it is Maisie who finds Dick "down and done for—masterful no longer, but rather a little abject; neither an artist stronger than she, nor a man to be looked up to— only some blind one that sat in a chair and seemed on the point of crying" (159; ch. 13). Kipling's intransitive application of the verb *crying* connotes the same infantilization as the simile that Brontë draws between blindness and the "weakness" of a child (441; ch. 37). Likewise, a comparison with the emotion that touches Jane's "heart to the quick" (434; ch. 37) can be found when, "filled with pity most startlingly distinct from love," Kipling's Maisie is "more sorry" for Dick than she has "ever been for any one in her life" (159; ch. 13). Thus, corresponding with the patriarchal notion of the castrating woman, in both novels it is the blindman's prospective lover who conjures up his disempowerment.

The notion of a link between vision and the masculine role raises issues of spectatorial identification, for Mulvey's work on cinema has defined the male protagonist as the bearer of the spectator's gaze, meaning that he frequently emerges as the representative of power in relation to woman as the spectacle. When applied to Brontë's novel this dynamic becomes inverted because Jane, rather than Rochester, emerges as the representative of power, the sighted character with whom the sighted Implied Reader identifies. This power relationship is alluded to in Sally Shuttleworth's study, as well as in Kleege's assertion that for Jane, "Rochester's blindness allows her to rise to power" (71), representing a deviation from Gilbert and Gubar's claim that Jane's power is drawn from within, "rather than from inequity, disguise, deception" (369). The departure from the classic feminist reading is sustainable because, implicit when Jane refers to Rochester by saying, "I stayed my step, almost my breath, and stood to watch him—to examine him, myself unseen, and alas! to him invisible" (426; ch. 37), it is through disguise and deception that the unseen spectator ensures not only inequity but also authority over the unseeing spectacle. The nature of this authority invokes a conceptual link with the Panopticon because, just as anyone who entered Bentham's central inspection tower could automatically assume authority over the unseeing prisoners (Bozovic), Jane assumes authority over Rochester and Kipling's Bessie does likewise over Dick: "There were droppings of food all down the front of his coat; the mouth, under the ragged ill-grown beard, drooped sullenly; the forehead was lined and contracted; and on the lean temples the hair was a dusty, indeterminate colour that might or might not have been called grey" (177; ch. 14). Dick's lack of concern for his appearance is typical of the blindman and provides a spectacle for Bessie's evaluating gaze. He is reduced to what Michel Foucault calls an "object of information" (*Discipline and Punish,* 200). Thus, although the scenario might be interpreted as subversive, a feminist reversal of the female character and the evaluating male gaze by which she is rendered passive, a concurrent implication is that people who do not have visual impairments are active and authoritative in relation to those of us who do have visual impairments.

There are several theoretical usages of the word *castration* that pertain to sexual matters explicitly, for, as well as to the removal of testes, the concept refers to "loss of the capacity" for erotic pleasure, or loss of the penis, as in the threats used to deter boys from masturbating (Rycroft, 15). The naming of Dick Heldar (i.e., penis handler) invokes the cultural link between blindness and masturbation, but both Kipling and Brontë evoke diminishments in respect of the capacity for erotic pleasure in their construction of the blindman. When extending the analysis of Rochester's castration into the area of erotic pleasure, then, one might consider Derrida's assertion that Samson loses "every phallic attribute or substitute, his hair and then his eyes" (*Memoirs of the Blind,* 104). This reference to Rochester's forebear is illustrative of the way in which phallocentrism and ocularcentrism are not only comparable but also interchangeable. In the unconscious, Karl Abraham claims, the "fixed stare" is "often equivalent to an erection" (352), a notion that informs and is informed by the idea that blindness is equivalent to castration. This dynamic is illustrated when Jane stays her step, almost her breath, and fixes Rochester in her stare:

> He descended the one step, and advanced slowly and gropingly towards the grass plot. Where was his daring stride now? Then he paused, as if he knew not which way to turn. He lifted his hand and opened his eyelids; gazed blank, and with a straining effort, on the sky, and toward the amphitheatre of trees: one saw that all to him was void darkness. He stretched his right hand (the left arm, the mutilated one, he kept hidden in his bosom); he seemed to wish by touch to gain an idea of what lay around him: he met but vacancy still; for the trees were some yards off where he stood. He relinquished the endeavour, folded his arms, and stood quiet and mute in the rain, now falling fast on his uncovered head. (426; ch. 37)

Given that he has already "stretched forth his hand as if to feel whether it rained," it might seem rather perplexing that Rochester should proceed with an "uncovered head," that he is referred to as "a man without a hat," but in psychoanalytic terms any such lack can be interpreted as a symbolic castration. It is therefore quite pertinent that Jane's "sightless Samson" (426; ch. 37) is rendered quiet and mute, that he is said to have descended without daring, to have moved slowly and gropingly. This castration is integral to its symbolic opposite in Jane because, while interpreting Rochester's behavior as helplessness, she refuses to assist him. Rather than relinquishing her fixed stare, her unconscious erection, she ponders and assumes spectatorial authority, as is illustrated by *her* assertion that Rochester *knew not* which way to turn—that is, by her ocularcentric appropriation of his epistemology.

The curiosity factor of the unseeing spectacle is evidently not always as overt as when Samson is forced to make "sport with blind activity" (*SA,* line 1328). The fact that Rochester is fixed in Jane's gaze as he merely steps outside his home illustrates that the most routine behavior of the blind-man is a source of pleasure for the unseen spectator. This pleasure is also illustrated in *The Light That Failed* by Maisie's reluctance to betray her presence:

Dick rose and began to feel his way across the room, touching each table and chair as he passed. Once he caught his foot on a rug, and swore, dropping on his knees to feel what the obstruction might be. Maisie remembered him walking in the Park as though all the earth belonged to him, tramping up and down her studio two months ago, and flying up the gangway of the Channel steamer. The beating of her heart was making her sick, and Dick was coming nearer, guided by the sound of her breathing. She put out a hand mechanically to ward him off or to draw him to herself, she did not know which. It touched his chest, and he stepped back as though he had been shot. (158; ch. 13)

While it is unlikely that someone who has a visual impairment would drop to her or his knees in order to identify a rug, especially in such a familiar setting, the point is that when Dick, the blindman, does so, Maisie is not only fascinated but also disgusted to the point of nausea, so overwhelmed that she can "hardly move her lips." Indeed, having "pressed herself up into a corner of the room," when she does "put out a hand," she does so "mechanically" (157–58; ch. 13). More than illustrating what Foucault calls the power of Panopticism (*Discipline and Punish,* 200), this combination of silence and visibility may be explained in terms of *jouissance,* which Bruce Fink defines as a pleasure that is "excessive, leading to a sense of being overwhelmed or disgusted, yet simultaneously providing a source of fascination" (xi). In these terms, Maisie's gaze—that is, her unconscious erection—lasts until the climactic point at which Dick responds as though he has been shot.

The interchangeability of phallocentric and ocularcentric perspectives illustrates Mary Devereaux's point that "the male gaze is not always male, but it is always male dominated" (339). Insofar as Jane's stare falls on Rochester and Maisie's on Dick, the traditional roles of the male gaze are reversed by Brontë and Kipling alike. However, the resulting depiction is ocularcentric and thus essentially patriarchal, because the reversal is predicated on the victim being unable to see. The subordinate role is feminine but allocated to Rochester and Dick owing to their symbolic castration; the dominant role is masculine but allocated to Jane and Maisie owing to their symbolic erections. Therefore, while the teleology of these inverted roles may be praised as a reaction to the objectification of women, we must recognize that a simultaneous point is being made about desire in men who have visual impairments. As if always scopophilic, love, the most profound of life experiences, becomes a superficial activity for which vision is requisite. Accordingly, Rochester tells Jane, "[I]f I were what I once was, I would try to make you care—but—a sightless block!" (430, ch. 37), much as Dick thinks of Maisie and says, "I couldn't be any use to her now" (140; ch. 11). The lamentation that underpins these claims is that Rochester and Dick are unable to deliver that in which Jane and Maisie are consequently unable to be caught: the male gaze. The patriarchal implication of this lament is that scopophilia is as necessary in male heterosexuality as is exhibitionism in the female counterpart—an example of ocularcentrism that renders male heterosexuality beyond the blindman.

The diminished capacity for erotic pleasure is a preliminary for the construct of dependency by which love is displaced in *Jane Eyre*. Rochester is "profoundly frustrated in his efforts to develop independence," according to Kirtley, and "consequently becomes almost wholly dependent on Jane, who plays the part of the good nurse until his sight is restored" (65). However, it should not be forgotten that Jane "enjoys" her new power over Rochester, as Kleege points out, because "his dependence on her makes him all the more attractive" (71), meaning that her actions are not selfless, the dependency is not parasitic:

> Mr Rochester continued blind the first two years of our union: perhaps it was that circumstance that drew us so very near—that knit us so very close: for I was then his vision, as I am still his right hand. Literally, I was (what he often called me) the apple of his eye. He saw nature—he saw books through me; and never did I weary of gazing for his behalf, and of putting into words, the effect of field, tree, town, river, cloud, sunbeam—of the landscape before us; of the weather round us—and impressing by sound on his ear what light could no longer stamp on his eye. Never did I weary of reading to him; never did I weary of conducting him where he wished to go: of doing for him what he wished to be done. And there was a pleasure in my services, most full, most exquisite, even though sad—because he claimed these services without painful shame or damping humiliation. He loved me so truly that he knew no reluctance in profiting by my attendance; he felt I loved him so fondly, that to yield that attendance was to indulge my sweetest wishes. (446; ch. 38)

Seemingly as a result of visual impairment, there are numerous services that Rochester requires of Jane, the execution of which she finds pleasurable in a "most full, most exquisite" way, thereby illustrating something of Albert Memmi's assertion that "there is in almost every dependency, even if it is apparently parasitic, some sort of symbiotic relationship" (66). The trouble is that Jane's conception of dependency does not accommodate Rochester's subjectivity. Whereas the dialectic of dependency results from a relationship in which the dependent is a provider and the provider a dependent, Jane does not recognize Rochester as a provider. The dependency is only reciprocal insofar as Jane receives pleasure and power in the act of giving. What lies beyond this dependency is a contentious point because, while stating with conviction that Rochester "loved" her "so truly," Jane is somewhat tentative in saying, "[H]e felt I loved him so fondly." Indeed, when articulating her own position in the relationship, Jane qualifies the verb *loved* with *felt*, displaces the adverb *truly* in favor of *fondly* and omits usage of the first person pronoun altogether. That is to say, she diminishes the emotion on three counts. Moreover, as is implicit in her dismay at the absence of "painful shame," "damping humiliation," and "reluctance in profiting" by "attendance," Jane cannot respect the man whom she ascribes no self-respect.

In *The Light That Failed*, Dick's diminished capacity for love is similarly exposed by a construct of parasitic dependency. Having lost his relationship with Maisie when he lost his sight, Dick initiates a relationship with Bessie by saying, "I'm afraid I must ask you to help me home" (174; ch. 14), reflecting later that she "can't care, and it's a toss-up whether she comes again or not, but if money can buy her to look after me she shall be bought" (179; ch. 14). What is more, echoing the moment in *Jane Eyre* when the eponymous protagonist addresses Rochester by saying, "I will be your neighbour, your nurse, your housekeeper" (430; ch. 37), Dick says to Bessie, "You'd better come and housekeep for me then" (180 ch. 14). There is some evidence that Bessie regards Dick as both provider and dependent when Kipling's narrator says, "Early in the afternoon time she came, because there was no young man in her life just then, and she thought of material advantages which would allow her to be idle for the rest of her days" (180; ch. 14). But that is not to say that her dependency is unlike Jane's, or that it is purely materialistic, for Dick's loss of sight instills in Bessie a "keen sense of new-found superiority" (175; ch. 14), the "utter misery and self-abandonment of the man appealed to her, and at the bottom of her heart lay the wicked feeling that he was humbled and brought low who had once humbled her" (177; ch. 14). Thus, like *Jane Eyre*, *The Light That Failed* is indicative of the way in which the blindman's dependency is integral to power and pleasure on which the sighted counterparts become dependent.

THE MELANCHOLIA OF BLINDNESS

The loss of the capacity for love, which is a precursor for the conception of parasitic dependency, is listed by Freud as a distinguishing mental feature of melancholia ("Mourning and Melancholia," 252). This detail is significant here because Brontë's Rochester is repeatedly ascribed "melancholy" (430, 433, 436; ch. 37), foreshadowing an assertion in *The Light That Failed* about the melancholy of blindness being a "weight of intolerable darkness" (140; ch. 11). In fact, not only the loss of the capacity for love but all the mental features of melancholia are relevant to the trope of the blindman. This list of mental features includes a profoundly painful dejection, an end of interest in the outside world, an inhibition of all activity, and what Freud calls a "lowering of the self-regarding feelings to a degree that finds utterance in self-reproaches and self-revilings, and culminates in a delusional expectation of punishment" ("Mourning and Melancholia," 252). Rochester's loss of the capacity for love is illustrated when he supposes that for Jane he can "entertain none but fatherly feelings" (430; ch. 37); his lack of interest in the outside world, when Mary tells Jane, "I don't think he will see you," adding that he "refuses everybody" (427; ch. 37); his general lack of activity, when he becomes a "fixture" (423; ch. 36); and his lowering of self-regarding feelings, when he says, "I was desolate and abandoned—my life dark, lonely, hopeless—my soul athirst and forbidden to drink—my heart famished and never to be fed" (429; ch. 37). Put briefly, the blindman suffers a miserable existence, an absence of joy in relation to which the lives of his counterparts are likely to appear joyful.

When considering the psychology of the blindman in more detail, attention might be paid to the way in which it corresponds with Freud's theory that the work of melancholia involves the internalization of the lost object, the result being a continuously critical presence in the ego: "the shadow of the object fell upon the ego, and the latter could henceforth be judged by a special agency, as though it were an object, the forsaken object" ("Mourning and Melancholia," 249). In accordance with this theory, we might infer that the blindman refuses to accept his blindness and seeks to revive his sight by internalizing the notion that it is necessary. This conclusion may be drawn about *The Light That Failed*, when Dick is said to have learned not to stir until advised to do so:

> [T]here was nothing whatever to do except to sit still and brood till the three daily meals came. Centuries separated breakfast from lunch, and lunch from dinner, and though a man prayed for hundreds of years that his mind might be taken from him, God would never hear. Rather the mind was quickened and the revolving thoughts ground against each other as millstones grind when there is no corn between; and yet the brain would

not wear out and give him rest. It continued to think, at length, with imagery and all manner of reminiscences. It recalled Maisie and past success,
reckless travels by land and sea, the glory of doing work and feeling that
it was good, and suggested all that might have happened had the eyes only
been faithful to their duty. (167; ch. 14)

The features of melancholia that are implicit in this extract include the loss
of the capacity for love, the profoundly painful dejection, the end of interest
in the outside world and the general inhibition of activity. Continuing with
the application of Freudian theory, then, we might infer that Dick revives
his sight by internalizing the notion that it is necessary for love, an interest
in the outside world and activity in general. In these terms, the melancholia
of the blindman may be said to result from the internalized object of sight
being at odds with the ego's sightless reality. The key point that is illustrated
by this psychoanalytic reading is that the reality of sightlessness is not melancholic intrinsically, only becoming so when permeated by ocularcentric
ideas, a scenario that is notable because the melancholia is integral to the
notion that sight is a necessary condition of vitality.

The lowering of the self-regarding feelings to a degree that finds utterance in self-reproaches and self-revilings, culminating in a delusional expectation of punishment, is the most significant feature of melancholia, being
the only one that is not also present in the state of mourning. The attribute
is portrayed in *Jane Eyre* when, for example, Rochester says, "I supplicated
God, that, if it seemed good to Him, I might soon be taken from this life"
(441; ch. 37). Indeed, in *The Light That Failed,* the fact that the lowering
of Dick's self-regarding feelings culminates in a delusional expectation of
punishment is explicit in the assertion that there poured into his soul "tide
on tide of overwhelming, purposeless fear—dread of starvation always, ter-
ror lest the unseen ceiling should crush down upon him, fear of fire in the
chambers and a louse's death in red flame, and agonies of fiercer horror that
had nothing to do with any fear of death" (167; ch. 14). The fear becomes
manifest when Dick is said to have "bowed his head, and clutching the
arms of his chair fought with his sweating self" (167; ch. 14), parodying the
moment when "straining all his nerves" Samson "bowd" and "shook" the
"two massie Pillars" (*SA,* lines 1646–50). The inclusion of this key feature
is notable because prior to Freud's early twentieth-century blurring of the
distinction between mourning and melancholia, the former was considered
a normal effect of loss and the latter a pathological disposition. That is to
say, *Jane Eyre* and *The Light That Failed* were first published at a time when

melancholia was widely defined in terms of alterity, indeed madness, a contextual factor that bolsters Rodas's suggestion that the identity of the madwoman migrates into the blindman ("Brontë's *Jane Eyre*").

The melancholia of the blindman is sustained by blindness-darkness synonymy, for whether the word *darkness* is used to denote a lack of light or sight, the connotation of misery remains the same. Rochester's "all" is reduced to "void darkness" (426; ch. 37), for example, before he is said to ask, "Who can tell what a dark, dreary, hopeless life I have dragged on for months past? Doing nothing, expecting nothing; merging night in day; feeling but the sensation of cold when I let the fire go out, of hunger when I forgot to eat; and then a ceaseless sorrow" (432; ch. 37). The motif can also be found in *The Light That Failed* because, having said that he is "blind" and "the darkness will never go away" (137; ch. 11), Dick asserts that it is "hard to live alone in the dark, confusing the day and night; dropping to sleep through sheer weariness at mid-day, and rising restless in the chill of the dawn" (167; ch. 14). The problem with blindness-darkness synonymy is that it is ocularcentric, it takes the visual perspective as a measure by which all others are judged, for it can only be from the subject position of people with vision that darkness looks like blindness. In other words, the synonymy does not accommodate the fact that the existence of a person without vision is, by definition, no more dark than it is light, that when sight loss is total, the bearer ceases to see not only light but also darkness.

Embedded with the melancholia of blindness is the Samsonian platitude that death is preferable to a life without sight. Accordingly, the eponymous protagonist of *Jane Eyre* is told that while Rochester is alive, "many think he had better be dead" (423; ch. 36), foreshadowing *The Light That Failed,* where it is asserted that blindness is "the living death" (126; ch. 10), a "death-sentence of disease" (129; ch. 10), that Dick is "dead in the death of the blind" (142; ch. 12) and that his life is "nothing better than death" (167; ch. 14). The allusion to *Samson Agonistes* is sustained by Brontë when Rochester says, "I supplicated God, that, if it seemed good to Him, I might soon be taken from this life" (441; ch. 37), much as by Kipling, when Dick is said to have "prayed to God that his mind might be taken from him, offering for proof that he was worthy of this favour the fact that he had not shot himself long ago" (170; ch. 14). Though corresponding in these evocations of suicide, Brontë differs from Kipling and Milton insofar as she does not depict the fatal act. It may seem as if Kipling is following suit when Dick persuades himself that suicide would be a "ludicrous insult to the gravity of the situation as well as a weak-kneed confession of fear" (170; ch. 14), which is why Kleege likens the character to Oedipus. However, bearing in mind the classic formula advanced by Emile Durkheim, that "the term suicide is applied to any death which is the direct or indirect result of a positive or negative act accomplished by the victim" (42), the detail to note is that Dick makes his final journey expecting to be shot, that on reaching his destination he says, "Put me, I pray, in the forefront of the battle" (208; ch. 15). In other words, because deliberately standing in the line of fire is every bit as suicidal as pulling down the building in which one stands, Dick's fate is linked with Samson in a way that Rochester's is not.

Although Brontë differs from Kipling and Milton insofar as she omits the suicidal act, the salient point is that the conclusion of *Jane Eyre* nonetheless endorses the ocularcentric belief that a person cannot live happily ever after without sight. For a "Christian God who is supposed to temper justice with mercy," as Kleege puts it, permanent "blindness would be too harsh a punishment" (70). Furthermore, the conclusion illustrates that the blindman's castration is integral to the sighted capacity for love and erotic pleasure, for Rochester recovers his sight sufficiently to produce a son: "[T]he sky is no longer a blank to him—the earth no longer a void. When his first-born was put into his arms, he could see that the boy had inherited his own eyes, as they once were—large, brilliant, and black" (446; ch. 38). This transformation invokes a parallel with Spivak's assertion that the emergence of Jane Eyre as the white individualist heroine requires the sacrifice of the Other in the form of "the mulatto woman" (*In Other Worlds*), for the emergence of Rochester as Jane's companion requires the sacrifice of the Other in the form of the blindman. Thus, by the end of the novel it becomes apparent that the misery of the blindman is integral to the happiness of not only the sighted woman but also the sighted man whom Rochester becomes.

CONCLUSION

In considering the multitude of diminishments with which Brontë associates visual impairment, I have isolated some of the many ways in which the characterization of Edward Rochester corresponds with that of Dick Heldar, as well as some of the ways in which both characters are foreshadowed by Samson. The ocularcentric basis of this unity and its resonance with psychoanalytic discourse have raised various feminist issues. Indeed, exemplifying Spender's definition of patriarchal knowledge, the trope of the blindman is premised on the notion that the experience of only part of the human population needs to be taken into account and the outcome imposed on the whole. Like Kipling, Brontë portrays someone who has a visual impairment but takes into account only the experience of people who do not have visual impairments. The result is a diminished character who augments the status of the sighted protagonist, a functionality that corresponds with feminism only insofar as the former is male and the latter female. That is to say, while inverting the patriarchal schema that Simone de Beauvoir has described as men taking the subject position and women being treated as an objectified Other, Brontë actively endorses the binary opposition of normativism and disability. This scenario has been found to be a concern for feminist as well as literary disability scholars because the subject position that Jane occupies is bolstered by the objectification of the disabled Other; it is indicative of disempowerment rather than empowerment.

In accordance with the Derridean assertion that deconstruction is an openness toward the Other, which is the basis for Corker and Shakespeare's reading of disability as an integral part of normativism, I have inverted numerous binary oppositions, analyzing the blindman's diminishments and exposing links with the augmentations of his sighted counterparts. I have suggested that the grotesque portrayal of haptic perception underpins the implication that physical beauty is appreciated by purely visual means, that the symbolic castration invokes the figure of the castrating woman and her symbolic erection, that the unseeing spectacle elevates the controlling status of the unseen spectator, that the dependency of the blindman necessitates the dependability of his sighted counterparts, that his melancholia defines their happiness and, finally, that the emptiness of his living death is fundamental to the fullness of their lives. In brief, I have privileged the construct of disability over that of normativism and, more specifically, the blindman over his sighted counterparts, the result of which is a new perspective on *Jane Eyre* that will supplement the corpus of feminist readings. Moreover, while there can be no denying Chow's assertion that the process of feminization must be understood as "the emergence of a discursive network in which forces of class and race as well as gender become imbricated with one another" (144), I have demonstrated that disability must also be added to the list of significant forces. Indeed, heralded by Kirtley, Kleege, and Rodas, among others, the conclusive point is that the taxonomy of feminist, Marxist, and postcolonial approaches to *Jane Eyre* can be supplemented by an approach that is appreciative of disability, from which we may infer that there must be an absence that, in a Derridean sense, requires supplementing. After all, Brontë may be excused for the regressiveness of her approach to disability on the grounds of historicity, but the same cannot be said of literary scholars who have written since the disability movement gathered momentum in the late twentieth century.

Chapter 3

"ON THE SPECTRUM"

Rereading Contact and Affect in *Jane Eyre*

JULIA MIELE RODAS

IN HER notorious piece appearing in *The Quarterly Review* of December 1848, Elizabeth Rigby comments on the "sheer rudeness and vulgarity" of the recently published *Jane Eyre* and cuts acutely at the narrator (440), observing:

> We hear nothing but self-eulogiums on the perfect tact and wondrous penetration with which she is gifted, and yet almost every word she utters offends us, not only with the absence of these qualities, but with the positive contrasts of them, in either her pedantry, stupidity, or gross vulgarity. She is one of those ladies who put us in the unpleasant predicament of under-valuing their very virtues for dislike of the person in whom they are represented. One feels provoked as Jane Eyre stands before us—for in the wonderful reality of her thoughts and descriptions, she seems accountable for all done in her name—with principles you must approve in the main, and yet with language and manners that offend you in every particular. Even in that *chef d'oeuvre* of brilliant retrospective sketching, the description of her early life, it is the childhood and not the child that interests you. The little Jane, with her sharp eyes and dogmatic speeches, is a being you

neither could fondle nor love. [. . . .] As the child, so also the woman—an
uninteresting, sententious, pedantic thing [. . . .].

It is a punishing review, but it brings home an essential point for all readers, even those who feel profoundly attached to the text: there is some quirk
in the narrative character that irks, that stands clear of our affection, that
resists our sense of intimacy. No matter what we may see *Jane Eyre* as being
"about," no matter how we may approach the text, there is no getting away
from the fact that the affect and social conduct of the narrator are highly
unusual. From its first publication in 1847 and persistently throughout the
century and a half that has followed, critics and theorists have commented
on the idiosyncratic nature of Jane's feelings and reactions, on her unconventional approach to relationships, and on the singularly remote, withdrawn, or unattractive quality of her social intercourse. There may be many
fruitful approaches to understanding Jane's affect and demeanor, including
widely disseminated postcolonialist and feminist readings that interpret the
protagonist's behaviors in terms of government and politics. This chapter
suggests, however, that a new approach to Jane's sociality enables a reading
of the heroine as an individual on the autistic spectrum, and that such an
interpretation, in turn, invites crucial new questions about the narrative of
Jane Eyre and its apparent politics.

"A QUEER, FRIGHTENED, SHY LITTLE THING": JANE EYRE AND ANTIPATHIES

A sampling of the copious critical and theoretical literature surrounding
Jane Eyre demonstrates a common theme running through even the most
disparate approaches to the text. In addition to that which appeared in
the *Quarterly*, another early negative review of the novel, an anonymous
piece from *The Christian Remembrancer*, says of the narrator, "Never was
there a better hater" ("Jane Eyre: An Autobiography," 439). In his lauda-
tory 1847 review, George Henry Lewes cites the book's "strange power of
subjective representation" (437). Other critics have followed suit in recognizing the idiosyncratic nature of the narrator, of the text, and frequently
of the author as well. In 1916, Virginia Woolf's interpretation of *Jane Eyre*
cues the reader first to think of Charlotte Brontë, "unhappy and lonely, in
her poverty and her exaltation." Woolf compares Brontë's writing unfavorably with that of Austen and Tolstoy, characterizing it as "narrow," "con-
stricted," and comparatively unidimensional. The impressions of writers

like Brontë, she adds, are "self-centered and self-limited," "close packed and strongly stamped between [. . . .] narrow walls. Nothing issues from their mind which has not been marked with their own impress. They can learn little from other writers, and what they adopt they cannot assimilate." Cora Kaplan sums up Woolf's assessment of "Brontë's heroine [as] located at the margins of bourgeois culture and normalcy, her social and psychic condition made to seem both voluntary and deeply eccentric" (*Victoriana*, 18). In his 1950s reading of *Jane Eyre* as gothic, Robert Heilman abstracts the narrator's character: "as a girl she is lonely, 'passionate,' 'strange,' 'like nobody there'" (460). He comments that she is "so portrayed as to evoke new feelings" and observes that Jane joins Rochester at Ferndean in a "closed-in life."[1] Terry Eagleton's *Myths of Power* (1975) interprets Jane's "self [as] a free, blank, 'pre-social' atom" (491). In the early 1970s, Adrienne Rich writes about Jane's extreme disconnectedness, her lonely and orphaned state, as a fundamental metaphor for the condition of women in patriarchal society. Other feminist approaches, like Gilbert and Gubar's *Madwoman in the Attic* (1979), ask the reader to understand Jane Eyre in terms of a "secret self." From the mid-1980s, Gayatri Spivak's groundbreaking postcolonialist reading is deeply critical of the "isolationism" of the narrator and of the like response Spivak sees the text as inspiring in its readers. So, for instance, Spivak reads Jane as occupying a space of "self-marginalized uniqueness," as preserving "her odd privilege," likewise observing that the text draws the reader in to become Jane's "accomplice" in this position (246). For Spivak, narrative details of the narrator's interactions with domestic space and her personal negotiation with the dominant sociality of the culture described are part of "the unexamined and covert axiomatics of imperialism in *Jane Eyre*" ("Three Women's Texts," 257). Following Spivak, Nancy Armstrong positions *Jane Eyre* within a tradition of domestic fiction that "detached the desiring self from place, time, and material cause," thus creating in their "universal forms of subjectivity" a dangerously antisocial narrative mechanism (187). And Sally Shuttleworth also proposes that *Jane Eyre* "can be read as a quintessential expression of Victorian individualism" (182, qtd. in Kaplan, *Victoriana*, 30). But perhaps most striking, for the present purposes, are the observations of R. A. York, who speaks directly to the narrator's characteristic "silence." In his *Strangers and Secrets: Communication in the Nineteenth-Century Novel* (1994),

---

1. The isolation of Ferndean has been a favored theme of many other scholars as well, including Shannon; Gilbert and Gubar; Roy; and Nestor. Yoshiaki Shirai reads Ferndean as a kind of "Wardian case" that "encloses Jane and Rochester" and preserves them from "noise" (129).

York demonstrates that Jane is "fundamentally uncommunicative for much of the novel," that "she retains a distaste for contact [. . . .] throughout much of her life," and that "her replies can be brief and uncooperative in the extreme" (62). Whatever other purpose or meaning such silence, secrecy, isolationism, rudeness, or resistance to contact may have, whether interpreted from the standpoint of Christian values, within a Freudian framework, from the context of Marxist or feminist politics, or of postcolonialist theory, the fundamental idiosyncrasy of Jane's affect, what one critic identifies as her "social freakery" (Chen, 374), remains a quality that confronts the reader at every turn.

From the very outset of Jane's life with her uncle's family, the Reeds, she is regarded as difficult and temperamental. Aunt Reed complains of Jane's affect even from babyhood, saying of the infant Jane, "I hated it the first time I set my eyes on it—a sickly, whining, pining thing!" (232; ch. 21).[2] Her reaction to the baby is uncharitable, certainly, but it is nonetheless worthy of examination, for it is not merely jealousy for her own children or class prejudice that dampen Aunt Reed's affection for her infant niece; it is clearly something in the baby's very being that irks her, some real but insubstantial irritation that lies behind her statement: "I would as soon have been charged with a pauper brat out of a workhouse" (232; ch. 21). Jane's unhappy childhood is so familiar that it has become almost a cliché; her aunt despises her and her cousins exclude her. Ultimately, Mrs. Reed's assessment, provided in the opening pages of the narrative, is almost diagnostic in its cruel precision: Jane is explicitly lacking "a sociable and childlike disposition" (7; ch. 1). There is certainly no love lost between them. Writes Jane:

I was a discord in Gateshead Hall: I was like nobody there; I had nothing in harmony with Mrs. Reed or her children, or her chosen vassalage. If they did not love me, in fact, as little did I love them. They were not bound to regard with affection a thing that could not sympathise with one amongst them; a heterogeneous thing, opposed to them in temperament, in capacity, in propensities; a useless thing, incapable of serving their interest, or adding to their pleasure; a noxious thing, cherishing the germs of indignation at their treatment, of contempt of their judgment. (15–16; ch. 2)

Jane is lonely and ill-treated by both her own account and that of others, the

2. The version of the primary text referred to in this chapter is Charlotte Brontë, *Jane Eyre* (Oxford: Oxford University Press, 2000).

servants whispering to one another of her wrongs but agreeing at the same time that something in the child's demeanor resists affection or attachment. The housemaid, Abbot, comments that "if she were a nice pretty child, one might compassionate her forlornness; but one really cannot care for such a little toad as that" (26; ch. 3); so, too, Abbot remarks to her fellow servant that Jane is "an underhand little thing: I never saw a girl of her age with so much cover" (12; ch. 2). In an uncharacteristic moment of frankness, the young Jane once approaches the more favored of these two maids, her nurse Bessie, with an impulsive embrace and an open plea against being scolded. But Bessie's reaction to this momentary impulse serves further to affirm the sense of Jane as withdrawn and forbidding: "'You are a strange child, Miss Jane,' she said, as she looked down at me: 'a little roving, solitary thing [. . . .]. You're such a queer, frightened, shy little thing. You should be bolder. [. . . . D]on't be afraid of me. Don't start when I chance to speak rather sharply: It's so provoking'" (39; ch. 4).

But it is not boldness, exactly, that Jane lacks. An unpopular orphaned child who will physically and verbally attack those who persecute her, despite their advantage in age, size, and power, cannot comfortably be understood as merely shy or shrinking. The assaults that Jane makes on her older cousin John, and more especially on his mother, are breathtaking, moments of triumph for the beleaguered narrator and for those readers who identify with her browbeaten childhood. Jane's famous speech to Mrs. Reed, rejecting her aunt and calling her to account for the terrible injustices the narrator had suffered, cannot easily be figured into the withdrawn character with which the reader is otherwise confronted. Aunt Reed remains baffled by Jane's behavior almost a decade later and is troubled by the child's outburst as an "uncanny" experience. Mrs. Reed revisits this encounter repeatedly, on her deathbed, still trying to configure Jane's behavior into a meaningful context. She refers to Jane's "disposition" as "very bad," "impossible to understand," and "incomprehensible" (239–40; ch. 21). Confronting the narrator in adulthood, Mrs. Reed laments:

> I could not forget your conduct to me, Jane—the fury with which you once turned on me; the tone in which you declared you abhorred me the worst of anybody in the world; the unchildlike look and voice with which you affirmed that the very thought of me made you sick, and asserted that I had treated you with miserable cruelty. (239; ch. 21)

For Mrs. Reed, it is as though "an animal that I had struck or pushed had looked up at me with human eyes and cursed me in a man's voice." For the socially conventional Aunt Reed, Jane is an enigma, "something mad," a "fiend," a being scarcely human, her affect and the extraordinary quality of her sociality locating her outside the explicable boundaries of human social contact:

> I have had more trouble with that child than any one would believe. Such a burden to be left on my hands—and so much annoyance as she caused me, daily and hourly, with her incomprehensible disposition, and her sudden starts of temper, and her continual, unnatural watchings of one's movements! I declare she talked to me once like something mad, or like a fiend—no child ever spoke or looked as she did; I was glad to get her away from the house. (231; ch. 21)

But if the narrator's character is enigmatic for her aunt, Jane is equally at a loss to understand her own inability to please. She is conscious that others do not like her, but she also suffers miserably from the coldness and exclusion she experiences. Though resentful of her treatment as a child, Jane is nevertheless bewildered, filled with painful wondering at the implicit rejection she experiences:

> Why was I always suffering, always brow-beaten, always accused, for ever condemned? Why could I never please? Why was it useless to try to win any one's favour? Eliza, who was headstrong and selfish, was respected. Georgiana, who had a spoiled temper, a very acrid spite, a captious and insolent carriage, was universally indulged. [. . . .] John, no one thwarted, much less punished [. . . .despite his violent and destructive behaviors]. I dared commit no fault; I strove to fulfill every duty; and I was termed naughty and tiresome, sullen and sneaking, from morning to noon, and from noon to night. (15; ch. 2)

Even in adulthood, nothing beholden to her aunt, Jane continues to seek the affection she feels she deserves, apologizing to the woman who had made her life a misery and arguing, "I should have been glad to love you if you would have let me" (240; ch. 21). Aligning with the textual observations of various critics, Jane's experiences in childhood, confirmed from a variety of perspectives within the novel, clearly define a person with an unusual sociality and personal affect. The person thus described, while baffling to others and often personally bewildered by social conventions and the unspoken expectations of interpersonal contact, may be identified within literature of the twentieth- and twenty-first centuries as "autistic."

DISCOVERING AUTISM:
THEORIES, DEFINITIONS, IDENTITIES

Coined in the early 1940s, the term *autism* was developed independently by two doctors—Hans Asperger and Leo Kanner—working autonomously continents apart (the former in Austria and the latter in the United States). Early work with autistic children by famed child psychologist Bruno Bettelheim and popular representations of profoundly autistic people have resulted in a widespread but false understanding of autism often in extreme negative terms, as completely disabling and as a "tragedy" for those affected. Although popular ideas about autism are shifting, the commonest sense of the autistic individual remains that of a person who is nonverbal, of low intelligence, and frequently violent, characteristics which have been disseminated through a wide variety of sources. Advertising for personal injury lawyers claims massive settlements in autism cases, indirectly informing the public unconscious and adding to the sense that autism is a calamity. Popular sources of electronic information—government websites, online encyclopedias, and commercial databases—describe children as "suffering from autism," as silent and unresponsive, and popular print sources report an autism "epidemic." In addition, grassroots health-care activists who see the recent "explosion" in diagnosed autism as resulting from environmental factors, especially the irresponsible overuse of childhood immunizations, urge political and social action but also typically portray autism in the bleakest light. Even positive representations of autism (usually as Asperger syndrome) are often poisoned by conventions that transform the autistic character into a sentimental icon or a stereotype of spectacular skill without full human identity in order to create what Stuart Murray calls an "effect of wonder at the level of human difference" (30).

Medical or therapeutic professionals working with autistic clients are also sometimes responsible for making devastating global claims about autism, as lamentable for their bias as for their inaccuracy. One recent text designed to guide therapeutic work with autistic adults claims, "In autism the prerequisites for creativity are not present. The adult with autism cannot extend the known, or bring together understandings to create new ones, because the known remains confined to the specific context in which it was learnt. [. . . .] Autistic thinking is of a non-imaginative kind" (Jordan and Powell, 78–79). This understanding of autism in negative terms, as deficit, is most infamously propagated in Bettelheim's classic book-length study on autism, *The Empty Fortress* (1967), a failed Freudian approach that sees autism as a prison and that ruthlessly blames parents (and mothers especially) for what the writer understands as a form of childhood psychosis. Even sympathetic accounts of autism written by family members frequently reinforce the idea that the person "inside" the autism is living an experience of imprisonment. Writing in 1999, Wendy Robinson, for instance, explains of her relationship with her autistic son, "We never broke down the wall and retrieved the person that could live independently and be socially aware" (244). All together, popular notions of autism give the impression that the withdrawn, insular, autistic self is profoundly damaged, incapable of feeling, dangerous, and diminished in capacity for thought or creativity.

This sense of autism not only diverges radically from the lived experience of many autistic people,[3] but it is also clearly contrary to the writings of Kanner and Asperger that first defined and delineated autistic personality. Key to this misunderstanding is a failure to look closely at the very word first coined to describe the single defining feature of different autistic persons. Though later writers frequently comment on the amazing coincidence of Asperger and Kanner coming up with the word *autism* independently, there is actually nothing strange about this, since *autism* literally means "selfness" and is the primary characteristic of the personality described. Thus, the principal feature of autism is an unusual degree of inwardness, aloneness, or independence, sometimes—but not always—to the exclusion of others from direct verbal exchange or eye contact. The "cases" first described by Kanner in his seminal article, "Autistic Disturbances of Affective Contact" (1943), are far from fitting the popular stereotype of autism today. Kanner's subjects span a broad range of intelligence, skill, and social awareness. In the brief theoretical section that follows his clinical analyses, Kanner suggests that:

---

3. Negative stereotypes of autism are an ever-present challenge, even within literature that is otherwise sensitive and well-informed. As autism becomes an increasing social presence, however, there is greater recognition of the assets and contributions of people on the spectrum. A recent article in *WIRED* magazine notes the spike in autism diagnoses in California's Silicon Valley and attributes the surge to the concentration of techie "geeks" whose intermarriage and reproduction have genetically reinforced the incidence of autism. While considering the disadvantages that arise in such a situation, Silberman nevertheless recognizes that autism is linked to specialized forms of intelligence and productivity, quoting Temple Grandin's observation, for instance, that NASA is likely "the largest sheltered workshop in the world," commenting on the prevalence of autistic types in "the halls of academe," and noting: "It's a familiar joke in the industry that many of the hardcore programmers in IT strongholds like Intel, Adobe, and Silicon Graphics—coming to work early, leaving late, sucking down Big Gulps in their cubicles while they code for hours—are residing somewhere in Asperger's domain."

[The] fundamental disorder is the children's *inability to relate themselves* in the ordinary way to people and situations from the beginning of life. Their parents refer to them as having always been "self-sufficient"; "like in a shell"; "happiest when left alone"; "acting as if people weren't there"; "perfectly oblivious to everything about him"; "giving the impression of silent wisdom"; "failing to develop the usual amount of social awareness"; "acting almost as if hypnotized." This is not, as in schizophrenic children or adults, a departure from an initially present relationship; it is not a "withdrawal" from formerly existing participation. There is from the start an *extreme autistic aloneness* that, whenever possible, disregards, ignores, shuts out anything that comes to the child from the outside. Direct physical contact or such motion or noise as threatens to disrupt the aloneness is either treated "as if it weren't there" or, if this is no longer sufficient, resented painfully as distressing interference. (41)

Indeed, Kanner's brilliance lies in his ability to recognize the single defining feature across a diverse range of other characteristics, lighting on the "autistic" quality of the children studied, despite a wide range of verbal capabilities and apparent intelligence. As autism expert Leon Eisenberg comments, "The genius of [Kanner's] discovery was to detect the cardinal traits [. . . .] in the midst of phenomenology as diverse as muteness in one child and verbal precocity in another" (qtd. in Rutter, 51). Kanner was highly conscious of the intelligence of many of the children he observed, and he noted particularly that all the subjects with whom he initially interacted came from unusually intelligent, highly educated, and/or exceptionally productive families, noting a relationship between the personality of the child and the exceptional nature of the family, and thus pointing not only to a potential genetic component to autism but also to a possible understanding of autism as linked to other idiosyncratic aspects of cognition or intelligence. In other words, despite his (sometimes cruelly) clinical approach to the autistic personality, Kanner's groundbreaking article allows room for interpreting autism in positive terms.

The increasing incidence of autism in recent decades, or at least the increasing rate of diagnosis, has worked to refresh and complicate the understanding and definition of autism for many people. Specifically, the introduction of Asperger syndrome to the *Diagnostic and Statistical Manual of Mental Disorders* (*DSM-IV*) and the subsequent proposed integration of Asperger syndrome into the diagnostic criteria for "Autistic Disorder (Autism Spectrum Disorder)" for the American Psychiatric Association's

DSM-5, has broadened diagnostic criteria, encouraging an understanding of autism/Asperger as existing on a "spectrum," defined primarily by patterns and behaviors having to do with conventional sociality.[4] So, for instance, in determining the presence of autism/Asperger syndrome, the *DSM* asks that, among other items, diagnoses consider the following:

1. failure to develop appropriate peer relationships
2. lack of social or emotional reciprocity (e.g., not actively participating in simple social play or games, preferring solitary activities, or involving others in activities only as tools or "mechanical" aids)
3. marked impairment in the ability to initiate or sustain a conversation with others
4. use of idiosyncratic language
5. lack of varied, spontaneous make-believe play or social imitative play appropriate to developmental level
6. abnormal functioning in social interaction
7. lack of spontaneous seeking to share enjoyment, interests, or achievements with other people

While not an exhaustive compendium of the diagnostic criteria offered in the *DSM,*[5] this list offers some sense of how subtle and ambiguous autistic behavior may be. Even if the individual assessed does not meet the standard for diagnosis, autism experts (including autistic people) speak of individuals as having autistic traits or characteristics. Autism is thus understood— within the medical establishment and by a popular community experienced

---

4. The defining of autism has been a hotly contested issue both among clinicians and within families and autism communities. Though many feel that broader diagnostic criteria are warranted, there has been persistent disagreement as to whether "autism" and "Asperger syndrome" ought to be understood as discrete categories. Both Kanner and Asperger use the term *autism* to describe their observations, and, while Asperger's work tends to look at individuals who are—in clinical parlance—considered to be "high functioning," there is certainly room in Kanner's initial study for the inclusion of the amply intelligent and the highly verbal, the key distinction made in the *DSM-IV* between autism and Asperger syndrome being one of verbal development and ability (a distinction that is elided in the proposed *DSM-5*). Kanner notes of those children who made up his initial eleven "cases": "Even though most of these children were at one time or another looked upon as feebleminded, they are all unquestionably endowed with good cognitive potentialities" (47). For the purposes of this chapter, which grounds itself in the earliest theorizations of autism, no distinction between autism and Asperger is deemed necessary and none is made from this point forward.

5. These diagnostic criteria are abstracted from the *DSM-IV,* the approved version of the manual at the time the present volume went to press; while incomplete, edited, or partially paraphrased, the apparent intended sense has not been altered; substantial changes to diagnostic criteria will appear in the *DSM-5,* scheduled for release in May 2013.

with autism—as existing along a spectrum, with some individuals having barely discernable social idiosyncrasies, some having active social and intellectual lives that play out exclusively through nonimmediate contact (e.g., through writing or within electronic communities), and with others who demonstrate no apparent contact with or interest in the "outer" world. Autism, Asperger syndrome, and related sensory and affective "conditions" are thus often encapsulated by the global diagnostic term ASD, or autism spectrum disorder. Along this spectrum, the manifestation of affective idiosyncrasy is as diverse as any other human quality. In other words, autistic people are not *always* visual, or *always* nonverbal, or *always* savants; the range of personalities and interests is as various as in any other demographic pool. And the degree of what is seen as "function" (i.e., the ability to interact seamlessly with ordinary people) in some autistic persons has led many to conjecture that there is a diagnostic crisis within the medical establishment. By embracing such a broad array of social and affective behaviors, some argue, it seems that diagnosis may become either impossible—or inevitable.

For many, the debate over diagnosis—especially insofar as it concerns the criteria of the *DSM*—is paramount, since the diagnostic pronouncement is immediately concerned with the distribution of material resources. However, for a larger portion of the population and for the purposes of fiction, formal diagnosis is beside the point. If an individual, no matter how eccentric, thrives without medical or therapeutic intervention, there is much to be said for resisting medicine, the disciplinary framework that exists, in many respects, for the tyrannical purposes of normalizing what is seen as irregular.[6] (A growing "neurodiversity" movement resists the pervasive misreading of autism as "defect" and insists on the cultural and social value of people on the spectrum, without the dubious benefit of intervention.) Likewise, for a fictional character, formal diagnosis can bring no benefit. At the same time, while diagnosis may not always be advantageous, coming to an understanding of autistic personality and a recognition of autistic characteristics, both within ourselves and in the world around us, can contribute to a more complex sense of identity and an enriched political consciousness. Thus, the suggestion of this chapter—that Jane Eyre is an individual on the autism spectrum—is intended not as an end, not as an incarceration of the character within the rigid framework of diagnosis, not as a gesture that cuts off meaning and interpretive possibility, but instead as a device to reopen

6. The thinking for this chapter is indebted in general terms to the work of scholars in disability studies. This passage in particular is obviously influenced by the work of Michel Foucault, but the observation that "normalcy" may be a tyrannical social force echoes the work of Lennard Davis.

discussion of the novel's politics and to challenge what seem to be some of our larger presuppositions regarding the political and social meaning of the individual.

JANE EYRE/AUTISM AUTOBIOGRAPHY

To some extent, the analysis of Jane's childhood offered earlier begins to effect this shift, but a brief rereading of the narrator's adult experiences within the context of recently published autism auto/biography creates a more textured sense of Jane's autism. Literature by and about autistic persons has proliferated in recent years, from the exploratory essays of neuropsychologist Oliver Sacks[7] in the 1970s, 80s, and 90s to Temple Grandin's groundbreaking autobiography, *Emergence: Labeled Autistic* (1986), to Donna Williams's best-selling *Nobody Nowhere* (1992), to the more recent productions of writers like Mark Haddon, Dawn Prince-Hughes, Daniel Tammet, and Keiko Tobe. As this genre grows and offers increasing clarity regarding the diversity of autistic personality and experience, readers can also begin to recognize certain shared themes and ideas within the literature. These frequently include: A feeling of misunderstanding and being misunderstood by others in everyday interactions; a powerful and elaborate sense of connection in some special arena or skill area (e.g., numbers, color, animals, drawing/painting, languages); the experience of being excluded, especially in childhood when rigid social structures prevail; and a sense of peace and satisfaction that comes with order and ordering, both in material and in logical terms.[8] As one rereads *Jane Eyre* in the context of this emerg-

7. While a controversial figure within disability studies—critiqued most notably by Tom Shakespeare and Thomas Couser—Oliver Sacks has made a brilliant, if flawed, contribution to the understanding of neurodiversity and very often writes of autism (and disability more generally) in terms of creativity, talent, and giftedness, countering the deficit model that is elsewhere so entrenched an aspect of medicalized disability. Moreover, Sacks has himself been regarded as an individual on the spectrum (Sacks, "Face-Blind," 37), a powerful reason for including his perspective despite criticism of his work.

8. The theme of peace and autistic ordering cannot be fully developed here; however, one might briefly consider the joy that Jane claims in the thorough cleaning of Moor House in anticipation of the Christmas holiday—"to *clean down* Moor House from chamber to cellar; [. . . .] to rub it up with bees-wax, oil, and an indefinite number of cloths [. . . .] ; [. . . .] to arrange every chair, table, bed, carpet, with mathematical precision," etc. (390; ch. 34)—a passage which may fruitfully be compared with one from Donna Williams's *Nobody Nowhere*, describing her work as a department store clerk: "It seemed almost unbelievable that I would be expected to do the thing I loved most: put things in order. There were numbers to be counted and ordered, there were colors and sizes and types of article to be grouped; every department was kept separate from every other department and called by a different name; it was a world of guarantees" (82–83).

ing literature, maintaining a consciousness of these commonalities and the ways that autism is perceived and represented "from the inside," Brontë's novel and Jane's story gain a familiar hue, and add increasingly to the sense that the "disconnected" governess may be understood as a person "on the spectrum" (161; ch. 16).

Having already touched on Jane's experience of exclusion in childhood, an account that dovetails suggestively with narratives offered in modern autism autobiography, it may be helpful to reconsider the general character of the adult Jane with a sense of autism in mind. With an interpretive gesture alert to autistic possibilities, all kinds of minor details and episodes, all manner of quirky characteristics take on new significance: Jane's "Quakerish" appearance; her sense of aloneness at Lowood, even after many years of residence; the feeling of peace and wholeness she seems to derive from nature, from gardens, from plants instead of people; her silent impatience with a talkative roommate ("a teacher who occupied the same room with me kept me from the subject to which I longed to recur, by a prolonged effusion of small talk. How I wished sleep would silence her" [85; ch. 10]). The episode of homelessness between her residences at Thornfield and Moor House, failing to take valuables with her, forgetting the morsel of luggage she does take along, forgetting her newly discovered connections, are all strongly reminiscent of homeless experiences depicted by Prince-Hughes and Donna Williams, who describe a sense of panic that induces them to leave places of comparative security. Think of Jane's sincere but formal affection for Adèle, the consideration of the girl's well-being as though from a distance. Jane's early period of engagement with Rochester, she provoking him into sparring with her continually, actively, and consciously resistant to more tender forms of affection, hints at a fear of conventional contact, a reluctance to connect sexually that is also a recurrent theme explored in autism literature.[9] Even Jane's discreet relationship with Pilot, her acknowledgment of Rochester's dog as a seeming peer, as an individual worthy of respect, demonstrates an autistic sensibility, a connection to animals that echoes that of many autistic persons.

It makes sense to explore further the appearance of Jane's autism by looking more closely at the impression of missed connection that frequently arises between autistic and nonautistic people. Nonautistic people often attribute this sense of disconnect to a mistaken belief that individuals with autism have little or no feeling, but, indeed, the contrary is more likely true. Autistic persons typically experience intense sensations and emotions but

9. See, for example, Sacks's "An Anthropologist on Mars," Williams's *Somebody Somewhere*, and Prince-Hughes.

may habitually reduce the *appearance* of feeling or shield the self from a barrage of overwhelming external stimuli (including dialogue and other forms of communication) in order to preserve an integrated sense of identity. For "high functioning" autistic persons, this shielding may take the form of exceedingly effective social performance that can leave both self and other with a sensation of loss or failure. This experience is described over and over in autism auto/biography. Donna Williams, for instance, writes of employing fully formed but nonintegrated performance personalities to engage with the world on her behalf, often leaving her teachers, family, and employers baffled and enraged (*Nobody Nowhere*). Dawn Prince-Hughes, seeking to engage in a love relationship, speaks of conducting an intensive field study of human sexuality, developing "protocols" and applying "data" that lead her to some problematic conclusions, including the explicit idea "that my own sexual pleasure was irrelevant" (80–81). Needless to say, her spectacular sexual performances, while bringing much gratification to her lovers, do not result in mutual satisfaction.

Within *Jane Eyre,* there is substantial evidence that Jane, too, participates in similar autistically informed social exchanges. In adulthood, as Jane exerts increasing control over her passionate emotional life, reducing her affect and concealing her deeply rooted feelings with ever greater success, experienced readers tend to contextualize this process in terms of cultural history, understanding the narrator's extreme self-control, her apparent poise, as meshing with historically appropriate social conventions. Readers know, as Jane does, that a Victorian gentlewoman must not evidence feelings of passion, must not put herself forward, must not be seen to harbor ideas or opinions that are beyond her limited social scope. Because the reader sees Jane's self-control from the inside, though, he or she is always aware of the roiling passions and rarely notices or questions the narrator's most obvious autistic characteristic, the silence and flattened affect, the autistic remoteness that other characters evidently experience. This is quite apparent in the festive drawing room scenes in which Jane is clearly portrayed as dreading to appear before company: Rochester and Mrs. Fairfax both anticipate Jane's objection to participating in social gatherings and the latter offers friendly advice on how best to avoid the crowd:

> I'll tell you how to manage so as to avoid the embarrassment of making a formal entrance, which is the most disagreeable part of the business. You must go into the drawing-room while it is empty, before the ladies leave the dinner-table; choose your seat in any quiet nook you like; you need not stay long after the gentlemen come in. (169; ch. 17)

In these scenes, the reader typically sees Jane as planting herself quite literally on the margins: "I sit in the shade—if any shade there be in this brilliantly-lit apartment; the window-curtain half hides me" (173; ch. 17). Even in the social exchanges that feel more natural to the reader, however, Jane's affective idiosyncrasies are evident upon close reading. When she addresses Grace Poole, for instance, after the fire in Rochester's room, hinting at what she thinks is a shared secret, Jane may look arch to the reader, but for outsiders—all the other characters with whom the governess is interacting—her manner must seem haughty, even bizarre. Leah, a witness to the dialogue between Jane and Grace Poole, must find the governess's behavior inexplicable, as she whispers closely with a servant far beneath her, a person for whom she has always shown contempt. Even Grace's reaction—Jane tells us that "there was something of consciousness" in the expression of the servant's eyes—suggests the possibility that she finds Jane's intimations a little weird (154; ch. 16).

In fact, Mrs. Fairfax, the one person at Thornfield who is truly Jane's social equal and with whom she would seem most naturally to fall into companionship, obviously finds Jane strange and bewildering, despite the older woman's warm feelings. The scene in which Jane first asks Mrs. Fairfax about Rochester's character offers a telling sample of many of their other interactions. After prodding the housekeeper repeatedly for some concrete, meaningful, detailed sense of Mr. Rochester, Jane ultimately gives up unsatisfied, commenting to the reader:

> There are people who seem to have no notion of sketching a character, or observing and describing salient points, either in persons or things: the good lady evidently belonged to this class; *my queries puzzled, but did not draw her out.* Mr. Rochester was Mr. Rochester in her eyes; a gentleman, a landed proprietor—nothing more: she inquired and searched no further, and *evidently wondered at my wish* to gain a more definite notion of his identity. (105; ch. 11; emphasis added)

Jane's queries puzzle Mrs. Fairfax, but they do not elicit information, and because Jane does the telling, it is Mrs. Fairfax who here appears deficient, lacking in natural curiosity or powers of observation. Narrated from without, however, it is easy to see how Jane's distant sense of Mrs. Fairfax's puzzlement and wonder might be translated into an understanding of the governess's queries as peculiar or socially untoward.

Even in her most passionate exchange with Rochester himself, the one person who "gets" her, who connects with the real, the unperformed Jane, she demonstrates an unusually perceptive understanding of her apparent affect and an incisive sense of how others must read her. In the dialogue that leads up to this first engagement, Jane shouts angrily at Rochester, repeatedly affirming that she *does* have feelings and pointedly announcing that she is not "an automaton" (253; ch. 23). It is an assurance that seems fitting to the reader, who shares Jane's rage and frustration over Rochester's teasing and erotic game playing, but it bespeaks as well a powerful underlying defensive posture, an insistence on her identity as a feeling human being despite persistent social misreading.

Another scene that speaks compellingly of Jane's autistic affect is that in which her marriage to Rochester is called off, she is exposed to Bertha Mason, and she is then left to manage her feelings in solitude. While the reader is offered an understanding of Jane as a person in shock, her absolute lack of affect and effective communication in this process are also strongly suggestive of an autistic personality. Upon the public announcement in the church that Rochester is already married and that his wife is living, Jane's reaction is all internal: "My nerves vibrated to those low-spoken words as they had never vibrated to thunder—my blood felt their subtle violence as it had never felt frost or fire; but I was collected, and in no danger of swooning" (289; ch. 26). When presented with the violent spectacle of Rochester and Bertha, Jane continues silent and apparently calm, Rochester observing that she "stands [. . . .] grave and quiet at the mouth of hell, looking collectedly at the gambols of a demon" (294; ch. 26). And when, at last, Jane emerges from the solitude of her chamber, to which she has immediately after retreated, Rochester observes, "I have been waiting for you long, and listening: yet not one movement have I heard, nor one sob: five minutes more of that death-like hush, and I should have forced the lock like a burglar. So you shun me?—you shut yourself up and grieve alone! I would rather you had come and upbraided me with vehemence. You are passionate. I expected a scene of some kind. I was prepared for the hot rain of tears; only I wanted them to be shed on my breast: now a senseless floor has received them, or your drenched handkerchief. But I err: you have not wept at all! I see a white cheek and a faded eye, but no trace of tears.'" Even Jane's forgiveness here is offered silently: "I forgave him all," she writes, "yet not in words, not outwardly; only at my heart's core" (298; ch. 27).

Like contemporary autistic autobiographers and autism writers, Jane also demonstrates a strong sense of attachment to a specific arena existing apart from social convention and obligation. For some autistic persons, this realm is numerical, linguistic, or animal, with myriad overlappings of interest or savant talent. While the sphere of human social interaction may seem to the autistic person to operate by codes that are invisible and unfathomable, the area of special talent is typically experienced as enriched, having a depth or dimension beyond that experienced by neurotypical individuals.[10] So, Daniel Tammet writes of his synesthetic experience of the numerical world, where numbers have for him distinct personalities, including explicit identifying colors and size/shape characteristics. Oliver Sacks describes a conversation in prime numbers between savant twins, like two connoisseurs, each savoring the purely numerical exchange ("The Twins," 201–4). Dawn Prince-Hughes is finally able to decode and replicate human social behaviors through an intense intuitive relationship with gorillas. For a great number of autistic persons, however, the area of enriched skill and interest is visual in nature. Countless autobiographical sources attest to this widespread visual orientation among autistic persons. Temple Grandin writes specifically about "thinking in pictures"; Stephen Wiltshire, an accomplished artist from childhood, has had significant public success, including the publication of book-length collections of his work; and another visually oriented autistic person, the incompletely identified "José" from Oliver Sacks's "The Autist Artist," is seen to harbor an astonishing visual intuition, his drawings "richly expressive" and filled with roguish humor despite the fact that he is regarded by the attendants of his institutional home as an "idiot" and "hopelessly retarded" (214). For many autistic persons, the visual world simply feels more real, more concrete, more authentic than the seemingly random social interactions of a babbling humanity.

Given this context, it is not difficult to see how Jane's unmistakable visual orientation and artistic skill help to locate her on the spectrum. Indeed, Jane's visuality has provided fertile ground for critical and theoretical exploration. Among the many who have observed the narrator's exceptional visuality, Antonia Losano has described the crucial connection between Jane's visual and narrative proclivities, and Carla Peterson sees Jane's favoring of landscape over verbal caption as a feminist gesture. From the moment Jane introduces herself, leafing through Bewick's *History of British Birds* "for the letter-press of which," she declares, she "cared little" (8; ch. 1), the reader is confronted with the narrator's devotion to the visual and her ability to concentrate herself entirely, to enter into an almost altered state when visually occupied. The report Jane makes to Rochester about working on the pieces he finds in her portfolio is telling: "To paint them," she says, "was to enjoy one of the keenest pleasures I have ever known. [. . . .] I sat

10. Describing this aspect of autism from the context of a medical model, Sacks writes, "'Isolated islands of proficiency' and 'splinter skills' are spoken of in the literature'" ("Autist Artist," 219).

at them from morning till noon, and from noon till night: the length of the midsummer days favoured my inclination to apply" (126; ch. 13). Again and again, artistic creation is seen as Jane's solace, a firm place to stand in unstable or unfriendly territory. Revisiting the "hostile" home of her youth, the mature Jane is once again shunned by her cousins, but she finds "occupation and amusement" in drawing, winning the unsought admiration of Georgiana and Eliza, who come to recognize Jane as a social equal because of her evident artistic gift (ch. 21). Generally dismissive of feminine beauty, Jane's artist self connects eagerly with the "model" in qualitatively different terms from those of the social human subject. Otherwise uninterested in the charms and social graces of Rosamond, her cousin St. John's love object, Jane nevertheless feels "a thrill of artist-delight at the idea of copying from so perfect and radiant a model. [. . . .] I took a sheet of fine card-board, and drew a careful outline. I promised myself the pleasure of colouring it; and, as it was getting late then, I told her she must come and sit another day" (369; ch. 32). Like many other autistic personalities, Jane feels secure in her visual sense and her work as an artist, even when the demands of interpersonal contact challenge or threaten her individual autistic integrity.

THE POLITICS OF PRIVACY: PRESERVING AUTISTIC AUTONOMY

It is around the idea of autistic integrity that it becomes possible to reread one of the great issues of *Jane Eyre*. While millions of readers have relished the text and countless critics have analyzed its merits, there remains a sense for many readers, amateur and professional, that the narrator's general remoteness and her ultimate retreat to Ferndean, in particular, are subjects for justifiable critique. Many theorists—Gayatri Spivak and Nancy Armstrong most notably—have suggested that Jane's "individualism" (or the individualism she is seen to represent) embodies a kind of antisocial selfishness, that her aloneness and the appeal of such aloneness for the reader represent a dangerous indulgence, a shuffling off of social and political responsibility that is damaging to others, possibly even murderous. Read as a manifestation of political isolationism, Jane becomes a culpable character, a passive agent of imperialism, a feminist reactionary who rejects the need for political solidarity. The difficulty with such an interpretation, even while it contributes to our understanding of the text and of our world, is that it fails to consider that the individual, even when she acts alone, is a political creature. Jane's aloofness and social idiosyncrasy are not a belligerent confrontation of outsiders; the making of her home at Ferndean is not a wholesale rejection of humanity; and, most decidedly, her marriage to Rochester does not make her responsible for the imprisonment and death of the Creole Bertha Mason or of the imperialist outrages perpetrated by her husband's family. The putting forward of such claims is to suggest a similar critique of tremendous political progressives like Jean-Jacques Rousseau or Henry David Thoreau, whose lives both point to the political importance of solitude.

I would argue, in fact, that individuals in retreat or acting independently have been among the chief proponents of political and social change. When, in "Civil Disobedience," Thoreau explains his refusal to pay taxes, his non-involvement is described as a perfectly deliberate political act:

> It is for no particular item in the tax bill that I refuse to pay it. I simply wish to *refuse allegiance* to the State, to *withdraw and stand aloof* from it effectually. I do not care to trace the course of my dollar, if I could, till it buys a man a musket to shoot one with—the dollar is innocent—but I am concerned to trace the effects of my allegiance. In fact, I *quietly* declare war with the State, *after my fashion.* (131; emphasis added)

Like Rousseau and like Thoreau, like Emerson and Wordsworth, Jane is a writer, influencing the greater world through her publication, but even without this very concrete contribution, her privileging of her own autism, her recognition and accommodation of this foundational aspect of her identity, should be acknowledged as a legitimate political gesture. Collective political action is a necessary and productive means of effecting social change, but the insistence that every individual act collectively is nothing short of totalitarian.

In acting to preserve the autistic self, Jane's behavior may be regarded as an active form of resistance to the autistic outcomes that predominate in her world. For Jane Eyre, in her aloneness, is not an only in the tale she narrates. Having explored the parameters of autistic personality, it becomes possible to mine the text further for additional examples of individuals on the spectrum. Unsurprisingly, Jane's cousins also demonstrate autistic characteristics: The single-minded St. John, a gifted linguist, makes a virtue of denying his love for Rosamond and courts his cousin Jane even though his affection for her appears purely theoretical or "ceremonial" (398; ch. 34); Jane's rigid and narrow-minded cousin Eliza approaches life according to a deliberate "system," whereby she divides each day into "sections" and assigns to each its "task" (236; ch. 21). Apart from these is Bertha Mason, imprisoned—

speechless—in the windowless attic room at Thornfield, a tempting human "enigma"; clearly, the so-called madwoman demonstrates what Leo Kanner identifies as "disturbances of affective contact." And for each of these individuals, Jane points to a punishing conclusion: St. John closes the text with a passionate expression of longing for his own death ("even so come, Lord Jesus!" [452; ch. 38]); cousin Eliza, despite her "sense," is "walled up alive in a French convent" (242; ch. 21); and Bertha, of course, is dead by her own hand. Without the strength and will to resist the world and to build a functional private space, the autistic individual is prone to imprisonment and extermination. Resistance to the encroaching world, and to tyrannical expectations of compulsory sociality, is necessary to autistic survival and self-determination. From this perspective, Jane achieves tremendous political stature, becoming a model for effective resistance to social control, her private fecundity seeding possibilities for oppressed and marginalized peoples, especially autistic persons, outside the sphere of her immediate control.

Chapter 4

FROM INDIA-RUBBER BACK TO FLESH

A Reevaluation of
Male Embodiment in *Jane Eyre*

MARGARET ROSE TORRELL

AS ROCHESTER and Jane have one of their earlier fireside chats, he explains that he has become "hard and tough as an India-rubber ball" and asks whether she believes there is hope for his "re-transformation from India-rubber back to flesh" (125; ch. 14).[1] She opts not to respond directly to him, wondering if he has ingested too much wine, but the text itself, peopled with "hard" male constitutions-turned-flesh by narrative, participates in answering his question. This uncloaking of male bodies in *Jane Eyre* functions rhetorically to question both gender and ability hierarchies, thereby performing an intervention into cultural attitudes about masculinity and disability that gestures toward a nonhegemonic model of masculinity, one which is complemented as opposed to conflicted by physical disability.

That the novel, written and narrated by women, tells the story of women's empowerment is nearly incontrovertible. However, that this empowerment occurs in concert with—not at the expense of—a progressive reconceptualization of masculinity and embodiment has not yet been fully recognized. As masculinity theorists have argued, masculinity and feminin-

---

1. The version of the primary text referred to in this chapter is Charlotte Brontë, *Jane Eyre* (Mineola: Dover Publications, 2002).

ity are social constructions and exist in a binary relationship to each other. Alterations in feminine identity impact the binary and cause a corresponding shift in masculinity (Connell, 84). Thus, when the boundaries of woman's identity are redrawn in the novel, the borders of manhood, the other side of the binary, are also adjusted.

Because embodied status is one of the main dividing lines of gender, attributing disability and embodiment to male characters is a means of accomplishing this alteration. Gender and embodied identity are traditionally conceived along an axis where masculinity is associated with a denial of embodiment and femininity is connected to corporeality. Jane's narrative both represents and destabilizes this conventional pairing, calling attention to it and freeing the axis of gender and ability so that a greater variety of gendered and embodied combinations form, among them a reaffirmation of identity as embodied, regardless of gender. As a result of this intervention in discourse, alternate models of masculinity are offered, some of which can more easily pair with physical disability and embodied status. This revision of masculinity, like the rewriting of femininity, performs valuable cultural work. While some ableist residue persists in Jane's discourse, the various constructions of male embodiment in the novel make progress in offsetting gender binaries and reworking some of the pejorative terms of embodied and disabled identity.

This exploration of the novel's retransformation of men into flesh begins with a baseline study of the discourse of male disembodiment in theory and in the text. Jane's narrative forms a counterdiscourse to these constructions, indeed transforming "hard, tough," seemingly disembodied masculine exteriors into flesh by a rhetorical manipulation of the established terms of gender and embodiment. The second section of the chapter examines one of the discursive maneuvers through which such a change might occur, considering the possibility that Jane repurposes a patriarchal, ableist discourse to assert a position of privilege for herself. The final section of the chapter identifies another discursive maneuver that repositions the terms of gender and embodiment in a more emancipatory way: with a nod to the frayed and diffusive nature of discourse that allows contradictory readings of the novel to exist side-by-side, I perform a new reading of Rochester's embodied masculine identity that emerges out of the discursive friction between the competing notions of gender and embodiment showcased in the text. His embodied masculinity relies on a correlating construction of embodied femininity; as I show, when embodiment is attributed to both sides of the gender binary, the result is that both gender and ability hierarchies are offset, and the power generated by them is attenuated. This prepares the way for an embodied manhood that is a rather radical alternative to the conventional model of disembodied and oppressive masculinity.

The Double Bind/ary of Gender and Embodiment

Jane Eyre is a novel of competing discourses about gender and embodiment. This section foregrounds the significance of male embodiment in the novel by examining the construction of male disembodiment in theory and in *Jane Eyre*. The subsequent sections take up two possible ways of reading Jane's response to these constructions. For the purposes of this chapter, I use the word *embodiment* to mean the understanding of the self and/or other selves as bodies. Embodiment is conceptually developed by an awareness of various visceral realities such as bodily processes, sensations, physical manifestations of strong emotion, and pain. As reflected in the work of such theorists as Peter Stallybrass, Allon White, and Martha Nussbaum, embodiment is often associated with nebulous corporeal boundaries, with the leaky and permeable, with the excretion of bodily fluids and a susceptibility to various forms of penetration from the outside. Embodiment frequently is a reminder of the "animal" or "mortal" nature of humanness.

There is almost a complete overlap between embodiment and disability; embodiment is in fact often read as the opposite of an ideal state of health in which the boundaries of the body are under careful control and visceral realities would therefore be invisible to others and virtually unnoticeable to oneself. Embodiment and disability, on the other hand, both involve the conscious awareness of oneself as a body. If there is a difference between embodiment and disability, it is perhaps a matter of timing: embodiment is a universal state (we—all of us—are bodies) and disability is a current identity for some, an eventual identity for most others. Perhaps because embodiment and disability are often reminders of our animal and mortal status, they have been interpreted through discourse as highly undesirable, facts to be anxiously denied as opposed to embraced. As a means of accomplishing this denial, embodiment and disability are often conflated, perceived pejoratively, and, as Nussbaum demonstrates in "'Secret Sewers of Vice': Disgust, Bodies, and the Law," broadcast on marginalized people as a way of maintaining the privileged status of dominant social groups.[2]

2. Nussbaum attributes the existence of the disembodied/embodied binary to people's strong desire to eschew thinking about themselves as mortal. As a result, they project characteristics of embodiment onto others: "We need a group of humans to bound ourselves against, who will come to exemplify the boundary line between the truly human and the

The flight from embodiment, then, forms a discourse that is a foundation for ethnic, class, gender, and other oppressive social divisions. While many of these are active in *Jane Eyre*, the focus here is on the construction of gender. The conflation of "female" with embodiment and disability in patriarchal discourse is evident, as Rosemarie Garland-Thomson observes, at least as early as Aristotle's *Generation of Animals*. She powerfully explains the insidiousness of the double binary: "I want to suggest that a firm boundary between 'disabled' and 'nondisabled' women cannot be meaningfully drawn—just as any absolute distinction between sex and gender is problematic. Femininity and disability are inextricably entangled in patriarchal culture" (*Extraordinary Bodies*, 27). By extension, male privilege is gained by a comparative disassociation from the body. The mechanism works by way of discursive sleight of hand. Like the magician who directs his audience's attention to his scantily clad assistant so that he can perform his trickery undetected, the emphasis on women's embodiment detracts attention from the male body, encasing it in a protective cloak of invisibility and normativity. Calvin Thomas sketches out how this construction operates: "the repression of the abject vulnerability of the male body—as repression necessary for the construction of heteronormative masculinity—demands a displacement of that vulnerability and all that it materially entails, onto the feminine" (63). In fact, the practice of projecting corporeality onto women in order to emphasize male "hardness" and comparative disembodiment is so common that Paul McIlvenny lists it as one of the foundational elements of dominant masculinity:

> [C]ontemporary hegemonic masculinity in relation to the male body often emphasizes ability, superhuman strength and stamina, physical violence, unemotionality, hardness, autonomy, potency, assertiveness, authority, the abjection of other bodies (the feminine, the homosexual, the grotesque), and the shame of failure. (103)

---

basely animal. If those quasi animals stand between us and our own animality, then we are one step further away from being animal and mortal ourselves. Thus throughout history, certain disgust properties [associated with embodiment]—sliminess, bad smell, stickiness, decay, foulness—have been repeatedly and monotonously associated with, indeed projected onto, groups by reference to whom privileged groups seek to define their superior human status" ("Secret Sewers of Vice," 29). Davis, in "Constructing Normalcy: The Bell Curve, the Novel, and the Invention of the Disabled Body in the Nineteenth Century," notes that during the nineteenth century, such constructions were particularly active as various social changes triggered a desperate desire for people to assert that they were "normal."

Even physical characteristics that are associated with the male body, such as physical strength and muscular power, become understood as features of the idealized body under perfect control. The "hard" male body is constructed, by way of comparison to other bodies, as disembodied—that is, less associated with the visceral realities of embodiment.

The insistence on male strength, toughness, and infallible physicality coupled with the connection of women to markedly weaker, faulty bodies has historically been a means of maintaining gender inequality. R. W. Connell notes that when advances in women's equality or other social changes trigger a masculinity crisis, a characteristic response is for there to be a greater emphasis on the hard, muscular male body. This configuration of the male body, Connell argues, functions as a way to suggest "men's superiority and right to rule" (84, 54–55).[3] *Jane Eyre* comes out of a time of particularly intense gender flux, one of those points in history during which there was a crisis in masculinity that resulted in the reinforcement of gender boundaries. In Victorian England, women's equal rights movements, industrialization, and class redefinition among other factors contributed to rethinking of gender and thereby promoted the production of cultural narratives that emphasized female and denied male embodiment. On the one hand, dominant masculinity became associated with emblems of ideal health— for example, strength, vigor, physical and emotional control. On the other hand, there was an increased construction of women as embodied. Thus, as Helena Michie puts it, the Victorians didn't just "inherit" the double binary of gender and embodiment but indeed "perfected it" (408–9) in response to a change in gender roles that threatened preexisting social hierarchies. As a result, differences in male and female embodiment were emphasized to maintain a clear division between the sexes. As Michie writes, there is "a historically unprecedented sense of the differences between the sexes that expressed itself, among other ways, in corporeal terms" in Victorian England (409).

A double binary is thereby set up in which a central difference between male and female identity occurs at the crossroads of disembodiment and

---

3. For more on the male/disembodied vs. female/embodied dichotomy as it plays out historically during times of crises in masculinity, see, for example, Breitenberg's *Anxious Masculinity* which examines how social changes in the sixteenth and seventeenth centuries produce an acceleration of masculinist discourse and Theweleit's *Male Fantasies* which explores the reinforcement of the gender dichotomy in Germany by men involved in the Freikorps movement in the wake of World War I. Bordo, in *The Male Body*, in addition to Thomas and McIlvenny who are mentioned above, are among the critics who observe this dichotomy in more contemporary times.

embodiment. Although embodiment is natural and normative, the preference given to masculine disembodiment is actually quite binding—that is,
both stubbornly reinforced and severely restrictive. That this double binary
is active in *Jane Eyre* is clear: the most central male characters are mouth-
pieces for masculinist narratives that elevate the status of men by emphasizing male disembodiment and female embodiment. For example, as the
novel opens, John Reed verbally assaults Jane. In fits of patriarchal postur-
ing through which he enacts his position as "master" of the household, he
tells her she is a "bad animal" (9; ch. 1) and later reports that she is a "mad
cat" (26; ch. 2), emphasizing her ties to her animal nature. The embodiment of Jane is carried forward by Mr. Brocklehurst, who announces to
the pupils and teachers at Lowood that Jane is a source of contagion and
sickness: because Mrs. Reed is afraid that Jane's "vicious example should
contaminate" the purity of the Reed children, Jane is discharged to Lowood
so that she can "be healed, even as the Jews of old sent their diseased to the
troubled pool of Bethesda" (63; ch. 7). Rochester also emphasizes Jane's
embodied status and is curiously more forthright about linking her with illness when he is in the guise of the gypsy fortune teller: "You are cold; you
are sick; and you are silly," he insists, reading her lonesomeness as a type
of sickness and feminine folly (187; ch. 19). Other comments about Jane
by Rochester associate her with something for him to control and own,
such as his configuration of her as "pet lamb" to his "shepherd" (204; ch.
20), a construction that—like John's—associates Jane with the animal. Even
St. John's religious beneficence is built on such constructions: for example,
when Jane all but rejects his marriage proposal and prepares to return to
Rochester, St. John slips a note under her door in which he exhorts her to
pray to avoid temptation. He cautions, "the spirit, I trust, is willing, but the
flesh, I see, is weak" (393; ch. 36).

It is worth noting that at moments when Jane threatens the position of
male characters, they increase their emphasis on her embodiment. These
instances are microcosms of cultural dynamics in which movements toward
female independence trigger a crisis in masculinity that leads to an acceleration in embodied constructions of women. For example, it is when Jane acts
independently of St. John's wishes for her and opts not to spend her life in
India with him that he connects her decision to a weakness of her flesh (393;
ch. 36). Later, he is still concerned about whether Jane is following spirit or
fleshly desire even after he receives news of her marriage (420; ch. 38). The
embodied construction of women is likewise exacerbated when men are in
the threatened position of having their cloak of invisibility cast from their
bodies. For example, when Jane confronts Rochester about the shadowy fig-

ure who tramples her wedding veil, Rochester discredits Jane by suggesting fallibility in *her* perception. When she asks who the woman is, he reassures her that she is merely Jane's hallucination: "The creature of an over-stimulated brain; that is certain. I must be careful of you, my treasure: nerves like yours were not made for rough handling" (268; ch. 25). His response is to suggest, rather forcefully, Jane's inherent unreliability, easy excitability, and general frailty, a sense he maintains even as she argues against it (266–67; ch. 25). Through the discursive sleight of hand which emphasizes her embodiment, Rochester's flaw remains hidden, his cloak still intact.

BACK TO FLESH:
JANE'S COUNTERNARRATIVES OF MALE EMBODIMENT

The main male voices in the novel thus reproduce traditional patriarchal configurations by drawing on a double binary that emphasizes male disembodiment through an ableist and masculinist rhetoric that associates women with embodiment. However, Jane's narrative disrupts such oppressive configurations: the story she tells is one in which embodied status is attached to men as well as to women. Her narrative thereby functions as a counterdiscourse that troubles gender and ability binaries active in the text and culture.

In the two remaining sections of this chapter, I explore two ways that such a counterdiscourse might be deployed in the text. This section considers the possibility that Jane draws from a discourse of embodiment that is used to marginalize women and applies it to men (as well as to other women[4]); in essence she repurposes tools of gender oppression to situate herself in a less embodied and therefore more socially privileged position. This reading of the novel is in line with the recent disability studies inspired scholarship of David Bolt and Chih-Ping Chen. In the final section of the chapter, I probe Jane's counterdiscourse for more emancipatory configurations of gender and embodiment.

As we explored in the previous section, John Reed, Mr. Brocklehurst, Rochester, and St. John tell a tale of Jane's embodiment through their spoken words; however, the story she tells in her narrative is one which empha-

---

4. The depiction of female "others" in *Jane Eyre* has received comparatively more critical attention than the construction of male characters. For more on the gendered politics of the portrayals of women in the novel, see Spivak, who considers Bertha as "a figure produced by the axiomatic of imperialism" ("Three Women's Texts," 247) and Chen, who examines Bertha and Blanche through the dynamics of the freak show.

sizes their corporeality and human fallibility. This embodied construction of them attenuates the power inherent in their embodied construction of Jane. For example, seemingly in response to John Reed's "bad animal" comment, Jane connects her cousin with corporeal characteristics, telling us "he was not quick either of vision or conception" (9; ch. 1) and depicting him in highly physiological terms that verge on the grotesque: he has "a dingy and unwholesome skin [. . .] heavy limbs and large extremities. He gorged himself habitually at the table, which made him bilious" and is generally in "delicate health" (9; ch. 1). This portrayal is continued throughout the novel, as John is aligned with other embodied and more female attributes of the time, such as excessive, uncontrollable impulses, eventually leading to his presumed suicide and his family's ruin (209; ch. 21). Mr. Brocklehurst's mission is to perform a type of disembodiment on his all-too-corporeal female charges—"to mortify in girls the lusts of the flesh" (61; ch. 7). However, the telling arrival of his own very well-coifed daughters and his stingy, hypocritical treatment of the Lowood pupils suggest, to turn his own discourse on himself, a heavy inclination toward the lusts of his flesh (61; ch. 7). Likewise, at the novel's close, St. John is not the spiritual, work-driven, unfeeling machine he makes himself out to be, but he is instead mortal, fallible, and enfleshed (422; ch. 38).

Rochester's introduction in the text, when he falls from the horse and must rely on Jane's help (109; ch. 12), is a model for several other moments that emphasize his connection to his body and situate Jane as a type of caregiver. For example, when Bertha sets fire to his bed, he is at first just a body—that is, he is inert flesh, completely unable to be aroused despite Jane's efforts to wake him. He is then soaked in fluids from his ewer and basin. Both are full—the ewer (or pitcher) with water, the basin with what must be "used" water—and so whatever bodily residue the basin water has washed off Rochester, Jane now casts back at him, a rather appropriate reminder of his embodiment. Finally, with a temporary realization of his own frailty, Rochester understands that he is helpless without Jane's intervention (142; ch. 15). Later, Rochester's shock at the news of Mason's arrival affords Jane another glimpse beneath the armor of his disembodiment. Unable to speak in full sentences, his breathing undergoing spasms, his face extremely pale, too weak to move by his own power, he again relies on her physical support (193–94; ch. 19). Rochester's blindness and amputation maintain these dynamics (and are the focus of the last section of this chapter).

Further, Rochester's earlier family and personal history also situate him outside of more traditional masculine roles. He is a second-born son who is not poised to inherit his father's fortune and the reputed victim of his father and brother's manipulations. As such, he is somewhat removed from the system of masculine privilege. In addition, his early marriage to Bertha and his various affairs belie a character aligned with strong physical passion, one that he cannot completely offset by projecting illicit sexual natures onto his assorted female partners. Likewise, although he defends his treatment of Bertha by depicting her as insane and monstrous, details in his own depiction reveal, as Julia Miele Rodas argues in "Brontë's *Jane Eyre*," that he is very similar to his first wife.

Thus, if John Reed, Brocklehurst, St. John, and Rochester all don similar discursive masks of masculinity in an effort to render their bodies transparent, Jane's accounts reveal the flesh that lies beneath their discourse of denial. Rochester may request Jane's help with escaping from his India-rubber exterior; however, her narrative suggests that his disembodied identity, like that of the other male characters who put on a cloak of invisibility in their attempts to embody her, has been maintained by a social discourse that by its very nature is unstable and illusory.

For most of the novel, Jane's reconstruction of John, Brocklehurst, St. John, and Rochester appears to be predominantly accomplished through an inversion of the gender binary that maintains the hegemonic structure of the ability binary. When the privileged side of the gender binary is associated with embodiment, the seemingly stable terms of the double binary become unfixed, allowing alternative models of gender and ability to establish themselves. Embodied status is attributed to men and, following the pattern, Jane is by comparison situated in a less embodied and therefore more socially valued position. Because both sides of a binary exist in synergistic relationship to one another, the construction of men as embodied refashions both male and female identity. As Calvin Thomas argues, in fact, there is a "certain feminist urgency" in "the project of male embodiment" because the association of men with their bodies undermines a construction that has historically powered oppressive gender divisions (71). According to this reading, the masculinist discourse governing gender difference is thereby interrogated, but ableist assumptions about embodiment appear to remain firmly in place.

This argument is taken up by disability studies scholars who are rightly suspicious of how disability is portrayed in the novel. They convincingly contend that the process of reassigning gender positions results in a perpetuation of ableist thinking. For example, Bolt, in his study of Rochester's blindness, powerfully demonstrates that the text reconstructs women's positions by placing the stress on male as opposed to female embodiment: "Male and female roles may well be inverted in the novel, but the underpinning hierarchies of normativism over disability and 'the sighted' over 'the blind' remain intact" (271). Along a similar line, Chen insightfully argues that by the end of the novel, Jane is not only in the more masculine and able position but that, as the narrator, she puts Rochester on display, almost like the host of a freak show would exhibit and capitalize on the physical alterity of the performers: "The subversion of freak show power relations concludes with the reinstatement of power hierarchy. Gender inequality and social marginality faced by a woman are 'corrected' only by the reversal of the gendered roles of the host and the exhibit" (383). For both Bolt and Chen, then, *Jane Eyre* questions gender hierarchies but raises the status of Jane by way of attributing more embodied identification to men. Jane's role as caregiver to Rochester, active at their first meeting and carried through to the novel's end, especially supports such a reading. The caregiver is in a position, as Garland-Thomson observes, of using the disabled body to "organize a more empowered and prestigious selfhood" (*Extraordinary Bodies,* 90). In this reading, *Jane Eyre* thereby replaces social discourses that suggest women's inferiority with a counterdiscourse that suggests male inferiority. In doing so, it transmits and perpetuates disempowered, pejorative conceptions of disability.

This reassignment of embodied identity to empower women has also been observed in other nineteenth-century literature. For example, Hugh McElaney's study of disability and freakery in Louisa May Alcott's work suggests that the disability of male characters in Alcott's and other nineteenth-century American women's writing is often a punishment for a male child's "excessive manifestations of masculinity" (148). By disabling young males, McElaney posits, the female writer asserts the comparative supremacy of women who are written as able-bodied and therefore less embodied than these male characters (156–57).

Rochester's own shifting status from blind man to partially sighted man replicates the ability binary in another way, as Elizabeth Donaldson and Bolt both demonstrate. Donaldson reads Rochester's return to partial sight as a reassertion of normalcy after his blindness ("The Corpus of the Madwoman," 110). As such, Rochester's disability becomes a point of assuring readers of their own wholeness, both because he gets some sight back, thereby allowing the reader to envision a happy ending, and because he remains disabled, thereby ensuring the presumably nondisabled reader of her own wholeness and normalcy. As Bolt also argues, "by the end of the novel it becomes apparent that the misery of the blindman is integral to the happiness of not only the sighted woman, but also the sighted man who

Rochester becomes" (285). These readings underscore the insidious connections between embodiment and disempowerment. Rochester's status as a blind man is used to privilege the relative disembodiment and consequently elevated status not only of Jane and the reader but also of the partially sighted Rochester.

The reading of the novel I have been considering in this section suggests that Jane's growth and empowerment are dependent on her ability to repurpose the tools of oppressive discourse to her advantage. While gender construction may become more mobile in her narrative, the pejorative terms of embodiment appear to be far more difficult to budge. However, they are not completely inflexible, and in the final section of this chapter I provide another reading of the novel that diverges from previous interpretations, one in which both the terms of gender and ability are reconfigured.

DISPERSED DISCOURSES:
TOWARD AN ALTERNATIVE READING OF
EMBODIMENT AND GENDER

My reading of *Jane Eyre* in this section demonstrates a model of gender reconstruction that agitates the abled–disabled binary at the same time that it questions the gender binary. In essence, when Brontë sets about to transform men back into flesh, the terms of gender and ability binaries are not reversed but indeed dismantled. The goal in this section is to explore how gender and embodiment identifications are altered when embodiment is attributed to both sides of the binary. After examining the shifting nature of language and the status of Jane's embodiment, this section specifically focuses on disabled masculinity theory and its application to Rochester, since his embodiment and masculinity are especially remarkable pairings.

By way of transitioning into the final section of the chapter, I would like to call attention to the dispersive nature of language and discourse, both to theorize the sometimes oppressive/sometimes empowering workings of gender and ability in the novel and to qualify my reading of Rochester, even before I begin it. Language has an expansive quality—it can be used to advance a kind of emancipatory thinking necessary for social justice— and at the same time it is also limited (the binary nature of the linguistic structure itself presupposes the existence of latent hierarchal relationships). James Wilson and Cynthia Lewiecki-Wilson recognize the multivalent properties of language in "Disability, Rhetoric, and the Body":

Language's effects are dispersed, uneven, and contradictory. People wield language for many purposes, but at the same time language's effects also spill or seep out, beyond the immediate container of the situation and intention for which it was crafted. Language can only be partly harnessed as an instrument of agency, never wholly so, for it always carries along many other material histories and purposes and the arbitrary and differential traces of its systematic functioning. If language can be said to transform economic systems, institutions, and social practices, then its power flows diffusively in uneven currents. (3)

Wilson and Lewiecki-Wilson are both cautious and optimistic about the power of language. Language can be used in the service of emancipatory thinking, but "never wholly so"; it is almost always inflected by remnants of the power structures it is employed to interrogate. Likewise, liberatory models of identity can be advanced through counter discourses, but these are rarely free of the imprint of social hierarchies. In fact, the model of male embodiment in the novel I have so far discussed is liberatory in the sense that it reseats hierarchical gender identifications, but at the same time it is oppressive because it accomplishes its work by reproducing ability hierarchies. Similar inversions take place in the construction of socioeconomic class, where, for example, Aunt Reed's prolonged illness might be read as narrative backlash for her trenchant embodied constructions of her niece. Jane herself employs such a strategy to uphold her womanly virtue by way of contrast to the French Adèle, the Creole Bertha, and the continental mistresses of Rochester, forging "foreign" women's connection to various lusts of the flesh in order to elevate her white English womanhood.

These are just some of the places where oppressive thinking may "seep out" by way of the disembodied–embodied binary, even as the novel challenges such constructions of women by men and even as the narrative works toward situating embodiment as a more normative state. In acknowledging the "diffusive" and "uneven currents" of language, I hope to validate readings of the text based on the limits of discourse, as I have done so far, as well as to discover moments where discourse has more expansive potential, moments in the text where language does begin to work more holistically out of the oppressive master narratives of a culture, as I do below.

Before turning to the analysis of Rochester, I will briefly address the issue of Jane's embodiment because it has an impact on how her constructions of male corporeality might be interpreted. Specifically, the notion that Jane enforces her own disembodiment when she links men to their bodies might be reconsidered. To follow the India-rubber metaphor, when Jane shows

Rochester's hard, tough exterior to be merely a self-constructed discursive mask, she does not don that same mask to render her body invisible. In fact, her narrative suggests the futility and hypocrisy—indeed the danger— of denying one's connection to the body.

Thus, although Jane does not consistently align herself with disabled identity, her concept of herself is inextricably tied to her body. Because she tells her story by way of recollection, the plentiful moments of bodily awareness in her narrative reflect a fairly unified sense of her corporeal identity from the standpoint of a grown woman. Only six sentences into her narrative, as she recalls her experiences as a girl of ten, she remarks on her "physical inferiority" to her cousins and her painfully cold "nipped fingers and toes" (7; ch. 1). Soon after, the head injury caused by John's attack on her results in pain, bleeding, and unconsciousness and has long term effects on her health, making her feel "physically weak and broken down" (19; ch. 3). The deprivations she experiences at Lowood are likewise described in embodied terms. The cold "nipped" and hunger "gnawed" her (46; ch. 5). Exposure to the snow causes her torturous pain, and she describes her "wretched feet flayed and swollen to lameness" (72; ch. 9). Jane is also prone to a restless excitement that is described in physical terms. For example, she "felt the pulses throb in [her] head and temples" as she considers her options for departing Lowood (82; ch. 10). Several times during her narrative, Jane emphasizes her small frame, pale complexion, and her "irregular," "marked" features (94; ch. 11). It is these that Jane compares unfavorably to Blanche Ingram's classic beauty to attempt to check her own growing interest in Rochester (153–4; ch. 16). This embodied portrayal is maintained through to Jane and Rochester's reunion, where, upon the anticipation of being with Rochester again, Jane's body is so uncontrollable she cannot hold her trembling frame still—emblematically, the water spills from the glass on her tray and her "heart struck [her] ribs loud and fast" (404; ch. 37). Her pregnancy and motherhood carry her embodied status to and beyond the novel's close. It is also worth noting that other female characters, such as Mrs. Reed and Helen, are configured as embodied alongside Jane.[5] To be sure, additional studies of Jane's embodiment (and that of other female characters) are needed to more fully articulate how the textual presence of women as bodies alongside of men as bodies can impact the gender-embodiment binary; these observations are starting points.

5. Interestingly, Helen's religious leaning allows her to accept her own embodiment and forecast a sense that all bodies are "corruptible" and mortal (55; ch. 6).

In this brief account of Jane's body, the suggestion is that when she contradicts masculinist discourses by asserting male embodiment, she leaves the discourses that equate femaleness with corporeality intact. The result is a narrative that tells the story of embodiment across gender identification, one that thereby rewrites the terms of corporeal identity alongside a reinscription of gender. No longer exclusively associated with the disparaged side of the binary, embodied status begins to shed its association with the anomalous, disempowered, and exclusively female and is situated as a more normal and natural condition of being. Attributing embodied status to men as the privileged side of the binary (while maintaining women's embodiment alongside of it) offers a recasting of masculinity apart from its association with social dominance and oppression. It is this formulation of masculinity in scholarship and *Jane Eyre* to which I now turn my attention.

It is challenging to conceive of an embodied masculinity because the gender/ability binary continues to remain in place, although not without increasing critical interrogation, in contemporary thinking. The root of the challenge is that masculinity and embodiment are understood as incongruous states. Thomas Gerschick explains the nature of this contradiction: "for men with physical disabilities, masculine gender privilege collides with the stigmatized status of having a disability, thereby causing status inconsistency, as having a disability, erodes much, but not all, masculine privilege" ("Toward a Theory," 1265). As a result, the contradictory nature of masculinity and disability has been known to cause disabled men to internalize a sense of failure at not meeting traditional masculine standards ("Sisyphus," 123). In fact, the relationship between female embodiment and masculine disembodiment is so potent that it is usually the case that a reversal of the terms of embodiment often presumes a correlating reversal of the terms of gender. Judith Halberstam elaborates: "The male body is feminized when sick and the female body is masculinized when healthy, invigorated, and active" (354). It seems that even in contemporary culture, physical disability is at odds with masculine identity and tends to act as a demasculinizing agent.

Yet as difficult as it is to conflate these socially contradictory identities, male embodiment has been singled out by masculinity studies and disability studies alike as an inroad to alleviating gender and ability oppression. Scholars working in these areas advocate for a type of male transformation into flesh—for the study of men as bodies that are fallible, mortal, leaky, and subject to cultural inscription. As Thomas explains, "*one* possibly productive way to analyze male power and hegemony, and to reconfigure male identification and desire, involves a specific sort of attention to the 'matter' of the male body and to the materialization of that body *in writing*" (62). Connell goes further, suggesting that "a politics of social justice" for gender inequality necessitates "re-embodiment for men, a search for different ways of using, feeling and showing male bodies," including placing male bodies in more traditionally female situations and roles (233). The notion of masculinities—masculinity in many forms, especially as it intersects with other cultural identities—reinforces the potential multiplicity of this gender category. Disability studies researchers such as Gerschick, Adam Stephen Miller, and Russell Shuttleworth have shown how some disabled men successfully access such alternative notions of masculinity and embodiment. For example, they expand their "masculine repertoire" so that they can more flexibly accommodate feminine roles when it is advantageous to do so (Shuttleworth, 175), and they craft their masculine identity "along the lines of their own abilities, perceptions, and strengths" (Gerschick and Miller, 265). This leads to positive experiences of disabled masculinity—indeed, to a diversity of disabled masculinities.

These insights from masculinity studies and disability studies theorists begin to unravel the cloak of invisibility from the male body, establishing in its place a proverbial and emancipatory coat of many colors. Locating the male body in various experiences, forms, and conditions erodes the primacy of masculinity as a disembodied identity, showing these to be cultural constructs that have little bearing on lived experience. This conception of men as bodies, then, is a way out of the gender and ability binary because it makes progress toward detaching disempowerment and emasculation from embodied status.

These maneuvers are accomplished because of the dispersive nature of discourse. The double binary may seem so locked in place that masculinity and embodiment are an impossible pairing. However, the terms of ability, like the terms of gender, are based in discourse and can thereby be redefined by counter discourse. Judith Keegan Gardiner argues this point: "The conflation of emasculation, castration, feminization, and femininity is a political maneuver, not a psychological law, and masculinity and femininity have different meanings and uses in male and female bodies and in differing cultural contexts" (15). We have been trained to read the intersection of embodiment and masculinity as an undesirable loss of power because we have also been trained to associate embodiment with femininity and weakness. Gardiner reminds us that these constructions are dependent on culture and political system, noting also that their connection does not occur cross culturally. Thus, the grouping of disability, embodiment, femininity, weakness, and death, like the grouping of their opposites, is a function of a discourse that maintains social hierarchies and can therefore be challenged through critique and counter discourse. With this in mind, the task before us is how to understand embodied masculinity not as disempowering and emasculating, but instead as a catalyst for more expansive thinking about gender and ability.

To be sure, the first accounts of Rochester's disablement suggest the presumed incongruity of masculine and embodied identity. The host of the inn (who was also butler to Rochester's father) provides the initial report, projecting severe pity on Rochester's current state. With one eye "knocked out," "the other eye inflamed [so that] he lost the sight of that also," and one hand crushed and amputated, Rochester is "now helpless, indeed—blind and a cripple" and as such "quite broken down" (401; ch. 36). With no available alternative masculine identity to assign to Rochester, the host can only read his change in body as a loss of status. Rochester's life has become so tragic, so unplaceable in the schema of social value, that the host reports that "many think he had better be dead" (400; ch. 36). When Jane first observes the disabled Rochester coming out of the door at Ferndean, groping, uncertain, his movements fall short of any masculine ideal (403; ch. 37), reflecting Shuttleworth's observations that the nature of one's disability may make it impossible to perform the expected movements and comportment of dominant masculinity (167). Upon Jane's reunion with Rochester, we find that he himself has subscribed to the masculine ideal of his time. Unable to align his disabilities with his masculinity, he feels degraded and puts himself into social isolation. He can no longer think of himself as attractive or eligible for romance or marriage. Concerned that Jane would "suffer [. . .] to devote [herself] to a blind lameter like [him]" (406; ch. 37), he fears his arm ("a mere stump—a ghastly sight") and his "cicatrized visage" will revolt her (408; ch. 37). Understandably, she does initially feel some sorrow mixed with pity at seeing him again, and she seems particularly taken by his sadness and powerlessness (410; ch. 37).

However, undercurrents in Jane's narration assert Rochester's masculinity and indeed his sexual desirability alongside his disability. To her, he is muscular, manly, and sexy. Despite a change in his countenance, she finds that he has maintained his "athletic strength" and "vigorous prime" (403; ch. 37). As she observes his aimless, uncertain movements on Ferndean's doorstep, she can barely keep herself from going to him and "dar[ing] to drop a kiss on that brow of rock, and on those lips so sternly sealed beneath it" (403; ch. 37). While he may not perform masculinity in his movements, his stoic face is inherently masculine, and she wishes to kiss both brow and lips—suggesting her sexual attraction to him as a disabled man. In a subsequent construction of him, she writes of his crying in a way that also maintains masculine identification: "I saw a tear slide from under the sealed eyelid, and trickle down the manly cheek" (412; ch. 37). Here, she conflates the emotional and embodied (indeed the leaky) with the manly—as a result—a new composite of masculine traits begins to form.

Her desire for Rochester also accomplishes a rewriting of conventional notions of disabled masculinity. Under Jane's pen, he is not asexual, an object of disgust, a person to be shunned, but is instead someone who stokes her desire and allows her an outlet to experience it. This is a concept that is built into the caregiver interactions that appear throughout the text and culminate in the final chapters. The moments in *Jane Eyre* where Jane acts as caregiver/rescuer to Rochester are particularly erotically charged. Physical touch between them, especially before any declaration of affection is made, would ordinarily be impermissible in Victorian society, but in Jane's narrative it is sanctioned—made proper and presumably asexual—by the terms of the caregiver relationship. In the romance of Jane and Rochester, however, these moments are an outlet for the sexual desire Jane has for Rochester, allowing her the thrill of physical contact while upholding her virtue and purity under the guise of caregiving. For example, when Jane first encounters the intriguing stranger on the road, she says she "should have been afraid to touch a horse when alone," but the rules of Victorian female propriety suggest that she certainly should be even more afraid to come into close physical proximity with—indeed to be touched by—an unknown man, if not for concerns about her own safety then surely for concerns about her reputation (109; ch. 12). However, under the guise of "necessity," Rochester and Jane have their first physical encounter as he puts his arm around her and she helps him to his horse. This dynamic is repeated again at the other moments of her coming to Rochester's aid. All suggest erotically charged eruptions in their developing relationship.

A similar dynamic permits Jane to narrate the eroticism of her reunion with Rochester. The touch of his "wandering hand" which a few lines later becomes his "muscular hand" on her "arm [. . .] shoulder-neck-waist" is just as longed-for by her as when he subsequently "entwined and gathered [her] to him" (405; ch. 37). She really means it (in more ways than one) when she tells him "I am glad to be so near you again" (405; ch. 37). His "groping," "wandering [and muscular] hand" becomes a site of sexual virility and enacts an erotic touch that is desired by both Rochester and Jane. I therefore do not read this moment according to the stereotype of the blindman as lecherous (where "touch becomes a grope and ultimately a lecherous grip") as Bolt does (275), but instead as an erotic moment, desired by both parties, from which new associations between disabled masculinity and female sexual desire may "seep out" (Wilson and Lewiecki-Wilson, 3).

Thus, Jane's narration asserts Rochester's masculinity and sexual desirability alongside his disability, imbuing male embodment with new value. In addition, she also emphasizes a developing interdependence in their relationship that suggests a diffusion of the oppressive hierarchies attendant to both gender and ability. For example, on the second day of their reunion, as their love is confirmed through their dialogue, Rochester calls attention again to his "seared vision" and "crippled strength," likening himself to a decaying, ruined, lightning-struck tree. Jane answers him back, reinscribing the image with the more positive association of a "green and vigorous tree": "Plants will grow about your roots, whether you ask them or not, because they take delight in your bountiful shadow; and as they grow they will lean towards you, and wind round you, because your strength offers them so safe a prop" (415; ch. 37). Her reconstruction of him emphasizes his vigor, strength, and generosity, as well as his ability to be of use and support—all descriptors of masculinity, but not necessarily dominant, oppressive masculinity.[6] He thus may need her help (indeed, just a few lines later he says she will "have to lead [him] about by the hand" and "wait on" him), but he also will be her support.

This interdependence powers Jane's love for him even more, as she asserts: "I love you better now when I can really be useful to you, than I did in your state of proud independence, when you disdained every part but that of the giver and protector" (416; ch. 37). His dependence on her (perhaps because it is coupled by her dependence on him) allows a more equal distribution of power in the relationship and at the same time does not affect his masculine vigor, desirability, or strength. In fact, she tells him he has no deficiencies (416; ch. 37), an assertion that surprisingly counters ableist attitudes about embodment. The ending chapter confirms their interdependence is still strong after years of marriage. She asserts, "I am my husband's

6. There are several earlier readings of Rochester that understand his disability as an avenue toward freeing him from the pressures of dominant masculinity, but these analyses predate many insights later developed through disability studies. For example, Kendrick identifies the potential of Brontë's text to redefine masculinity by placing Rochester in positions that are removed from dominant social discourses of gender and class. Kendrick argues that Rochester "represents a man who is quite at odds with the dominant narrative of being an 'English Gentleman'" from the start (247), and from his final vantage point of social exile, he "rearticulates and redefines his position as a masculine subject" (235). Likewise, Wylie attaches a liberatory significance to Rochester's disability. As Wylie argues, Rochester recognizes that the terms of dominant masculinity are impossible fictions to live up to and in doing so, he becomes "a new type of masculine hero: one who is more in keeping with the flawed humanity of [Brontë's] own experience" (68).

life as fully is he is mine" and "all my confidence is bestowed on him, all his confidence is devoted to me; we are precisely suited in character—perfect concord is the result" (420–21; ch. 38).[7] It is a union based on interdependence in which no partner has greater privilege than the other, one that seems to have worked successfully out of the double binary.

Thus, three elements in Jane's reinscription of Rochester suggest a nascent liberatory model of embodied masculinity in her depiction of him. First, through Jane's narratives, Rochester's masculinity is asserted alongside his disability and embodiment. Even as he himself cannot yet read his new status according to the models of masculinity available to him, she redefines the borders of masculine identity to admit male embodiment. This redefinition of masculinity suggests, if we return to disability studies theories, a type of gender flexibility or expansion of the "masculine repertoire" (Shuttleworth, 175). Rochester retains more masculine and Jane more feminine attributes, so there is not a complete removal of the conventional terms of gender, but there is certainly more freedom to access elements of masculinity and femininity as necessary. Second, Jane's assertion of her desire for Rochester forges a connection between disability and sexual desirability that is absent in conventional thinking about disabled masculinity. Third, the interdependent nature of their union forecasts a dispersion of power that is a foundation for achieving greater social equality. Ironically, these new possibilities for understanding male corporeal identity may be more readily conceivable by Jane because she has experience with understanding herself as embodied, according to patriarchal constructions of female identity that have been projected onto her. Her narrative's rather sweeping overview of their happy marriage suggests that Rochester has adopted such a positive understanding of himself, most likely through her influence.

It is curious that Brontë (or God's mercy, according to the narrative) grants Rochester a return to partial sight in the last paragraphs of the novel as opposed to closing with him remaining blind. This is an admittedly ocularcentric turn, as Bolt asserts (285), and indeed represents an "uneven" current in the flow of the text and this reading (Wilson and Lewiecki-Wil-

---

7. Rochester and Jane's strong interconnectedness is depicted in a highly positive way, with the possible exception of her admission that she finds his willing and total acceptance of her help "sad": "And there was a pleasure in my services, most full, most exquisite, even though sad—because he claimed these services without painful shame or damping humiliation. He loved me so truly, that he knew no reluctance in profiting by my attendance" (421; ch. 38). However, in the context of Jane's narration, I favor reading her use of "sad" as evoking "grave" or "serious," which were earlier uses of the word. In that sense, she finds her role as helper pleasurable but also serious (that is, important and bearing heavy responsibility) because he trusts her implicitly.

son, 3), but it is not a completely ableist one. Rochester's fulfillment, sexual attractiveness, paternity, and interdependent relationship with Jane predate the return of his sight, so he is granted such positive identifications as a blind man. Further, his identities as a disabled man (a vision-impaired amputee) and as a fulfilled person are intact at the novel's close.

Overall, Rochester's is an unusually progressive portrait of disabled masculinity. He has achieved an integration of identity characteristics that counters traditional understandings of gender and ability: he is vision-impaired and an amputee; he embodies elements of femininity that are intermingled with undeniable masculine traits; he depends on Jane, but she, too, relies on him; he is sexually active in a happy marriage—a perpetual honeymoon, as he refers to it; he is attractive; he is, Jane reports, fulfilled and happy.

Among the "uneven currents" of the competing discourses of *Jane Eyre*, then, is a rewriting of the terms of gender and ability. Some narrative strands use disability to invert gender binaries and reflect ableist thinking, especially in the transformation into flesh of John Reed, Mr. Brocklehurst, and St. John Rivers. Other narrative strands, particularly those that construct the embodiment of Edward Rochester, work to diffuse both gender and ability hierarchies and anticipate more emancipatory blendings of models of identity.

While Rochester's "re-transformation [. . .] into flesh" may serve as an avenue to Jane's empowerment, it is thus not necessarily an expressway to his disempowerment. Instead, it is an inroad to an alternative, nonoppressive model of masculinity. His life may have been altered by accident, and Jane's narration is somewhat affected by elements of conventional thinking about the body, but to presuppose that he remains disconsolate due to his impairments is to embrace the mainstream, pejorative understanding of disability, to uphold traditional definitions of masculinity, and to miss an alternate, emancipatory reading of the ending of Brontë's text. Through the lenses of disability studies and masculinity studies, Rochester's "re-transformation [. . .] into flesh" is really a transformation of cultural attitudes about gender and ability; just as the India-rubber stretches into flesh, so too does the model of masculinity stretch to encompass new, more inclusive possibilities for male embodiment.

FROM CUSTODIAL CARE TO CARING LABOR

The Discourse of Who Cares in *Jane Eyre*

D. Christopher Gabbard

"ALL *JANE EYRE* LOVERS," writes Gail Griffin, "have been strangely drawn to Bertha Mason Rochester" (89), and this attraction is in itself noteworthy, given that, as Laurence Lerner puts it, she is a "minor character" who "does not speak a single word" (280). Initially, a disability studies reading of Bertha and *Jane Eyre* would appear unpromising, for both seem to offer examples of what David Mitchell and Sharon Snyder term the "negative image" school of "humiliating" literary depictions of people with disabilities (*Narrative Prosthesis,* 18). Cora Kaplan writes that this text "offers Bertha Mason no sympathy at all" ("Afterword," 310). David Bolt states that Brontë "actively endorses the binary opposition of normativism and disability" (286). And Kathleen Jones writes that Bertha "remains 'the monster,' 'the maniac'—a grim and hated figure [. . .]. It is with the greatest satisfaction that the author and reader reach the final dénouement—the fire, the death of the 'maniac' as she hurls herself from the burning building, and Rochester's freedom to marry Jane" (21). However, by observing that "even the most 'derisive' portrait harbors within it an antithesis, its own disruptive potential," Mitchell and Snyder also suggest the possibility of a "transgressive reappropriation" (*Narrative Prosthesis,* 35–40). Such a reading could turn the tables by asking, for example, not why the disabled

Bertha is killed off according to the stereotypical "cure or kill" formula, but why those charged with her care are not doing a better job of preventing her from harming herself.

Reading disability in *Jane Eyre* as a static element—as something almost exclusively associated with Bertha—will indeed yield a "negative image" interpretation; however, Bertha is merely the text's first disabled character. By reading disability dynamically, as a category that is disclosed slowly, and by attending to the interlocking but shifting roles of caregiver and disabled, one begins to understand that the text presents two phases of caregiving and disability—the first featuring Rochester and Bertha, the second Jane and Rochester. Narrated by Jane in the mid-1840s, when public policy reforms were being instituted for improving the treatment of mentally ill and disabled people, Brontë's novel can be understood as incorporating these reforms and reflecting negatively on Rochester's custodial care practices. In other words, the novel's closing chapters have Jane enact in miniature the spirit of the national reforms and, by so doing, Brontë's narrative thematizes the transition from one caregiving paradigm to another, from custodial care to caring labor.[1]

This transition from one paradigm to another can only be determined by attending closely to the text's subtleties of discourse. Ostensibly a *bildungsroman* focusing on the protagonist's mastery of communication, *Jane Eyre* paradoxically compels the reader to infer what the narrator does *not* say. Between the disclosure scene in the attic and her return to the ruined Thornfield, Jane does not record all or even most of her thoughts (ch. 26, ch. 36).[2] This chapter is concerned with Jane's unwritten thoughts as they pertain to

1. The terms *care* and *caregiving* should not be used uncritically. Kelly writes that "persistent use of the term 'care' without engaging with disability critiques signals an ignorance at best, or dismissal at worst" of the "oppressive legacies" and "potential for abuse" associated with the concept (7, 8). Disability critiques view care as a complex form of oppression because, in "the context of disability, care is haunted by the spectres of institutionalization, medicalization and paternalistic charities" (3). Kelly goes on to state that "[n]aming this ambiguous work [of providing support with dressing, bathing, etc.] is an ongoing debate" (2). To disassociate it from paternalistic charity, advocates have substituted such terms as *support work, attendant care, personal support,* and *personal assistance.* (Kittay uses the term *dependency worker.*) However, Kelly acknowledges that "[s]omething is lost when the concept of care is eliminated" (17), and she presents a case for a new model of "accessible care" that resembles Cushing and Lewis's caring labor model. Concerning *Jane Eyre,* terms such as personal assistant or dependency worker might be applicable to Grace Poole but would be inappropriate for Rochester and Jane, who fulfill functions vis-à-vis disabled spouses within a familial rather than paid context. For this reason, this paper will employ the terms *care* and *caregiver.*

2. The version of the primary text referred to in this chapter is Charlotte Brontë, *Jane Eyre,* 2nd ed., ed. Richard J. Dunn (New York and London: Norton, 1987).

her development from the attic scene, in which she panics at the sight of the disabled Bertha, to the Ferndean section, in which she exhibits tranquility regarding Rochester's disability. In part, I present the case that Thornfield's attic functions for Jane as, what Mary Louise Pratt terms, a "contact zone" (6). This zone entails a space of encounter between two groups who have been separated geographically and who are unfamiliar with one another. Such contact produces change. In this case, the contact zone facilitates the meeting of the able-bodied Jane and the disabled Bertha and changes the former. Jane does not speak explicitly about this change, but the reader can surmise that what inaugurates her subsequent transformation is her direct encounter with Bertha and that what advances it further are her periods of wandering on the heath and convalescence at Moor House, where she learns the difference between the Rivers' *caring labor* and Rochester's grudging and negligent *custodial care*. In sum, this chapter argues that *Jane Eyre* is less a *bildungsroman* centering on Jane's mastery of communication than one of her moral education about disability and that what instigates this moral development is her close contact with Bertha.

Of course, thinking of Bertha as any kind of constructive influence other than as a cautionary tale runs against the conventional wisdom, for few (if any) critics have entertained the possibility that Bertha presents Jane with anything positive or useful. For example, in the influential *Madwoman in the Attic,* Sandra Gilbert and Susan Gubar assert that "Bertha does [. . .] provide the governess an example of how *not* to act" (361; emphasis added). Critics do not consider Bertha a catalyst of Jane's moral development because Jane herself says nothing about it. However, I argue that this moral development takes place within a discursive gap and use the concept of the implied interlocutor to provide an inductive reading of Jane's silence and Bertha's nonverbal world. By way of the implied interlocutor, one can conclude that Jane develops morally through her contact with Bertha and, more importantly, grows in her understanding and acceptance of diversities of ability and their requisite ethical considerations.

BERTHA'S IMPLIED INTERLOCUTOR

Jane Eyre has been understood as portraying its protagonist's efforts to gain recognition as a modern liberal subject. As Suzanne Shumway points out, the novel "rests upon a valorization of, as well as an investment in, language and its powers" and mainly consists in "the story of a woman's search for subjectivity through language" (159, 161). Janet Freeman concurs, stating that "the power of speech" in the novel "is supreme. It enables Jane to take more and more control of her life" (686). Sally Shuttleworth agrees, maintaining that from "the opening paragraphs [. . .] it becomes clear that the narrator [. . .] is a figure involved in the processes of self-legitimation" through the acquisition of "rational discourse" (153, 164). Pursuing a related line of inquiry, Julia Miele Rodas argues that reading Jane as an individual on the autistic spectrum contributes to an understanding of her childhood struggles and increasing control in adulthood "over her passionate emotional life, reducing her affect and concealing her deeply rooted feelings with ever greater success" ("On the Spectrum"). Disadvantaged by gender and class, Jane, from the beginning, strives to acquire a voice that will allow her to take her place in society. The advantages of rising socially accrue to her when she learns to practice linguistic self-control. This development becomes manifest through Jane's increasing facility with words against the foil of Bertha's supposed inability to communicate. Indeed, recognizing the role of increasing language facility in Jane's social ascent, critics have commented on the pairing of the speaking Jane with the "silent" Bertha. Jane's early, unrestrained, explosive outbursts align her with Bertha, but as the novel progresses and as Jane gains control over her tongue, Bertha metamorphoses into her counterpoint. Shuttleworth observes that "Bertha's laughter and 'eccentric murmurs' constitute another narrative within the text, running in counterpoint to Jane's rational discourse" (164). While Bertha supposedly rages incoherently and eventually dies, Jane gradually modulates her tone and, by doing so, achieves self-determination and personal integrity, thereby empowering herself as the modern independent subject and achieving rough parity with Rochester. As Gilbert and Gubar note, by the Ferndean section Rochester "and Jane are now, in reality, equals" (368).

In contradistinction to Jane's mastery of speech is Bertha's supposedly nonverbal status. Jane affirms that, during the attic scene, Bertha uttered a "fierce cry" and "bellowed" (258; ch. 26), but she does not report having heard Bertha speak intelligibly. Bertha thus illustrates the model set forth by Catherine Prendergast, who notes that mentally ill people are often placed in "a rhetorical black hole" and that to "be disabled mentally is to be disabled rhetorically" (198, 203). In other words, "If people think you're crazy, they don't listen to you" (Prendergast, 203). Bertha is a character caught in the breakdown of communication due to what is, in essence, "a sociomedical condition, a secret family history of mental illness" (Donaldson, "The Corpus of the Madwoman," 102). Concerning such a person, Lucy Burke asks, "[w]hat does it mean [. . .] to represent someone who is unable to tell their own story?" (ii). Exploring this prospect would require reconceiving what it would mean for the nonverbal person to speak. For example, minutes before her death, Bertha vociferates loudly from Thornfield's rooftop. For the narration of Bertha's final moments, Jane relies upon the report of the host of the Rochester Arms (374; ch. 36), who informs her that he "witnessed, and several more witnessed" Bertha just prior to jumping, when "she yelled" and "was standing, waving her arms, above the battlements, and shouting out till they could hear her a mile off" (377; ch. 36). In this oxymoronic "second-hand eye-witness" account, the innkeeper describes hearing her voice but indicates neither one way nor the other whether her language could be understood. In sum, he does not stop to consider what Bertha is shouting or to whom. Yet Bertha's verbalization and frantic gesturing constitute a speech act, one that, considered dialogically, is meant for an addressee. Taking into account that this speech act is a message broadcast in a loud volume and from a high place—voluble enough to be heard "a mile off"—one reasonably could speculate that the intended recipients would be just about everyone within hearing (377; ch. 36). Her rooftop statement is delivered to a *generalized recipient,* one that is diffused over a wide social expanse.

Bertha's delivery to this generalized recipient implicates her as a speaker in a unique dialogic situation that can be explored by recourse to the notion of an extralinguistic realm of communication. Far from the usual interactions between addresser and addressee, this kind of discourse is one in which an atypical mode of communication predominates: Ato Quayson's *implied interlocutor.* This is a narrative device that unfolds as extralinguistic discourse for the purpose of disclosing a nonverbal character's participation in a dialogic setting. The concept is rooted in Mikhail Bakhtin's model of dialogism in which an addresser and an addressee exchange language between them. Put simply, anything a person says is a response to something already said and anticipates something that will be said in response. This model takes for granted that all parties in such interchanges are fully verbal. Quayson's implied interlocutor extends Bakhtin's model to disability studies by questioning this last aspect: two sides of an exchange exist but with one consisting of a nonverbal person and the other serving as his or her addressee or "implied interlocutor" (Quayson, 29). For the nonverbal person, there can be an "anticipation of an interlocutor even when the context of communication does not seem to explicitly denominate one" (29). Quayson further adapts Bakhtin's work by advancing the idea that "the addressee/interlocutor" does not have to be "a human character at all" (154). Instead, the interlocutor could consist of "a structure of societal and cultural expectations not attributable to any single source," that is, the cumulative cultural attitudes and/or ingrained prejudices circulating within the fictive social setting (154). Quayson explains "that for the disabled, that interlocutor may be an aggregation of attitudes" of the "normate," Rosemarie Garland-Thomson's term for "the corporeal incarnation of culture's collective, unmarked, normative characteristics" (Quayson, 151; Garland-Thomson, *Extraordinary Bodies*, 6). Lastly, and most importantly, such an interlocutor is unobtrusive, for it recedes into the background of the storytelling. In fact, the more it does so—becoming ever more naturalized and fluid—the more operatively influential it becomes (167).

Judging from the unvoiced thought processes that seem to rage incessantly within Bertha, one can surmise that she is engaged in some sort of ongoing conversation with an implied interlocutor. While it would be reasonable to assume that she seethes with anger against her estranged husband and his new love, it is equally reasonable to assume that she also reacts against the attitudes motivating these two, the same attitudes that demarcate her existence as a person with a mental disability, and that might best be interrogated by examining the attic scene. After the aborted nuptials, when Rochester leads "the three gentlemen" and Jane up to Thornfield's third story, he chooses to be a "guide" who puts Bertha on display in the titillating prospect of a freak show (257; ch. 26).[3] Until the wedding, Rochester has secreted Bertha in the attic, as he tells Jane later, due to a sense of shame and "dishonour [. . . because of his] connection with her mental defects" (272; ch. 27). However, after Bertha's brother Richard disrupts the ceremony, Rochester reverses his position: instead of hiding her, he now makes a spectacle of her. This spectacle begins when he injects a bit of theatrical panache into the act, "lift[ing] the hangings from the wall," thereby introducing "the brief *scene* with the lunatic" (257, 260; ch. 26, emphasis added). By pulling back what is in effect a stage curtain, Rochester transforms himself into a showman. As Hermione Lee points out, "the climactic unveiling of Bertha [. . .] is done as a dumb show with Rochester as Interpreter. He raises the curtain, goes on-stage for the fight, and then comments

---

3. Bogdan would argue that the display of Bertha technically does not qualify as a "freak show" because he defines the phenomenon as a "formally organized exhibition of people with alleged and real physical, mental, or behavioral anomalies for amusement and profit [. . . with the exhibition being] attached to organizations such as circuses and carnivals" (*Freak Show*, 10). Garland-Thomson observes that, whether one follows Bogdan's strict definition or not, "[w]hen the body becomes pure text, a freak has been produced from a physically disabled human being" (*Extraordinary Bodies*, 59). Garland-Thomson also points out that 1847, the year of *Jane Eyre*'s publication, is the year the word *freak* "become[s] synonymous with human corporeal anomaly" (*Freakery*, 4).

on the scene to 'the spectators'" (239). Rochester's transformation into both showman and "Interpreter" calls attention to his exclusive role in telling Bertha's story and especially to the discursive template he uses to guide the gentlemen and Jane through a reading of her body. As Robert Bogdan points out, because the chief task of the freak show exhibitor was to make certain that every spectator saw what he wanted them to see, every exhibit "was, in the strict use of the word, a fraud. [. . .] [E]very person exhibited was misrepresented" (*Freak Show*, 10). Because the evidently speechless Bertha does not tell her story, she is mediated through Rochester's account, which, given his bigotry about disability and his melodramatic tendencies, cannot be taken at face value.

Rochester's theatrical framing of Bertha reflects several historically resonant tropes having to do with the presentation of living human subjects in scientific and medical demonstrations, especially in the then "new" sciences of teratology (the study of monsters) and ethnology (the study of human race and ethnicity) and in the developing enterprise of exhibiting "freaks" as commercially viable entertainment. In fact, Rochester's propensities as a scientific naturalist come to light several chapters prior to the attic scene, when, during an evening outdoors and accompanied by Jane, his attention is captured by a moth. "Jane, come and look at this fellow. [. . .] Look at his wings [. . .] he reminds me rather of a West Indian insect" (218; ch. 23). The garden incident momentarily delineates him as an amateur naturalist and foreshadows the way that he will later direct the notice of the three gentlemen and Jane to the human West Indian specimen, Bertha.

This scientific rhetoric invokes what Margean Purinton terms the "techno-Gothic grotesque," a phenomenon of the period in which scientific and medical information were presented in theater-like settings, with aspects of drama being "appropriated by science" (301). Purinton argues:

> [Especially in cases in which a living human subject was placed on display, the] physicality of the techno-gothic grotesque was simultaneously a spectacular, extraordinary body, gothically designed for pleasure and culturally coded for education, display[ed] at the public "clinic" where theatergoers could participate in scientific and medical anatomizing. (302–3)

Living human illustrations served as a key component in these displays and were particularly useful for explicating both teratology and ethnology. Aspects of the "techno-Gothic grotesque" were particularly pertinent to the former: the "burgeoning nineteenth-century science of teratology" constituted a new approach to studying monsters that was far more systematic than it had been in previous centuries (Philip K. Wilson, 11). Indeed, with Isidore Geoffroy Saint-Hilaire's *Traité de Teratology*, published about a decade prior to the appearance of Brontë's novel, talk about so-called monsters rose to the level of a fad (Huet, 108). Perhaps inspired by Saint-Hilaire, Brontë has Rochester refer to Bertha as "a monster," and it is of her supposed *monstrosity*, especially, that he wishes to convince the three gentlemen and Jane (272; ch. 27).

Related to the era's new interest in monsters was the emergence of the science of ethnology. Richard Altick writes that "by the late 1840s, the infant science of ethnology" had come into formation and, with it, the need for "living specimens of barbaric or savage races" (268). The rise of ethnology merged with desire in London for spectacle, which could be satisfied at the Egyptian Hall and Bethlem Royal Hospital. At the Egyptian Hall, people from various European colonies became popular and profitable exhibitions: Sartje Baartman or "the Hottentot Venus" from South Africa, Tono Maria or "the Venus of South America," native Americans, and south African Bushmen were put on stage (Altick, 268, 272, 273, 275–79). An 1846 Egyptian Hall advertisement for "The Wild Man of the Prairies" closely resembles Rochester's presentation of Bertha: "Is it an Animal? Is it Human? Is it an Extraordinary Freak of Nature, or is it a legitimate member of nature's works?" (Altick, 265). At the city's main state-run insane asylum, the Bethlem Royal Hospital (or "Bedlam," as it was commonly known), public audiences could find similar displays of human oddity in the form of mentally ill residents. According to Allan Ingram, Bedlam had served since the seventeenth century as a venue for "spectacle, a place of entertainment," a practice that was ongoing at the time of *Jane Eyre*'s publication (2). Londoners went to Bedlam to gawk at the lunatics, paying a penny to peer into their cells. A vivid illustration of this practice can be found in William Hogarth's series of engravings, "The Rake's Progress" (1735): a Bedlam cell is portrayed in the eighth and last plate, and in it the crazed Tom Rakewell occupies the foreground while behind him several fashionably dressed women appear to be amused by his antics.

In the attic, Rochester inscribes Bertha's body with the discourses derived from naturalism, teratology, ethnology, the commercial exhibitions of exotics and "defectives," and Bedlam lunacy. As a result, Bertha's implied interlocutor can be located partially in this aggregation of discourses that determine how she is viewed. Moreover, the interlocutor can be situated in the other assumptions that surface as Rochester performs the combined roles of overburdened, caregiving spouse and freak-show barker:

"That is *my wife*," said he. "Such is the sole conjugal embrace I am ever to know [. . .]. And *this* is what I wished to have" (laying his hand on my shoulder): "this young girl, who stands so grave and quiet at the mouth of hell, looking collectedly at the gambols of a demon. [. . .] Compare these clear eyes with the red balls yonder [. . .] this form with that bulk." (258–59; ch. 26)

Rochester alludes to his fourteen-year "burden" of caregiving, his tone oscillating between self-pity and exasperation. Using Jane as a prop for comparison, "laying his hand on my shoulder," he draws together the implications of the study of monsters and exotic freaks to emphasize Bertha's lack of humanity. More exotic even than either Tono Maria, the Venus of South America, or Sartje Baartman, the Hottentot Venus from South Africa, is Bertha Mason—the Venus from Hell. Thornfield's attic room is the "mouth of hell," Bertha's behavior "the gambols of a demon," and her "red balls" the devil's eyes. Furthermore, he characterizes Bertha as a "bulk," metonymically referencing excessive behavior and an animalistic body. This "bulk" he contrasts with Jane's "form," meaning Jane's comportment, which accords "to prescribed or customary rules" regarding "etiquette, ceremony, or decorum" ("Form, n.15. a"). Rochester conflates corporeal difference with teratology and demonology. The implied interlocutor with whom Bertha must contend and to whom she shouts from Thornfield's rooftop sees her not only as monstrous but also as that ultimate incarnation of the Other—the devil.

THE ABLEISM OF ROCHESTER AND JANE

During his tenure as Bertha's provider, Rochester's negative attitudes about mental disability are reflected in the type of care he arranges for her. His normative framework of caregiving is an inherently dichotomous, asymmetrical, custodial one in which Bertha is, or, in his view, should be, the *passive* recipient of care. In other words, his approach parallels the "popular conception of the one-way flow of benefits in care relationships rooted in medical and charitable paradigms" (Cushing and Lewis, 174). Power and control accrue entirely to him. While Rochester's assumptions may have aligned with the prevailing standard in an earlier era, in which families of means either sequestered relatives with mental illness within their own homes or lodged them in private asylums, these assumptions invite scrutiny, especially when considered in light of 1840s efforts to reform treatment for mentally ill and cognitively impaired persons.

Situating the novel historically helps one to understand why Rochester's attitudes about mental disability and caregiving may not be shared or endorsed by the novel's implied author. Jane tells her story in the middle of the 1840s, an historical moment when the neglect and ill treatment of "lunatics" and "idiots" caught the public's attention, and when a number of liberal reforms were enacted with regard to improving their conditions (McCandless, 84–104; McDonagh, 209, 211). For example, the later part of the decade witnessed the founding of Britain's first asylum for idiots, Highgate, later renamed Earlswood, which Charles Dickens visited "on more than one occasion in order to draw inspiration for his novels" (Wright, 137). Hence, Rochester's approach to caregiving represents what a sizable segment of the reading public by 1847 would have recognized as reflecting outdated attitudes, the ones holding sway back in the 1820s and 1830s, when most of the story takes place. Sally Shuttleworth explains that the "system at Thornfield represents the vestiges of a prior era, when the 'animal' insane were kept hidden and mechanically restrained (as Bertha is after each attack) and no attempt was made at cure or recuperation" (160).

By 1847, a sizable portion of Brontë's reading public would have considered Rochester's caregiving manner to be archaic for three reasons. First, Rochester confines her to the equivalent of a tower—a windowless attic (264; ch. 27). Second, even though by the time of the novel's publication cures or at least ameliorations of mental illness were thought possible, he makes no provision once the couple has returned to England for her to be seen by physicians with expertise in mental illness (McCandless, 85; Sally Shuttleworth, 36–37).[4] Rather, he employs a single attendant, someone he found at the Grimsby Retreat, Grace Poole, and this lone attendant seems unable to perform the job adequately, for Bertha in the course of the story comes into possession of a knife, wanders Thornfield's halls at night (seemingly at will), and, on at least two occasions, lights fires. Hiring a single, "gin-sodden attendant" to supervise an ambulatory, physically powerful, forty-five-year-old mentally ill adult female would have been recognized by some contemporaries at least as reckless endangerment of the person cared for (Jones, 21). Improperly attended, Bertha brings about her own death, a death representing a catastrophically unsuccessful episode of caregiving. Moreover, by the 1840s, the public was starting to believe that lodging a

---

4. Neither Carter, the surgeon who dressed Mason's wounds, nor any typical rural or town physician, would have been recognized as being competent to treat Bertha's mental illness.

"lunatic" in a private home was backward, while accommodating him or her in an asylum was progressive, therapeutic, and humane (regardless of what is believed today in the wake of Foucault). In the 1820s and 1830s, several public and private asylums were operating in Yorkshire, and if Rochester were a progressive thinker, he would have lodged her in one of them. In sum, Rochester implicitly makes choices about Bertha's care that a portion of Brontë's audience in the late 1840s would have recognized as inadequate and outdated. As a consequence, given the reform mood, a number of readers would have identified his conduct toward the woman in his custody as negligent, abusive, and cruel—a dereliction of responsibilities.[5]

Calling into question both Rochester's outdated notions and his care-*less* practices is Jane, who strongly censures him. Following the attic scene, Jane tells him to modulate his tone when speaking of his wife, chiding him for being "inexorable for that unfortunate lady" and for speaking "of her with hate—with vindictive antipathy. It is cruel" (265; ch. 27). In the same scene, after Rochester asks her, "If you were mad, do you think I should hate you?," her reply is sharply critical: "I do indeed, sir" (265; ch. 27). However, what makes Jane *most* wary of Rochester's way of thinking and doing things is the fact that, just as he alludes to one set of pseudoscientific notions to explain Bertha to Jane, so too has he alluded to a second set earlier when explaining Jane to herself. Previous to their nuptials, he has told her that she suffers from "hypochondria" and has addressed her as "Little nervous subject!" (246, 248; ch. 25). Additionally, the night before the wedding, he dismisses her fear about a bedroom intruder by intimating that she is experiencing a nervous disorder. Her fear, he informs her, is the "creature of an over-stimulated brain; that is certain. I must be careful of you, my treasure; nerves like yours were not made for rough handling. [. . .] [T]here shall be no recurrence of these mental terrors" (250; ch. 25). Shuttleworth insightfully observes that Rochester is not "content with defining one wife as 'maniac'" but also must place "his future bride in that other category of female weakness, the nervous, hysterical woman" (171). However, Jane

5. Along these lines, Grudin points out that Brontë "was a devoted disciple of Harriet Martineau, who in 'The Hanwell Lunatic Asylum' [. . .] sought to eradicate" the cruel and negligent treatment that those with mental illness suffered (147). Brontë may have assumed that most readers would consider Rochester's practices slipshod and backward. "It is no wonder that the novelist was obliged to apologize for the message a literal reading of her novel seems to produce" (Grudin, 147–48). Concerning her portrayal of Bertha, Brontë writes the following: "I agree with [Miss Kavanagh and Leigh Hunt] that the character is shocking [. . .]. It is true that profound pity ought to be the only sentiment elicited by the view of such degradation, and equally true is it that I have not sufficiently dwelt on that feeling; I have erred in making *horror* too predominant. [. . .] [T]he truly good behold and compassionate [insanity] as such" ("To W. S. Williams," 3).

immediately refutes his explanation by stating, "Sir, depend upon it, my nerves were not at fault" (250; ch. 25). Producing the torn wedding veil, she demonstrates the basis of her fears. Having proven him wrong once, she has reason to not accept at face value whatever he says about Bertha.

And yet, however critical of Rochester's attitudes Jane may be, she is far from enlightened, at least at this stage of the narrative. In fact, it is not just Rochester who contributes to the aggregation of attitudes of the normate but Jane as well. As the fourth attic spectator, Jane recounts her first impressions of Bertha, and these betray her extreme nervousness in the presence of disability:

> [A] figure ran backwards and forwards. What it was, whether beast or human being, one could not, at first sight, tell: it groveled, seemingly, on all fours; it snatched and growled like some strange wild animal: but it was covered with clothing; and a quantity of dark, grizzled hair, wild as a mane, hid its head and face. (257–258; ch. 26)

Jane's description reveals more about herself than about Bertha. Her disgust and fear become evident in her impulse to animalize the mentally disabled woman, who becomes in her telling an inhuman "figure" scurrying "backwards and forwards" as though without direction or purpose. Commenting on the scene, Grudin asserts that "[e]ven to the relatively charitable Jane, Bertha is essentially subhuman, terrifying, and disgusting," and viewing her prompts Jane to see "something more deserving of annihilation than of charity" (147). Interestingly, Jane's vocabulary references the language used about Jane by Mrs. Reed: by employing the pronoun *it* and reducing Bertha to animal status, Jane inadvertently echoes her former guardian's words about herself. On her deathbed, the ailing Mrs. Reed says of her young charge, "I hated it the first time I set my eyes on it" (203; ch. 21), a characterization reinforced when, later, referring to the youthful Jane's episode of explosive anger, Mrs. Reed states that it was "as if an animal that I had struck [. . .] looked up at me with human eyes and cursed me in a man's voice" (210; ch. 21). Jane's visit to the dying woman calls attention to how hard she has struggled to free herself from dehumanization. Now, having been recently reminded of this objectification as "it" and "an animal," Jane reassigns these attributes to Bertha. Thus, Jane's use of Mrs. Reed's language to describe Bertha symbolically transfers these qualities from herself to another.

Transferring the dehumanization from herself to another, however, also signals the end of one phase of Jane's development and the beginning of another. As has been observed above, the principal skill that Jane learns to master in this *bildungsroman* is a modulation of language and tone; by the time the eponymous hero enters the attic, for all intents and purposes she has thereby achieved a considerable degree of self-determination and personal integrity, empowering herself as the modern independent subject. Therefore, by the time of the attic scene, Rochester and Jane have already become "in reality, equals" (Gilbert and Gubar, 368), a rough equality accomplished through Jane's linguistic accomplishment. However, contact with Bertha profoundly unsettles Jane because it forces her to confront something she heretofore had not anticipated—the limits of language. This confrontation instigates the final major phase of her maturation: the exploration of extralinguistic discourse. Whatever Bertha may vocalize during the attic scene, and whether those within hearing are capable or willing listeners, Bertha's presence is especially meaningful for the narrator. At the first sight of Bertha, Jane can acknowledge only an abject, subhuman figure lacking linguistic capability, the very capability that she has striven to master and that, Jane has come to believe, underwrites full membership in the human species. Seemingly devoid of intelligible speech, Bertha instantiates for her a disturbing humanoid form, human and subhuman combined, an embodiment of the animal-human nexus—an uncanny double. This encounter with the uncanny instigates a paradoxical reaction: while the meeting should reinforce the primacy of language for Jane, in effect it does the opposite, highlighting instead the fragility of the self she has assiduously constructed and challenging the very definition of the human. Because of Jane's encounter with Bertha, the questions of what it means to be human and how speech fits in as to resolving this issue become less certain, not more so. Jane has assumed language was worth mastering because doing so meant everything, but her sudden close proximity to an alternative verbal position raises the alarming possibility that a realm exists in which conventional mastery of language is of little use. Far from eliciting a sense of wonder, this revelation arouses revulsion.

JANE'S IMPLIED INTERLOCUTOR: FROM CUSTODIAL CARE TO CARING LABOR

This revulsion reflects the approach to disability in the earlier part of the novel that ends with Bertha's death. The aggregation of normate attitudes that underwrites Rochester and Jane's conduct earlier in the text comes under implicit scrutiny in the latter part of the narrative. Here, the subject-positions shift, with the former caregiver switching places to occupy the disabled position, and Jane, formerly a bystander, entering to become a caregiver. One could argue that, for Rochester, the hubristic ableist, to become disabled himself, constitutes poetic justice. However, to suggest such an idea would be to replicate the ancient prejudice—that disability serves as a punishment or symptom of wrongdoing. A more coherent and consistent way to address this role reversal is the recognition that, "as linguistic creations, the disabled in literature may trade a series of features with the nondisabled, thus transferring some of their significations to the nondisabled and vice versa" (Quayson, 27). Some characters, like Bertha, became disabled sooner than others, and, with Rochester eventually joining her in this category, his example validates the observations of those disability scholars who have "noted the provisional and temporary nature of able-bodiedness" (Quayson, 14). Bertha thus trades a series of features with the formerly nondisabled. As Rodas notes, "in the end [. . .] husband and wife both wind up participating in disabled identity" ("Brontë's *Jane Eyre*," 151). Neither immune nor invincible, Rochester must come to terms with both the vicissitudes of the body and his former ableism.

Jane, too, is drawn into the circle of disability by moving into the caregiver role. However, the novel's second phase of disability and caregiving will not replicate the mistakes made in the first. By the time Jane steps into the caregiving position (*vis-à-vis* a disabled life partner) once held by Rochester, her attitude about the responsibilities it entails varies considerably from what his had been. In fact, her approach differs radically, for hers is rooted in what Pamela Cushing and Tanya Lewis term a "philosophy of relational mutuality" (174). What Jane effects with Rochester is, using Cushing and Lewis's language, "a shift from custodial care to 'caring labor'" (180). As they observe, "Sharing power [between caregiver and disabled] is a radical ideal in a field where workers are tacitly trained to value 'compliance' over agency in their charges" (186). The relational mutuality approach aims to build a relationship of reciprocal respect by mitigating dependency and achieving parity between the person with a disability unable to live independently and the person undertaking his or her care.

The vehicle for this transition from one model of care relationship to the other is the alteration in Jane's worldview that occurs between the time she views Bertha in the attic and that of her return to the ruined Thornfield. Jane's psychological development after the attic scene supplants the novel's earlier preoccupation involving the narrator's mastery of language and tone. Her growing respect for and comfort with extralinguistic discourse commences with her initial, panicked reaction at the sight of Bertha, a point at which her uncritical, ableist assumptions about the human and about discourse and disability become painfully apparent and against which her later behavior can be contrasted. By the time she returns to Thornfield after wandering on the heath and staying with the Rivers, she has grown in her tolerance for extralinguistic discourse, in her appreciation of divergent levels of ability, and in an understanding of dignified caregiving. The evidence of her "education" can be read in her willingness to act in accordance with the principles of relational mutuality once she is reunited with the disabled Rochester at Ferndean.

Because the phase between the attic scene and her Thornfield homecoming is so important, it will be necessary to retrace several of her steps. After Jane flees Thornfield, three episodes unfold by which she learns what it means both to see the world through Bertha's eyes and to be seen in the world as Bertha. In the first of the three episodes, Jane becomes implicated in Bertha's supposed animality. Recounting what she saw in the attic, Jane reports that "it [Bertha] groveled, seemingly, on all fours" (257; ch. 26). However, soon after she leaves Thornfield, and yet prior to boarding the coach, she falls and is reduced to "crawling forwards on my hands and knees" (283; ch. 27), a description strongly reminiscent of Bertha "grovel[ing], seemingly, on all fours." Thus, as Shuttleworth points out, Jane "mirror[s] Bertha's animal posture" (166). Earlier, this chapter examined Jane's unwitting deflection of Mrs. Reed's attempt to dehumanize her by assigning the same animalizing language and objectivizing pronoun *it* to Bertha. Yet, with the phrase *crawling forwards on my hands and knees*, she lapses back into the bestial position into which she had attempted to substitute Bertha, thereby rendering the earlier transference unsuccessful.

In the second episode, after wandering from the heath into a village, Jane feels a sense of "moral degradation" because people regard her as "an ordinary beggar" (289; ch. 28). The villagers avoid her, even shun her as a pariah, perhaps concluding that she is "crazy." As was noted earlier, "If people think you're crazy, they don't listen to you" (Prendergast, 203). In these circumstances, Jane simply cannot approach the villagers and explain she is as rational as they are, for the very attempt would confirm their initial unfavorable assessment. Bertha's character is momentarily superimposed over her own on account of this public perception of her mental incapacity: she steps into Bertha's role as a mentally deranged spectacle and, by so doing, takes on the role of reviled Other. Thus, she experiences firsthand an alterity far more profound than anything she previously has encountered.

The third episode is anchored in a moment long prior to her leaving Thornfield. Upon learning of her impending marriage to Rochester, Mrs.

Fairfax attempts to caution Jane, and the latter rebuffs her, asking "Am I a monster?" (233; ch. 24). As it turns out, Jane's question is far from rhetorical, for several chapters later she undertakes an action that alludes to nineteenth-century British literature's most well-known monster, Victor Frankenstein's creation in Mary Shelley's *Frankenstein; or, The Modern Prometheus* (1818). After leaving Thornfield and wandering on the heath, Jane comes upon Moor House and, approaching it stealthily, creeps up to a window and reports observing the family within through an "aperture" (292; ch. 28). This action parallels the one Victor Frankenstein's humanoid performs when he discovers a remote dwelling and through an "imperceptible chink" secretly observes the De Lacey family (100; ch. 11). The similarity between these scenes serves to mitigate the reader's sense of Bertha's monstrousness by intimating that Jane, too, possesses a share of this quality. This mutual apportionment blurs any simple binary between the monstrous and the "normal." For a moment, Jane's identity blends with the monstrousness of Frankenstein's creation and, by implication, with that of Bertha.

In these three episodes, the parallels with Bertha are unmistakable, and it would be reasonable to suppose, given her quickness of association, that the narrator herself glimpses some of these similarities. And yet, she does not acknowledge recognizing them, nor, indeed, does she reference Bertha at all between chapter 27, when she leaves Thornfield, and chapter 36, when she returns and learns of her demise. In fact, Jane never once names Bertha in the novel: "Bertha" is a name uttered only by others. The closest Jane comes to speaking of her directly is in conversation with Rochester, when, before leaving, she refers to her in the line, "Sir, your wife is living" and in back-to-back sentences: "Sir [. . .] you are inexorable to that unfortunate lady: you speak of her with hate [. . .]. It is cruel—she cannot help being mad" (267, 265; ch. 27).

Though the reader can assume that Bertha and everything associated with her must cross Jane's mind, the narrator does not inform the reader about having such thoughts. Indeed, it becomes downright curious that, over the next nine chapters after leaving Thornfield, she never once speaks of or even alludes to her rival. While Bertha is the text's most obvious nonverbal character, Jane too, for long stretches, and depending on the subject, can be said to be nonverbal. Hence, Rodas has proposed that Jane's unusual communication and affect are suggestive of autism. For the purposes of the present chapter, however, Jane's language gaps can productively be understood as suggesting an implied interlocutor. Quayson observes that the implied interlocutor is not necessarily confined to situations in which a nonverbal disabled character such as Bertha appears: "all literary characters," disabled or not, "in the end interact with an implied interlocutor" (154).

Of course, it could be objected that to suppose a narrator is engaging in an unrecorded conversation with an implied interlocutor is pure speculation, for, by the very definition *unrecorded,* no evidence can be produced to support the claim. However, it is helpful to consider that, in the case of Jane at least, the implied interlocutor serves as a variety of structural irony. Just as a naïve narrator does not fully comprehend the events he or she narrates, and just as an unreliable narrator cannot be fully trusted, so a narrator with an implied interlocutor discloses less than everything he or she thinks. As a narratorial device, Jane's implied interlocutor to some degree serves the purpose of avoiding redundancy: the reader can perceive the existence of an implied interlocutor through the dynamic that not everything needs to be uttered for Jane's views to be made known. In other words, the reader can imagine what her thoughts must be, given her recent history and current circumstances. For example, the reader does not need to be told that Bertha in the attic and Rochester's manner of dealing with her occupy Jane's mind. Also, a reader expects the implications of these spectacles to weigh on her, especially as she wanders the heath, where she is homeless, shunned by the villagers, and needing care. More to the point, a reader anticipates her apprehensions concerning the type of care (or lack of it) she is likely to receive, based on the models of caregiving presented by Mrs. Reed, Mr. Brocklehurst, and Rochester. In fact, the very excuse she makes on behalf of the villagers (they "knew nothing about my character" [289; ch. 28]) intimates that it is a response to these unrecorded anxieties.

In addition to avoiding redundancy, this device sharpens the contrast between her hopeless plight on the heath and the *deus-ex-machina* solution of Moor House, the very juxtaposition of which renders her so receptive to the relational mutuality model. This receptivity can be measured by the extent to which Jane becomes part of Moor House and embraces its philosophy. She goes from being a stranger looking through an "aperture" at its occupants to becoming literally a part of the family (292; ch. 28). Diana, Mary, and St. John accept her into Moor House despite the fact that she is a stranger to them, an Other, even a potentially "crazy" one. Demonstrating skill and respect as they nurture her back to health, they showcase a type of care based on the relational mutuality principle. Having been well cared for during this period, Jane comes to understand the difference between humane and dignified treatment of people in positions of dependency versus Rochester's scorn and disregard.

By the time Jane goes back to Thornfield, she has embraced the caring labor model of relational mutuality. And yet, as with so much else in this part of the narrative, she does not acknowledge the development. Wide gaps emerge in the storytelling, one of which concerns the fact that she returns to Thornfield expecting to find Bertha alive but about which she says nothing to the reader. Moreover, she goes back to Rochester even though his proposal—that they live together unmarried—has not become any less "sophistical" during her stay with the Rivers (267; ch. 27). Because it would be absurd to suggest that she is *not* aware of the implications of returning, her lack of disclosure further substantiates that she engages *sotto voce* with an implied interlocutor. Whatever her expectations regarding a reunion with Rochester, she cannot help but understand that his wife will continue to require care and that this care hitherto has been inadequate and inhumane. While Jane most certainly does not return to Thornfield for Bertha's sake, it is plausible to infer that it cannot be far from her mind while in transit that the manner of the wife's care would have to be reformed. However, she arrives too late to accomplish this, learning instead that the woman shouted from the rooftop before to jumping to her death (377; ch. 36). Jane is as silent about what she thinks of Bertha's final speech act and demise as she is about her prospects upon returning to Thornfield.

Whatever Jane's thoughts, her subsequent behavior and attitude reveal a great deal. For example, she adopts an upbraiding tone with Rochester soon after, when, alluding to the difference between his approach to caregiving and that of the Rivers, she tells him, "I have been with good people; far better than you: a hundred times better people; possessed of ideas and views you never entertained in your life" (385–386; ch. 37). In assuming the caregiver role with him, she will play it in the same way these "good people [. . .] a hundred times better" would do it. Consequently, she inaugurates in the novel's second phase of caregiving what amounts to reform measures, ones that align with those being implemented historically on a wider social scale. For example, rather than equating people with disabilities with the subhuman, as Rochester had done, Jane will acknowledge their full humanity, and this new attitude is evidenced when she tells him, "It is time some one undertook to *rehumanise* you" (384; ch. 37; emphasis added). Taking her at her word, it would be impossible for the reader to imagine Jane making a degrading spectacle of Rochester as an exotic, subhuman specimen in any way resembling the manner he did with Bertha. Thus, when he asks, "Am I hideous, Jane?" and she replies, "Very, sir: you always were, you know," her line is both humorous and telling (385; ch. 37). She is referring not just to his postfire physical configuration but also to the monstrousness of his former ableist attitudes and negligent practices.

It could be objected that Jane falls into the category "of those who care passionately—rather than compassionately" (Flint, "Disability and Difference," 165). However, Eva Feder Kittay notes that for caregiving to be "well-done," it must be characterized by "care, concern, and connection" (31). Either way—passionately or compassionately—the responsibilities and occupations of caregiving are taxing enough, as Jane acknowledges when she finally sends Adèle away to boarding school: "my time and cares were required by another—my husband needed them all" (396; ch. 38). As Kittay observes, "the care of dependents *is work*" (30). Jane's position with her husband is the mirror image of what Rochester's had been with his wife, namely, of one spouse caring for the other.[6] The comparison of the way Rochester and Jane fulfill their roles vis-à-vis a life partner underscores the preference for a caregiver who cares *passionately* over one moved by compassion, an emotion that can corrupt into pity. Most importantly, one of this novel's core themes is the passion (or lack of it) in the individual who cares for those living dependently. Jane's reform mode brings into consideration the novel's other, positive examples of caregivers: not just Mary, Diana, and St. John Rivers but also, and most particularly, Maria Temple. Conversely, Jane's approach implicitly critiques those who are cruel and negligent: Mr. Rochester, of course, but also Mrs. Reed and Mr. Brocklehurst.

By recourse to the implied interlocutor, the reader can infer that Jane grows in her understanding and ethical appreciation of disability. She overcomes the panic the disabled woman initially elicited and becomes able and willing to gain knowledge from her. Indeed, to argue that Brontë's novel is a *bildungsroman* of moral development instigated by an inarticulate woman with a mental disability is counterintuitive, given both the text's preoccupation with language and its characterization of a "madwoman" that easily could fall into the "negative image" school (Mitchell and Snyder, *Narrative Prosthesis*, 18). Yet Jane's attitude regarding disability clearly changes from the contact zone of Thornfield's attic to the closing section at Ferndean. Three interpretive maneuvers open up this transgressive reappropriation: (i) utilizing the implied interlocutor to disclose concealed aspects of Jane and Bertha; (ii) superimposing the narrative's timeline over its historical one; and (iii) taking into account the reform movement unfolding at the time of

6. Jane's fulfilling the caregiving role more satisfactorily than Rochester did replicates the gendered pattern so characteristic of such activity, for women disproportionately assume the caregiving position. For the feminist critique of care, see Kittay and Kelly.

publication—the novel's narrative instant. Telling a story that unfolds over several decades, Jane brings the fictional histories of Bertha, Rochester, and herself into the historical present of 1847. By doing so, she *looks back* and, by doing so, *looks askance* at the caregiving practices that once held sway at Thornfield. The protagonist's reformed caregiving practices enacted in the narrative's present (the mid-1840s) vis-à-vis her spouse vastly improve upon those carried out by Rochester with *his* spouse one-to-two decades in the past. Thus, at the conclusion, rather than the story of disability coming full circle, gesturing toward an ever-repeating cycle, the ending points to a new beginning, to the hope of reform.

"I BEGAN TO SEE"

Biblical Models of Disability in *Jane Eyre*

ESSAKA JOSHUA

CHARLOTTE BRONTË was an adept commentator, absorber, and interpreter of biblical material, and it is no surprise, given both the ubiquity of biblical allusion in *Jane Eyre* and the extent of the novel's concern with disability, that her biblical intertexts engage with disability. Theologians and scripture scholars have frequently read biblical disability as a condition that has a negative personal and social impact. Commenting on the Hebrew Bible, Saul Olyan observes that the "stigmatizing association of disability with weakness, vulnerability, dependence, and ineffectuality constitutes an exceedingly widespread literary topos in biblical texts" (8). People with disabilities are commonly associated, in biblical narratives, with "the poor, the afflicted, and the alien, on account of a perception of shared vulnerability and weakness" (Olyan, 128), and disability in the Bible is often a marker of low social status as much as it is a physical or mental condition. In a groundbreaking essay collection, *This Abled Body: Rethinking Disabilities in Biblical Studies* (2007), David Mitchell and Sharon Snyder point out "the skepticism with which disability-studies scholars have traditionally approached religious frameworks" that interpret disability ("Jesus Thrown Everything Off Balance," 174), but suggest that, in spite of the "alarming array of ways in which disability prompts cultural disavowal" in biblical

111

narrative (174), "disability-studies based analyses can guide reform-minded readers to alternative applications of Christian narrative traditions" (183). This chapter examines Brontë's alternative application of biblical disability in order to establish how these biblical references inflect Brontë's overall presentation of disability in *Jane Eyre*.

BIBLICAL MODELS OF DISABILITY

Motivations for the study of disability in the Bible are varied but have been neatly schematized in *This Abled Body* as "redemptionist," "rejection-ist," and "historicist" (4–5; Avalos, 91). A redemptionist approach seeks "to redeem the biblical text, despite any negative stance on disabilities, by recontextualizing it for modern application" (Avalos, et al., 4; Avalos, 91). Rejectionists oppose this, arguing that "the Bible has negative portrayals of disability that should be rejected in modern society" (4–5). Historicists situate biblical texts within their surrounding cultures, and "without any overt interest in the consequence of the conclusions for modern applica-tion" (Avalos et al., 5; Avalos, 92).[1] Scholars often, as Avalos, Melcher, and Schipper point out, "combine, in varying proportions, at least some of these approaches" (4). Olyan, for example, presents a balance between an his-toricist agenda that seeks to identify "the various taxonomic categories" of disability in the Hebrew Bible and a redemptionist-rejectionist reading that recognizes stigmatization where it occurs yet sees the God of the Hebrew Bible as "an advocate for disabled persons, just as he is for other categories of persons represented as weak and marginal" (Olyan, 126). This recent work has aimed at revising traditional scholarly approaches that concen-trate on the diagnosis of disability and illness, and at exposing ideologically informed interpretative strategies that have limited the definition of disabil-ity to a hybridized medico-religious model.

Disability-studies scholars often approach biblical writings with some unease and focus their attention on how to provide a coherent response to the multiplicity of ways in which the Bible presents disability. Henri-Jacques Stiker and Nancy Eiesland, for example, attempt to resolve some of the con-trasting viewpoints by positing a division between approaches to disability in the Hebrew Bible and in the New Testament. Eiesland's *The Disabled*

1. Avalos uses these various terms to describe the reclamation or rejection of the Bible as a whole. When I use his terms, I mean to signify Brontë's choice to include or exclude biblical narratives that are redeemable or not redeemable and do not mean to suggest that Brontë is redeeming or rejecting the Bible as a whole.

God outlines the ways in which biblical texts present an overwhelmingly negative attitude toward disability. This, she argues, can result in a disabling theology. In rejectionist mode, she identifies three central biblical themes associated with disability. First, in appearing to conflate disability with sin, the Bible offers an understanding of disability that sees it as a punishment for immorality or pride, and as an imperfection that does not reflect the image of God; it also presents disability as "un-wholeness" (72). Second, disability in the Bible, Eiesland argues, is associated with "virtuous suffering" (72) and operates as a form of trial through which a person becomes pure and accepting of God. As Pauline Otiento observes, along rejectionist lines, this theme "encourages passive acceptance of social barriers for the sake of obedience to God" (2). Finally, disability is associated with social ostracism, charity, and healing: "Failure to be 'healed' is often assessed as a personal flaw in the individual, such as unrepentant sin or a selfish desire to remain disabled" (Eiesland, 117). In redemptionist mode, Eiesland presents a new thesis, that the resurrection of Christ's tortured body is an important symbol not of the "negation or erasure of our disabled bodies in hopes of perfect images, untouched by physical disability" (107) but of the "hope that our nonconventional, and sometimes difficult, bodies participate fully in the imago Dei" (107). Simon Horne, conversely, offers a continuity of vision between the Hebrew Bible and the New Testament.[2] Horne argues that the "central paradox of the New Testament is that 'within inability is striking capability'" (88). Disability functions as a kind of paradox that is a surprising and aesthetically pleasing occurrence in narrative because of its unexpectedness; it is not simply a condition that "Jesus eliminates" (88). Disability is, for Horne, a strong indicator of the coming to discipleship: "characters with impairments embody the process of full discipleship and particular qualities, such as obedience, persistence, and trust" (98). There is a range of motivations behind this revisionism. Principal among these is the theological need to produce a sense of a benevolent and just God from a set of narratives that are meant to be a guide to living ethically, and the need to find justification for an inclusive Church. These pragmatic goals are important for disability scholars because to "contemplate the mechanisms of stigma," as Mitchell and Snyder point out, is to begin the process of providing "ourselves with the opportunity for changing perceptions and alternative ways of comprehending disabled lives today" ("Jesus Thrown Everything Off Balance," 176).

---

2. Stressing this kind of continuity is not a commitment to thinking that accounts within both Testaments are incompatible.

JANE EYRE AND BIBLICAL MODELS OF DISABILITY

Chapter 6

Although *Jane Eyre* has long been understood to have moral education as one of its central concerns, it is only in recent years that there has been sustained discussion of the biblical sources of the novel. Focusing on Brontë's rewriting and renewing of biblical texts with attention to gender politics, Keith Jenkins suggests, following Joan Chard, that Brontë's selection and manipulation of biblical allusion provides a basis for understanding *Jane Eyre* as a form of spiritual autobiography. Brontë, Jenkins argues, breaks the biblical stories down into their component parts and manipulates them into a *bricolage* that challenges patriarchal authority. He makes the case that the gender reversals apparent in the ascription of male biblical roles to female characters and vice versa, and the undermining of God's providential role in controlling human action in favor of a larger degree of human self-determination, work to strengthen Brontë's social agenda in the novel: to argue for greater self-determination for women. Brontë's uses are sometimes "surprisingly casual" (Jenkins, 134), and scripture is often deployed negatively to emphasize a theological position with which Brontë does not agree (e.g., Calvinism). Catherine Tkacz highlights Brontë's technique of contrasting uses of a single Bible passage, her process of embedding scripture within speech, her amalgamation of ranges of Bible passages, and her evocation of scripture both with and without direct quotation. Tkacz is interested in Brontë's method, rather than the theological explanation for her selectivity, and proves that Brontë's assimilation of biblical material is extensive and that it plays a significant role in characterization, plot, imagery, commentary, and narrative comment. I argue elsewhere (Joshua, "Almost my hope of Heaven") that the biblical allusions have a distinctly anti-idolatry theme that points to the novel's distrust of false Messiahs.

To extend understanding of disability in *Jane Eyre*, I will use a methodology similar to that used by Jenkins and Tkacz: that of employing biblical allusions to explicate aspects of the novel with which these allusions connect. Brontë's approach to the Bible's representation of disability is highly selective. She emphasizes the spiritual worth of disability and the role of a person with a disability as an agent for the power of God. In essence, Brontë locates her discussion of biblical disability around one central question: what is the relationship between the physical body and the spiritual self? The nature of this relationship is explored more particularly through two further questions: What is the theological significance of sight and blindness? What is the theological significance of madness? Through redemptionist selectivity, Brontë dissociates stigma and disability, choosing biblical quotations that imply that disability is a symbol of being saved and that it is a route to salvation. Although there has been much discussion of the theological significance of the novel, critics have approached disability not through the biblical allusions to it but through a more secular understanding of the conditions the novel presents. Nonetheless, the meanings critics associate with the disabilities included in the novel are theological: Edward Rochester's disability is seen as a punishment for his immoral behavior, for instance. It seems fitting, then, to explore the possibility of whether Brontë's biblical allusions to disability in any way contribute to a theological understanding of the condition. The novel's positive characterization of disability, which I demonstrate by examining its use of certain biblical texts, rules out the punishment interpretation, an interpretation which is plausible only on the assumption—always unargued—that disability is something negative.

THE RELATIONSHIP BETWEEN THE PHYSICAL BODY AND THE SPIRITUAL SELF

In general, Brontë rejects the idea of the equation of spiritual cure with physical cure, preferring to dwell on the benefits of disability for spiritual insight, and on the experiences of people with disabilities who demonstrate great faith. St. John Rivers warns Jane to remember the fate of Dives "who had his good things in this life" (423; ch. 35 [Luke 16.19–31]).[3] Dives, the rich man, is punished in the afterlife; Lazarus, the man covered in sores who begged at his gates, is rewarded, and his impairments do not disqualify him from recompense in Heaven. To reject St. John's proposal would be to live as Dives in the luxury of not being a missionary's wife. Jane is urged to become Lazarus: her uncomfortable life, St. John urges, will make her fit for Heaven.

This story exemplifies the novel's tendency to include biblical references to disability (or illness) that indicate unexpected salvation, though the reference is misapplied by St. John in his false assessment of Jane's spiritual worth and in his associating her with the indulgent rich man. As I have written elsewhere, "St. John's path is rejected by Jane, not because he places too much emphasis on the role of Christ, but because he overlooks the fact that prioritizing Christ does not entail refusing to allow a secondary place for human affection" (Joshua 100). The novel proposes that this is not the cor-

---

3. The version of the primary text referred to in this chapter is Charlotte Brontë, *Jane Eyre*, ed. Margaret Smith (Oxford: Oxford University Press, 1975).

rect spiritual path for Jane. Brontë undermines this reference by making St. John use Lazarus as a false example; nonetheless, this is a positive account of disability as an indicator of the spiritual reward to come, even if it is misapplied.

The link between faith and the healing of a physical disability is present when Edward makes implicit reference to Matthew 8, the passage in which the centurion's servant or son, who is "sick of the palsy" (v. 6), is healed by Jesus because of the centurion's faith.[4] In Matthew, the centurion expresses his faith by telling Jesus that he is a man of command and that he trusts Jesus's ability to heal by command: "Just say the word, and my servant will be healed" (v. 8). It is this vocation for command that Edward echoes when he cites Matthew 8.9 and excuses his tone by saying to Jane, "I am used to say 'Do this,' and it is done" (125; ch. 8). Edward's allusion signals that he has avoided a religious life. His echo of this passage may also hint that he supplicates for a healing—he is in charge of a sick wife, and it may be that his pursuit of Jane is a misguided form of healing. Like the reference to Luke 16, the passage indicates that Jesus will heal those who do not feel entitled to it. Matthew 8 is another form of elevation of those who are not tradition- ally regarded as worthy. The chapter is referred to again when Jane is dis- cussing St. John Rivers. He, like Edward, has a commanding nature and is in the role of centurion; but, unlike Edward, he is ostensibly a man of faith, and so the reference may hint at his problematic status as a future martyr. Jane says of St. John, "When he said 'go,' I went; 'come,' I came; 'do this,' I did it. But I did not love my servitude" (402; ch. 34.). Jane takes the hum- bler role of the centurion's servant, and the reference may hint at her patient wait for spiritual renewal.

Brocklehurst references what he perceives to be Jane's lack of spiritual wholeness by associating her with the healing of a physical disability. He announces that Jane's aunt has sent her to his school "to separate her from her own young ones, fearful lest her vicious example should contaminate their purity: she has sent her here to be healed, even as the Jews of old sent their diseased to the troubled pool of Bethesda; and, teachers, superinten- dent, I beg of you not to allow the waters to stagnate around her" (67; ch. 7). John 5.2–9, the passage referenced here, is an account of a man who had been ill for 38 years, and who is waiting to be healed at the pool of Bethesda.

---

4. Although it is conventional to use the names Jane and Rochester, I refer to characters of both genders consistently by their first names, where the first name is known. I think it is more appropriate, when discussing the egalitarian agenda of a novel, to use gender-neutral language than it is to follow a convention that has been for some time regarded as patronizing to women.

The healing is expected to take place when an angel disturbs the water. The man's mobility impairment prevents him from going into the pool quickly enough, and, since he has no one who is willing to assist him, he is unable to be healed. Jesus tells him that he does not need to enter the pool because he has cured him. John 5 explicitly represents disability as lack of wholeness and suggests that there are two ways for the man to be made whole: either by stepping into the pool or through a miracle performed by Jesus. In both cases, to be cured is to be made whole. Jesus links sin and catastrophe to disability or illness when he tells the man "sin no more, lest a worse thing come unto thee" (v. 14). Brontë distances herself from this irredeemable account of disability by giving the allusion to Brocklehurst: the healing of a physical disability is undermined as an indication of spiritual cure as the pool is not the cause of the healing in the biblical story.

Through her reference to Mark 5.24–34, Jane links herself to the healing of a physical disability that cannot take place. Here, she describes another self-interested character, Blanche Ingram, as "a great lady, who scorned to touch me with the hem of her robes as she passed" (187; ch. 18). Like her use of John 5.2–9, Brontë's use of Mark 5.24–34 is also ironic. Reflecting on what she supposes is a courtship being conducted between Edward and Blanche, Jane recalls the woman with the gynecological ailment ("an issue of blood" [Mark 5.25]) who is healed by Christ, whose robes she touches as he passes by her.[5] The association between Blanche and Christ may be part of the novel's motif of identifying characters as false Messiahs and is another example of disability as lack of wholeness in these contexts: Christ says to the woman "go in peace, and be whole of thy plague" [Mark 5.34]). Brontë uses the passage negatively, by emphasizing the impossibility of the healing (as Jane does not touch her), to signal that disability is not lack of wholeness.

In contrast, Brontë's reference to the Sermon on the Mount (Matt. 5.28–29) lends itself to a redemptionist reading and offers a more positive link between the spiritual body and the physical body than the reference to disability as the product of sin in John 5 and Mark 5. Having shut herself in her room to grieve over her aborted wedding, Jane converses with herself about what she should do next. She identifies that her conscience holds her "passion by the throat," warning her of the temptation with which she is faced: to become Edward's mistress. It tells her to be active in removing herself from moral danger, "[Y]ou shall tear yourself away; none shall help

---

5. Candida R. Moss makes a case for Jesus's discharge of power mirroring the leaky body of the woman. This is part of her wider discussion of impairment as a symbol of connection to God.

you: you shall, yourself, pluck out your right eye; yourself cut off your right hand: your heart shall be the victim; and you the priest, to transfix it" (307; ch. 27). The words of Jane's conscience echo, closely, those of the Sermon on the Mount, but with a reversal of genders: "For whosoever looketh on a woman to lust after her hath committed adultery with her already in his heart" (Matt. 5.28–29). As Tkacz points out, "the loss of the hand and eye is a 'profitable' sacrifice enabling one to avoid full punishment for uncountered lust" (10). Disablement is, here, an indicator of being in a position to avoid moral turpitude. This biblical fate is seen more explicitly in the symbolism of Edward's "mutilated" (441; ch. 37) left hand, and in the ultimate blindness in one of his eyes.[6] Jane's positive reference to the disabilities of Matt. 5.28–29 (307; ch. 27) points toward the possibility that Edward's disabilities could be read as an indication of his spiritual worth.

THE THEOLOGICAL SIGNIFICANCE OF SIGHT AND BLINDNESS

Edward's blindness has been read in various ways, most of which have been negative. From the identification of blindness with castration by Richard Chase, to the reading of blindness as symbolic of the author's fear of sex and her resistance to her supposed forbidden love for her father by Lucile Dooley, Edward's blindness is generally understood as a punishment, an affliction, or a humiliation.[7] We see the beginnings of a redemptionist approach to blindness in its association with a feminist equalization of power in *The Madwoman in the Attic* (1979) by Sandra Gilbert and Susan Gubar. They are lukewarm in their endorsement of the view that Edward's injuries are a "symbolic castration" (Chase, 467); they argue, instead, that his blindness is an attempt to make Jane "an equal of the world Rochester represents" (368), pointing out that the pair are only able to drop their "social disguises" once one of them is blind (368). For Peter Bellis, Edward's blindness signals the novel's shift from characterizing Jane's perspective as merely "an alternative source of visual power" (645) to presenting Jane as the dominant source—this is by virtue of the removal of Edward's challenging sight. When

6. Tkacz nevertheless reads Edward's disabilities as punitive, observing that "On one level the loss of his left hand and eye punishes him [Edward] for attempting bigamy; in gaining faith through his experiences, however, he finds that his loss proves profitable and, in regaining Jane and his sight, he discovers that justice is tempered with mercy" (12).

7. Robert Martin's *The Accents of Persuasion* calls Edward's blindness a "humiliation" (91), though he suggests that "the reader is never invited either to sentimentalize over him [Edward] or to disregard the brutal facts of his humiliation" (91).

Jane becomes her husband's eyes, Bellis sees her as dominating him (649), rather than identifying her as his aide. Sharon Marcus proposes an alternative version of this idea by seeing Jane as a prosthesis. But Marcus argues that Jane is fragmented by her role as aide: "Critics have often interpreted Rochester's blinding and mutilation as a form of symbolic castration, but Jane appears to adopt—rather than to triumph over—her husband's bodily fragmentation by transforming herself into a prosthetic part" (213). Marcus limits the attraction of seeing Jane as a prosthesis through this subordinating definition of the role of caregiver.

The question of whether Edward's blindness can be positioned as something positive has gained attention recently. David Bolt argues that, although the novel challenges gender hierarchies, "the underpinning hierarchies of normativism over disability and 'the sighted' over 'the blind' persist" (271). Georgina Kleege interprets Edward's blindness as "divine retribution for the sin of wishing to marry Jane when he already has a wife in the attic" and as an event that allows Jane to "rise to power" (70, 71). Kleege rejects the novel for this reason, classing it as one of the "old stories of blindness" (73) that make her "weary and a little afraid" (73). Marianne Thormählen regards Edward as a man "blighted by severe disabilities" (80), suggesting that it "goes against the grain of a present-day reader to regard them as Divine chastisement," but that Edward is fundamentally a man who has been "made aware of the power of God" and who "learns to repent" because he is "stricken" (80). Like Thormählen, Kate Flint follows Edward's own account of his religious conversion: "Divine justice pursued its course [. . .]. *His* chastisements are mighty; and one smote me which has humbled me for ever [. . .]. I began to see and acknowledge the hand of God in my doom" (*Jane Eyre*, 452; ch. 37). Edward asserts that his blindness is the result of retributive justice and that it is also the beginning of his spiritual sight. Flint observes that Edward's blindness is a "form of punishment that ultimately proves to be a means of illuminating the inward eye" (*The Victorians*, 80). Thomas Vargish also argues along these lines, suggesting that "Rochester's punishments are necessary to his spiritual salvation and therefore to his *rise* toward spiritual equality with Jane" (66, n8). Blindness can be seen, then, as part of his spiritual recovery; but it is, for these critics, still a divine punishment.[8] That Edward regards his physical blindness as a divine punishment is without question, but the issue here is

8. Flint and Vargish are close to my own view that Edward's blindness, when understood in the context of the novel's references to Messianism and idolatry, "symbolizes the abandonment of idolatry" and is "a positive symbol for his religious well-being" (Joshua, 95).

its meaning in the novel as a whole, rather than the character's own presentation of his viewpoint to another character with whom he has a particular and evident agenda. The novel's biblical allusions provide an important context that takes us beyond this negative view of the religious or moral meaning of Edward's blindness.

Edward's own admission that he sees clearly in a spiritual sense in his blind state ("I began to see and acknowledge the hand of God in my doom" [452; ch. 37]) alludes indirectly to John 9, a chapter that plays throughout on the meanings of seeing as sensory experience, as understanding, and as recognizing Jesus. Edward's words are closest to "whereas I was blind, now I see" (John 9.25), which means, at this stage in the biblical story: though I had been physically blind, I now have spiritual insight. In John 9.3, Jesus explicitly dissociates blindness from sin, asserting that the blindness in this man was not a punishment for his sins or for the sins of his parents, and that he has been made blind so "that the works of God should be made manifest in him." The narrative as a whole suggests that the blind man is the one person who recognizes that Jesus is the "Son of God" (John 9.35)—a Messianic title. John 9 explicitly states that blindness is not punitive and that it has a purpose that derives from God. In various ways, this healing narrative presents the positive religious significance of blindness: spiritual insight and innocence. In associating Edward with the idea that being blind is a necessary condition for spiritual insight, through the echo of John 9, Brontë signals Edward's recognition of his religious role.

This chapter of John is quoted more directly by St. John Rivers. Tkacz has explored thoroughly Brontë's preference for giving the same biblical allusions to pairs of characters who are in conflict as a way to signal her attitude to them. Edward's allusion contrasts with St. John Rivers's use in several ways. St. John concentrates on John 9.4. Emphasizing the importance of recognizing Christ's role in the world, he stresses to Jane the urgency of his missionary work by suggesting that "the night cometh when no man shall work" (423; ch. 35). This quotation closely ties the idea of working while it is day, that is, working while one can see, to a set of definitions of blindness and sightedness that are concerned with spiritual insight and the lack of it. This passage, which quotes Jesus's words about his mission, closely allies being able to see light and being able to do religious or other kinds of work. Through it, St. John warns Jane that he believes his mission to convert Indians to Christianity to be urgent. In echoing Christ's words, here, St. John implies that, because the "night" (or the end of his life) is on its way, it will be too late for her to demonstrate her spiritual worth. Jesus says, in this passage, that he and his followers must "work the work of him who sent me, while it is day; night comes, when no man can work. As long as I am in the world, I am the light of the world" (John 9.4–5). Jesus is both the person who works in the light and the light itself. St. John hints here at his false Messianic role: he measures Jane's allotted time to do her spiritual work as the same length as his own life, echoing Christ's instruction that everybody must work hard as long as he is in the world. Equally, the reference to sight focuses on what is, for Brontë, a negative component of the John 9 narrative. When Edward echoes John 9, his use of the passage places him in the role of discipleship and not in the religiously irregular Messianic role that he has formerly attempted to adopt. St. John uses the same chapter of John as Edward but aligns himself with its sighted aspects. Thus Brontë subtly suggests that St. John lacks spiritual insight in his pursuit of Messianic glory. The interplay of these positive and negative uses of spiritual sight and blindness, in the allusions to John 9 by Edward and by St. John, when taken together, signal that Edward is not being punished, as he and his critics are suggesting, but that his blindness indicates his spiritual worth and his discipleship.

Edward is compared with another biblical blind man, Samson.[9] In Judges, Samson sacrifices himself for the greater good of his people, and his blindness may be read as a means to the end of destroying God's enemies.[10] Samson's disability is read by some as an example of a punishment, but the biblical story is more subtle than this, and it may just as easily be supposed to be an example of a condition that leads to Samson's becoming an agent of God. Brontë's reference to the biblical Samson offers the parts of the tale that signify her redemptionist approach, and she combines a number of different aspects of this narrative in her three references to it in *Jane Eyre*. The first allusion is to Samson's temptation by Delilah. Samson, who has been a Nazirite from birth and has therefore been bound to the rules outlined in Numbers 6.1—to avoid wine and the fruits of the vine, to avoid cutting his hair, and to stay away from any corpse—is tempted, by his wife's charms, to break his oath. Forming part of a discussion between Jane and Edward on the past effects of female beauty on Edward's character, Jane replies to Edward's appreciation of her face, and to his embrace of her influence over him ("the conquest I undergo has a witchery beyond any triumph *I* can

9. I am grateful to Jeremy Schipper for discussing disability in the Samson narrative with me.

10. I am presenting a different argument from Bolt, who suggests that *Jane Eyre* is in conversation with Milton's *Samson Agonistes* rather than with the biblical source, and am departing from his view that the novel leaves "the underpinning hierarchies of normativism over disability and 'the sighted' over 'the blind' remain intact" (271).

win" [263; ch. 24]), with an enigmatic facial expression. When questioned about what she is thinking, Jane responds to Edward that she "was thinking of Hercules and Samson with their charmers" (263; ch. 24). Here Jane hints that Samson's (and Edward's) downfall is his sight—Samson's susceptibility to the physical charms of his wife Delilah, and to the conflict that this creates with his devotion to God. The sighted Edward is an echo of the sighted Samson at this point because he is overcome by Jane's particular kind of beauty. As Edward and Jane are discussing "women who please me only by their faces" (263; ch. 24), Brontë draws attention to Edward's temptation by Jane's physical appearance as well as by her character—her "clear eye and eloquent tongue" (263; ch. 24).[11]

Edward himself refers to Samson when he longs for the physical strength to convince Jane to become his mistress after the aborted wedding. He says, "By God! I long to exert a fraction of Samson's strength, and break the entanglement like tow" (306; ch. 27). The reference is one of the moments in the biblical narrative when Samson plays with the possibility of breaking his vows. He suggests (falsely) to Delilah that if she weaves seven locks of his hair with a "thread of tow," his strength will be broken (Judg. 16.9). When Delilah does this and Samson is set upon by the Philistines, Samson breaks the bonds with ease. Like Samson, Edward signals here that he both wants and does not want to break the vows he has made before God. Edward likens Jane's life, in classical terms, to a "silken thread" that has been smooth until this point, and that has now developed a "knot"—"The hitch in Jane's character," as Edward describes it (306; ch. 27). It is likely that he is not referring to his prior marriage as the sticking point—which is a hitch not in Jane's character but in his—but to Jane's commitment to her chastity. His wish is to break that commitment with the strength of Samson. But to use divinely sanctioned strength for ill by pursuing Jane as a mistress and committing adultery is clearly an indication that Edward is on the wrong religious path; it is his sightedness that leads him to this point.

The final reference to Samson is made by Jane and is to Samson's blindness and to the strength that has returned with his hair:

> But in his countenance, I saw a change: that looked desperate and brooding—that reminded me of some wronged and fettered wild-beast or bird,

---

11. Daniel Margalioth notes that "Delilah charmed Samson away from the right path, while Jane charms Rochester into it, but the mastery over the strong is the same, and so are the blinding results" (204). Jane's charms are a temptation to Edward, but it is difficult to see how he can be on the right religious path at this point. Edward's conversion occurs without Jane's mediation, though it may be a consequence of his love for her.

dangerous to approach in his sullen woe. The caged eagle, whose gold-ringed eyes cruelty has extinguished, might look as looked that sightless Samson.

And reader, do you think I feared him in his blind ferocity?—if you do, you little know me. (436; ch. 37)

Bolt suggests that Brontë's reference to a "caged eagle" (272) echoes Milton's *Samson Agonistes* (line 1695).[12] Although Milton's eagle, part of an epic simile describing Samson's triumphant death, is a free bird whose "cloudless thunder bolted on" (line 1697) the heads of the Philistine audience who have come to watch him profane himself with his performance in honor of their god, Brontë, nevertheless, appears to be using Milton as her source for the description of Samson's pitiable state. The biblical source contains no reference to Samson's self-pity, or to his being pitied by others, but this occurs extensively in *Samson Agonistes*. Bolt's identification of Milton as the source is significant, because it confirms that Brontë consistently has a redemptive approach to biblical passages about disability; this reference to Edward's pitiable state as Samson-like can be set aside as it is not a direct reference to the Bible. Moreover, Jane immediately corrects her pitying of Edward's blindness when she speaks directly to the reader, through her claim to be unafraid of his "blind ferocity" (436; ch. 37).

Brontë's references to blindness that come directly from biblical sources avoid presenting the condition as disabling or as an indication of low social standing, associating it instead with positive spiritual gains. Blindness is neither compensatory nor punitive. In the case of Edward Rochester, it is an indicator of spiritual insight, one that helps preserve him from spiritually misleading judgments and that represents his right relationship to God and to mankind. Brontë's use of Samson warns of the dangers of sight and of strength as a route to temptation, and, like her use of John 9, indicates a redemptionist agenda with regard to biblical texts. Her allusion to *Samson Agonistes* complicates this picture, in that, when she gives Edward and Jane moments of self-pity and pity, their recognition of the spiritual gain of blindness is in abeyance. In her reference to *Samson Agonistes*, Brontë is not drawn to the part that alludes to Samson as having his "inward eyes illuminated" (line 1689) but to the idea of the eagle. The eagle is triumphant in Milton's version, but it is, in this moment of doubt, a caged bird. In this Brontë may be echoing the earlier parts of *Samson Agonistes*, which dwell on Samson's captivity and self-doubt. Nonetheless, Brontë's overarching rea-

12. See also Martin, 98–99

son for including the Samson references is Samson's status as a biblical hero whose greatest feat as a warrior comes when he is blind, and who comes to see his blindness as the route to his glory.

THE THEOLOGICAL SIGNIFICANCE OF MADNESS

The issue of the role of the disabled body in signaling spiritual worth is taken up again through the reference to King Nebuchadnezzar's madness. On reuniting with Edward at the end of the novel, Jane refers to him as having a "'faux air' of Nebuchadnezzar in the fields" (441; ch. 37). There are three aspects of the stories associated with Nebuchadnezzar that may be relevant to the theological message of *Jane Eyre*: the King's spiritual pride and association with idolatry; his dream of a tree; and his madness in the wilderness and his recovery. Given that Jane's reference is explicitly to "the fields," it is likely that this is a direct reference to the King's madness; but, as in the reference to Edward's arm and eye, Brontë may be using the Nebuchadnezzar story in other ways too.

Nebuchadnezzar dreams of an image—with a golden head, a breast and arms of silver, thighs of brass, legs of iron, and feet of clay—that is destroyed by a huge stone (Dan. 2.31–35). The prophet Daniel interprets the golden head as standing for Nebuchadnezzar himself, hinting that the baser substances symbolize the degeneration of his kingdom under different leadership in successive years. Nebuchadnezzar is depicted here, and in the remaining stories in the book of Daniel, as "a foolish and arrogant self-idolater" (Barton and Muddiman, 565). Having dreamt of this idol, Nebuchadnezzar constructs it, inviting all the leaders of his provinces to worship it, threatening death by fire if they refuse (Dan. 3.6). The King attempts to unite a region with diverse religions through commanding the worship of this idol, but the Jewish leaders in his kingdom refuse and are thrown into "the burning fiery furnace" (Dan. 3.21). Being true to their faith, they are saved from the fire's effects (Dan. 3.25), but this is insufficient to convert Nebuchadnezzar. Next, the King dreams of being visited by a messenger from Heaven who tells him to fell a tall tree that provides shade and fruit, leaving a stump that will "be with the beasts in the grass of the earth" (Dan. 4.15). Daniel interprets the tree as referring to the King himself. The dream predicts that Nebuchadnezzar will be forced to dwell with the beasts as an animal until he recognizes the God of the Jews, after which time he will be restored to power. Nebuchadnezzar ignores the warning of the tree and is told directly by a voice from Heaven that he will be driven from his home and will live as an animal, until "his hairs were grown like eagles' feathers, and his nails like bird's claws" (Dan. 4.33). His "understanding" is removed from him, suggesting he has gone mad (Dan. 4.34). After his conversion, the King is restored to sanity and his kingdom and his greatness is even increased. He learns that "those that walk in pride [God] is able to abase" (Dan. 4.37). Just as the tree in Nebuchadnezzar's narrative is a warning, so it is a warning for Edward. Echoes of this return in the scene when Edward refers to his hand as a "mere stump" (441; ch. 37) and sits on a "dry stump of a tree" (445; ch. 37). The tree is referenced again in connection with Edward's disabilities when Jane asserts "You are no ruin, sir—no lightning struck tree: you are green and vigorous. Plants will grow about your roots, whether you ask them or not, because they take delight in your bountiful shadow" (450; ch. 37). Using the symbolism of Nebuchadnezzar's benevolent tree, Jane rejects Edward's assumption that he is more like the blasted chestnut and hints that, in his blindness, he has returned to glory as Nebuchadnezzar does at the end of his narrative.

Although the other parts of Nebuchadnezzar's narrative (the blasted tree, dreams, and idols) are clearly part of the novel's wider set of symbolic images, Nebuchadnezzar's madness is the part of his narrative that is most directly referenced by the novel. Edward places himself in the position of a false God, encourages Jane to see him this way, sees her in this way himself, and is therefore strongly associated with idolatry—the other important theme of Nebuchadnezzar's story. For instance, Jane says of Edward that she could not "see God for his creature: of whom I had made an idol" (277; ch. 24). From the moment Jane hears the Mighty Spirit—God's voice in response to her prayer—and becomes "enlightened," she renounces idolatry (425; ch. 35). Edward, coincidentally, renounces it at the same time, and his blindness symbolizes this rejection.

Tkacz is unequivocal in her assertion that the Nebuchadnezzar reference signals that Edward is in "proud defiance of God" and in need of "beneficial correction" (12). Nebuchadnezzar's madness is, for Tkacz, a punishment that ends "when his pride has been abased" (14). Elizabeth Donaldson sees Edward's "punishment" as "paralleling Nebuchadnezzar's [tree] dream," reading Edward's blindness itself as a kind of dream, suggesting that "the closed eyes of the sleeping dreamer seem temporarily blinded" and that by "[i]mprisoning and isolating the dreamer, the dream state represents the threat of inescapable interiority, or madness" ("The Corpus of the Madwoman," 109). But the Nebuchadnezzar story does not offer this kind of detail on the paralleling of dreaming and blindness, and Brontë is less committed to the idea of punitive disability than she might appear. Nebuchadnezzar's madness is punitive (when Daniel reveals to the King that he will go mad for a period of time if he does not convert, he means this will be a punishment from God if he does not "break off" his "sins by righteousness" and "show mercy to the poor" [Dan. 4.27]); and madness is linked here to a loss of status and power. Jane makes her comparison between Edward and Nebuchadnezzar in such a way as to undermine it, however. In his blind state, Edward is the forgiven Nebuchadnezzar.

Edward alludes to himself as sounding mad slightly later in the conversation. When recounting crying out Jane's name during his conversion experience, he notes, "If any listener had heard me, he would have thought me mad: I pronounced them with such frantic energy" (452; ch. 37). Given that Brontë aligns the description of Edward with the symbolism of Nebuchadnezzar's story, and given that her understanding of him as retaining his vigor and his central role as a provider of shade and strength in his blindness, we might make a case that Brontë presents disability here as no bar to power.

Bertha Rochester is, obviously, the character most associated with madness. Demonic possession is, in biblical narrative, an explanation for madness. Interestingly, Bertha is associated with demons rather than the demonically possessed of the Bible, who clearly have an identity that is separate from the demon. Bertha is called a demon on several occasions and Edward associates her with Hell, citing the Book of Revelation in connection with her. He explicitly sees Bertha's madness as a religious trial that he must overcome and uses biblical language in order to convey this impression (312; ch. 27). In his descriptions of Bertha, Edward summons up all of the negative aspects of the biblical models of disability. Her disability is strongly connected with sin—he describes her as "at once intemperate and unchaste" (310; ch. 27); he regards her as unclean, and her illness taints him, according to his perception of how the world might see it: "In the eyes of the world I was doubtless covered with grimy dishonour: but I resolved to be clean in my own sight—and to the last I repudiated the contamination of her crimes, and wrenched myself from connexion with her mental defects" (311; ch. 27). To portray life with someone who is mentally ill as hellish does not admit of a redemptive reading, it is clear, but Brontë is offering this model of disability as a way to characterize Edward's misguided approach to his religious test and his marital obligations. He believes himself to "have done all that God and humanity" (313; ch. 27) required of him, but he embarks on a life of dissipation until he finds hope that Jane is his savior and his idol, disregarding what Jane calls "the law given by God" by attempting to marry her (321; ch. 27). Edward returns to his religious path when he realizes his duty of care to Bertha. His attempt to save her from the fire, risking his own life, is an indication of this. Edward's association of Bertha with Hell makes explicit his disordered religious state—he has the wrong attitude toward disability at this stage in the novel.

CONCLUSION

Brontë makes no distinction between the Testaments and does not opt for the solution that Stiker and Eiesland offer—that of seeing the New Testament, or even Christ's disabled body, as redemptive. Instead, her selectivity connotes an inclusive theology of disability that presents it, as Horne does, as an indicator of coming to discipleship. *Jane Eyre* addresses the problem of stigma in many forms, and places disability as central to the theological and romantic resolution. This emphasis signals that biblical allusion is part of Brontë's attempt to establish the social and religious worth of people with disabilities in this novel. Brontë's use of biblical texts addresses the problematic associations that the Bible makes between disability and punishment, sin, disruption, and uncleanness. She throws into a negative light the biblical identification of disability as lack of wholeness, as being an outcast, and as indicative of insufficient spiritual worth. She does this in two ways: by associating negative passages, such as the healing of the man at Bethesda, with characters she moralizes against, and by associating passages that admit of a redemptionist reading with characters who show their spiritual worth. The biblical allusions to disability are remarkable in *Jane Eyre* for the consistency of their approach and for their function as indicators of the stage that the characters have reached in their spiritual growth. When the sighted Edward is on what the novel deems to be the wrong religious path, he is associated with the foibles of the sighted Samson; when he has experienced his religious conversion, he is the blind man who spiritually sees (John 9). Edward's failure in recognizing Bertha's sacral purpose (or his ethical obligation to her), by associating her with the unclean and unworthy, is part of the lesson he is required to learn.[13]

Biblical healings are controversial in disability studies, for the theology of cure that they may generate and for their reduction of people with dis-

13. It is interesting to note that Brontë's account of disability in *Villette* is much less sympathetic. Miss Marchmont is an eccentric invalid with a commanding nature who shows little sympathy for others, and a character known only as the "crétin" is described as deformed, animal-like, and mendacious. Brontë's later use of disability makes the strong connection between biblical references and disability and the consistency of the redemptive approach seem even more striking in *Jane Eyre*. I am grateful to Christine Went for reminding me of these references.

abilities to passive tools of God. Mitchell and Snyder note the scarcity of comment in modern theology and biblical studies on the fact that Christ's healing miracles resolve the difficulties that arise from disability through "the erasure of rather than the acceptance of disability" ("Jesus Thrown Everything Off Balance," 178). Brontë's positive use of people who are healed of their disabilities leaves her open to the criticism leveled by some critics that people with disabilities in the Bible are reduced to agents of God. But, one could just as well argue that to be an agent of God is the highest form of dignity within the Christian tradition. Brontë avoids this controversy by the careful selection of aspects of biblical narratives that identify disability as a route to salvation and as an indicator of faith. Her selectivity and manipulation of biblical allusions reveals a redemptionist agenda that helps to clarify the more ambiguous uses of disability in the novel, causing serious doubts about readings that suggest that Edward is punished, Jane has ascended in power over him, and St. John is saved. The biblical intertexts point to a nonpunitive understanding of disability that provides a strong basis for understanding Edward's disabilities not as a divine punishment but as a signal that he is righteous. Brontë takes her inspiration for Edward's disabilities from the hand and eye of the Sermon and the Mount, strongly underscoring that she believes them to be markers of redemption.

Chapter 7

ILLNESS, DISABILITY, AND RECOGNITION IN *JANE EYRE*

SUSANNAH B. MINTZ

ILLNESS AND DISABILITY pervade *Jane Eyre* according to what seem like typically metaphorical patterns. From the death of Jane's parents to typhus to the loss of Rochester's sight and hand, from minor figures like the unnamed students at Lowood school to the hero and heroine themselves, problematic bodies are repeatedly introduced and then rehabilitated or eradicated from the story in ways that bring presumed deviation under control. Illness tends to suggest the novel's assumption of a progress narrative. When Jane and Helen Burns get sick, for example, their conditions signify at once the problem of institutional corruption (as in families or schools) and the belief that compassion and benevolence will redress that failure, along with the conventional symbolism of the ill as both vulnerable and pure. Other cases, such as Mrs. Reed after her stroke, demonstrate the flip side of the illness dichotomy, where recovery is thwarted by "ill"-will, so that Mrs. Reed's inexorable physical decline manifests her unregenerate attitude and greed. The more static conditions of disability—madness, blindness, and disfigurement (though of course these too are subject to change)—would seem to mock the novel's faith in improvement, being resistant to the salutary effects of care. The troubled bodies of Bertha and Rochester thus call our attention to a different institutional framework, marriage, within whose boundaries the unsightliness of dysfunction can be hidden or recuperated. Fascinated by, and clearly somewhat anxious about, the nature of corporeality, *Jane Eyre* participates in what scholars have cited as a particularly Victorian preoccupation: the porous boundaries of the body, its internal unpredictability, its need for regulation, and its relationship to identity.[1]

Multiple instances of sickness and recovery haunt the novel as reminders of its complicity in the symbolic production of an ableist reality. At the same time, however, *Jane Eyre* reveals the cost of denying or suppressing difference—longing, in moments staged as confrontations with illness and disability, for alternatives. Making use of the psychoanalytic theory of recognition, this chapter argues that Brontë records the possibility of a form of interaction that acknowledges and accepts the frailties of the body. If, as Julia Miele Rodas writes, "disability in Victorian fiction indicates [. . .] a desire to experiment with places and roles" ("Mainstreaming," 373), in *Jane Eyre* that experimentation takes the form of encounters with bodily difference that point toward intersubjective respect. Rochester's impairments, for example, as perhaps the most notable in the text, have been read as an emasculation whose recovery is signified by the son he can partially see, but they may also be regarded as accidental injuries that have little bearing on his chances for a happy life. The neatly predictable outcome of the novel's marriage plot suggests that such injuries are intolerable unless compensated by legitimate class and relational status. But in Jane's concluding avowal that "Reader, [she] married him," we might also locate hope for an environment in which disability is *neither* hidden nor overly exposed as a way of managing the horror it supposedly represents. Far from covering over the problem of Rochester's body (and Jane's, for of course she has been damningly described as plain), marriage makes them at once obvious and inconsequential to relational success.

Such a reading of the central relationship in *Jane Eyre* suggests that the novel, attentive as it is to bodily shape, facial features, and extremities of sickness and injury, renders these as axes of heightened intersubjective possibility, where subjects are tested for their capacity to tolerate and respect. In his discussion of the origins of the novel as entangled with the inception of an able/disabled binary, Lennard Davis claims that "to truly acknowledge the existence of another identity dilutes the general category of identity" (*Bending Over Backwards,* 101). Yet recognition as defined by psychoanalytic theory insists that true acknowledgment of another's subjectivity is

1. See in particular Frawley; Holmes; Rodas; and Tromp.

possible—indeed, that it is the basis of political and cultural understanding. Jessica Benjamin has described recognition as an intersubjective space in which individuals "bridge difference," "hold multiple positions," and "tolerate nonidentity rather than wipe out the position of self or other" (*Shadow*, 107). To "recognize" is to take up a kind of "double position," in Benjamin's terms, from which the self maintains a sense of separateness without denying to the other an equivalent freedom of identity and self-expression—or, to put this another way, an individual acknowledges the other as a legitimate subject without losing selfhood to the coercive pressures of sameness. Anomalous bodies, tending to inspire both fascination and fear in the nondisabled and thus forcing the encounter with difference in an exaggerated way, may maximize what Benjamin calls the "continual misfiring of recognition, the very plurality that strains subjectivity" (*Shadow*, 101). But they also demand the hard work of acceptance—not only, or not even, of the apparently monstrous *other* but of the innately strange *self*. Brontë's novel represents such an ethic of understanding across the boundaries of plurality that is the foundation of recognition.

Representations of disease, disability, or atypical bodies throughout *Jane Eyre* complicate the idea that these are inevitably problematic conditions, rather than being incidental to problems of social arrangement. I use *incidental* in both senses of the word: the afflictions of the body are secondary to or less significant than the problems of this world, but disability is also attendant upon those problems and thus worthy of attention insofar as it underscores the need for social change. This is not precisely equivalent to the so-called social model of disability (articulated by Tobin Siebers, Tom Shakespeare, Paul Longmore and Lauri Umansky, among others)—that disability is a function of cultural, architectural, and sociopolitical arrangement, rather than a medical problem centered in the body—but it seems arguably a precursor of such arguments.[2] In its emphasis on intersubjective regard as a means of disrupting hierarchical binaries of dis/ability, too, the novel seems intriguingly forward thinking, reminding its readers of the need for more engaged ways of thinking about bodies, selves, illness, and relationships.

Jane Eyre has often been described as at once a naturalistic and a visionary novel, one whose story must be understood as having an imaginative rather than strictly mimetic logic. In Helene Moglen's words, "Brontë did not

---

2. The literature on the move from a medical to a social model of disability—and beyond these to phenomenological and even "posthuman" models—is extensive. In addition to Siebers, Longmore and Umansky, Couser, and Shakespeare, others who have written on this subject include Iwakuma, Hughes and Paterson, and Oliver.

write of what was, but of what could be" (107). Against the text's unsurprising participation in the structures of normalcy, then, can be set its depiction of what might obtain between people in a world where "irregularity"—a word that recurs frequently in the novel in reference to the shape and symmetry of people's bodies—does not need to be repaired. In the context of illness and disability, this overlap often takes the form of tension between *reasonable* bodily reactions to circumstance and *unreasonable* psychological reactions either to those bodies or to interpersonal engagement between differently embodied subjects. The novel openly displays troubled bodies—not to make them the intriguing or pitiable spectacles of readerly stare, but rather to return, time and again, to the scene of potential recognition.[3]

UNCOUPLING THE METAPHORICAL AND THE REAL

Some of the more obvious metaphorical associations of illness are disrupted in discussions of Jane's parents and Helen Burns. Jane's clergyman father, for example, who dies administering to the "poor of a large manufacturing town," would seem to represent a clash between spiritual uprightness and the injurious conditions of industry (21; ch. 3).[4] This situation clearly foreshadows Jane's future at Lowood School, where she and the other girls will also be exposed to a toxic institutional environment brought about by greed. The illnesses of Jane's parents and the virtuous Helen Burns thus seem to symbolize the plight of subjects vulnerable to forces greater than themselves, the combined injustices of patriarchy, class hierarchy, and social intolerance. Helen in particular seems an obvious instance of what Cindy LaCom has called the "typically ethereal," "sexless" and selfless invalid of nineteenth-century English novels (192). In this compacted metaphorical loop, piety is both sign of and compensation for severe illness, which is further cause for devotion (the injustice of sickness made comprehensible through the mechanism of faith); moreover, in different but simultaneous ways, illness and religious fervor make the individual unapproachable, untouchable by average folk whose recoiling from the threat of contagion can be masked as shame in the face of the other's incomparable goodness.

But to the extent that the novel is critical of the kind of zealous piety voiced by Helen, and later by St. John Rivers, her death as well as that of

3. Garland-Thomson's *Staring* offers a detailed taxonomy and cultural history of staring and a brief discussion of recognition in terms of specifically visual exchange (158–59).

4. The version of the primary text referred to in this chapter is Charlotte Brontë, *Jane Eyre*, ed. Richard J. Dunn. 2nd ed. (New York and London: Norton, 1987).

Jane's parents suggest that adherence to one totalizing discourse, such as religion, cannot simply be substituted for another, such as industry or class superiority. Innocence and moral purity do not provide existential protection; on the contrary, they seem almost to constitute naïve capitulation to explanatory narratives. "By dying young, I shall escape great sufferings," Helen tells Jane with a kind of abject logic; "I should have been continually at fault" (71; ch. 9). Unlike Helen, who "'live[s] in calm, looking to the end'" (51; ch. 6), and by implication her clergy parents, Jane is resolutely of *this* world, her sense of indignation and independence trained not on the consolations of the afterlife but on effecting change in the conditions of this life (again, unlike Helen, Jane "questioned" [71; ch. 9]). Jane's very survival, in fact, puts in relief the novel's more realistic politicizing of the deaths of Helen and the Eyres. ("It is possible," as Cindy LaCom argues, "to read disability both literally and as a metaphor that makes meaning" [199].) The living and working conditions Jane's parents and her Lowood classmates have encountered will inevitably take their toll on bodies, and if there is a problem to be solved, it is thus one of systems rather than individuals.[5]

In focusing our attention on the condition of bodies in social and material settings, Brontë situates much of the imaginatively charged work of her story in the threshold space between subjects, a space where recognition can obtain or fail. This relational moment, to quote Benjamin, "corresponds to the political question, Can a community admit the Other without her/him having to already be or become the same?" (*Shadow*, 94). The success or breakdown of recognition between selves thus has consequences beyond those individuals, leading to (because also informed by) attitudes of mutuality and respect or domination and negation within the social group. It is the ambiguous body, Brontë suggests—excessive or depleted, ill or frail, disfigured or disabled—that places these already complex social dynamics at a kind of maximum intensity, forcing a confrontation with difference but also encouraging alternative responses to what might be feared or misunderstood.

To be sure, *Jane Eyre* identifies nearly all its characters in terms of physical attributes, usually with powerful characterological assessments attached to those descriptions, what David Mitchell and Sharon Snyder call the "*strict mirroring relationship*" of body to subjectivity (*Narrative Prosthe-*

---

5. Writing of *Shirley*, Torgerson argues that while Bronte's "true empathy is with the plight of the middle class, not the lower classes" (54), the novel nevertheless maps out the possibility for social and public health reform through the metaphor of disease. A similar strategy seems to be at work in *Jane Eyre*.

sis, 58).[6] In juxtaposition, however, those judgments tend more to cancel or contradict each other than to uphold a consistent taxonomy of metaphorical meaning. In the early scenes of the novel, for instance, Jane's body takes on acute symbolic import in contrast to her cousin John, but it is not reliably clear what body types or tendencies mean. In her combination of physical vulnerability and intellectual resistance (manifested in a refusal to "remain silent" [5; ch. 1]), Jane seems representative of the middle classes bridled by a bloated, rapacious caste system, of which John, in turn, is the obvious emblem. Jane spares no rhetorical excess in her account of him: John is "large and stout for his age, with a dingy and unwholesome skin; thick lineaments in a spacious visage, heavy limbs and large extremities. He gorged himself habitually at table, which made him bilious, and gave him a dim and bleared eye and flabby cheeks" (7; ch. 1). His "disgusting and ugly appearance" is part and parcel of his violent nature (8; ch. 1); as Jane explains, "He bullied and punished me [. . .] continually: every nerve I had feared him, and every morsel of flesh on my bones shrank when he came near" (7; ch. 1). It could hardly be made more apparent that John's spoiled arrogance signifies the appetites, the privileges, of a system run amok.

Yet what does it mean that John also "ought now to have been at school; but his mamma had taken him for a month or two, 'on account of his delicate health'" (7; ch. 1)? Is delicate health not the particular burden of the morally good? Perhaps the difference is maternal coddling as opposed to orphanhood. Perhaps sickness is always the sign of untenable social relationships and beliefs about social value. Here again, bodily excess and extremity, however symbolically they point toward anxieties beyond themselves, are also literal. John's health, like that of Jane's parents or Helen Burns, is embedded in habit and the accidents of circumstance; surrounded by food and opportunity, John indulges himself, as Helen, weakened by deprivation, lacks the physical resources to withstand tuberculosis. Both are caricatures of inequity, yet neither is only that, since their respective physical conditions are also unremarkable in the context of the material worlds they inhabit. Jane, too, reminds us that there is no inevitable correlation between spiritual and physical "health," between the outline of the body and that of the "self," for while we might expect her to appear self-restrained and temperate in order to accentuate the symbolism of her brutish cousin John, she is instead a set of apparent contradictions: feisty, plain, subject to prolonged "absence" through illness, audacious, and per-

6. On the role of phrenology in *Jane Eyre,* see Mitchell and Snyder, *Narrative Prosthesis, passim;* Torgerson (1–17); Pickrel (167); and Donaldson ("The Corpus of the Madwoman," 103).

sistent. What, if anything, is thus inarguably good or bad in these physical representations? Jane's story repeatedly returns us to the possibility of embodiment simply being, rather than representing some puzzle that needs to be solved.

Jane Eyre also interrupts a stereotypical slippage between facial features and physique and temperament or psychology. Beauty may be fetishized, as when, for example, Jane extols the "perfect beauty" of Rosamond, that "earthly angel" (319; ch. 31). Yet beauty is also problematized by unexpected combinations of body and self. Ultimately, beauty guarantees characterological goodness no more than ugliness is the sure mark of a sullied soul. Neither Blanche Ingram nor St. John Rivers, both of whom have what Elizabeth Donaldson calls "classically beautiful bodies" ("The Corpus of the Madwoman," 103), is a particularly pleasant or forgiving person, and when Miss Abbot remarks that if Jane "were a nice, pretty child" she might be better cared for, the error is clearly Abbot's rather than Jane's (21; ch. 3). John Reed is ugly, but so is Rochester. In contrast to these two, it might seem surprising that Mrs. Reed, Jane's formidable aunt, is described as unexpectedly average: she is "stout" but "not obese," of "sufficiently regular" features, and with a "constitution [as] sound as a bell—illness never came near her" (30; ch. 4). "Robust" and "strong-limbed" as she is, Mrs. Reed exhibits neither the repugnant physicality of her son John nor the exaggerated beauty of her daughter Georgiana—who, in turn, with "her pink cheeks and golden curls, seemed to give delight to all who looked at her, and to purchase indemnity for every fault," though she is really no less despicable than her brother (12; ch. 2). Perhaps most unexpected are Brocklehurst's remarks before the assembled students at Lowood; he notes that "no signal deformity points [Jane] out as a marked character. Who would think that the Evil One had already found a servant and agent in her?" (57; ch. 7). But in so observing, the manager of Lowood unwittingly refutes his own belief in the metaphorical properties of body feature. With subtle irony, Brontë has one of her more detestable characters articulate a central principle of the novel: that the signs of the body bear no stable relation to personal character.

WHEN RECOGNITION SUCCEEDS OR FAILS

The novel thus suggests that while its characters are obsessively focused on physical features as manifestations of interiority and, by extension, social value or worth, they are not particularly accurate in their assessment of those metaphors. What are the implications of such inaccuracy for the

attainment of recognition between selves when that encounter is fraught
by anxiety about or intolerance of illness or disability? Bodies may matter
to interpersonal engagement in the story, but do they matter in predictable
ways?

As feminist readings have emphasized, one of the more significant relationships in *Jane Eyre* is between Jane and herself. She is described throughout the novel, and by different sources, as "strange," but she initiates this
epithet herself, during her banishment to the so-called red-room (10; ch.
2). In a mirror-moment that precedes the "species of fit" that renders her
unconscious (15; ch. 2), Jane encounters a "strange little figure there gazing
at [her], with a white face and arms specking the gloom, and glittering eyes
of fear" (11; ch. 2). This "tiny phanto[m], half fairy, half imp" seems an
obvious symptom of Jane's psychological struggle with her circumstances,
an emanation of both her anger and her sense of powerlessness in the face
of the Reeds' cruelty (11; ch. 2). The vision is also, I think, a mark of Jane's
inability to recognize herself as a legitimate, legitimately embodied, subject.
"I was a trifle beside myself," she says; "or rather *out* of myself" (9; ch.
2). The misrecognition has partly to do with being at such odds with her
relatives—in her words, "I was like nobody there," "a heterogeneous thing"
(12; ch. 2). That anxiety about unlikeness is here experienced as dissociation
from the image in the mirror; with the insult of a wound inflicted by John
Reed still stinging on her body, Jane cannot reconcile her outrage at being
wronged with the horror of her physical and emotional vulnerability.

At the same time, of course, readers will understand that heterogeneity
is precisely what differentiates Jane from others in the best sense, allowing
her to be more flexible and tolerant, less rigidly didactic or opinionated.
Her failure to take in her reflection as herself—a failure rendered in terms
of bodily anomalousness, of being "strange"—is thus a missed opportunity
to make contact with the diverse and less familiar parts of herself. It seems
important that Jane's first vivid experience of self-reckoning takes the form
of this frightful misrecognition, as if to insist on the powerfully internalized
effects of others' regard. The problem here lies not so much in a need to
integrate the contradictions of subjectivity into a unified "whole" (remembering the Victorian connection between a "whole" body and a "wholesome" soul [LaCom, 190]) but rather in Jane's inability to "contain shifting
and conflictual versions of self" (Mitchell, *Hope*, 105). From this perspective, the mirror-moment is significant less because it reveals Jane to be split,
her frustrations "acted out" through projection (the standard reading of the
scene since Gilbert and Gubar), than because it points toward the possibility of sustaining the tensions and contradictions of selfhood—its strangeness

and irregularity—*without* collapsing these through the negation of sameness. If this moment is originary, ushering Jane toward eventual realization of her adult selfhood, I would argue that the task it underscores is not one of subduing bodily unruliness in the service of psychological "health," but instead learning how to maneuver between subject positions that do not necessarily adhere to an orderly, unstrange whole.

Granting Davis's point that Jane's oft-remarked and lamented plainness makes her an unusual nineteenth-century heroine (*Bending Over Backwards*, 96), we might also consider that what really makes Jane "strange" is her refusal to acquiesce, to succumb to others' desires or authority. But could *strangeness* not also seem plain—that is, does the novel not reclaim the anomalous from the borderlands of recognition? The spectacle of Jane's night in the red-room, her nervous shock and subsequent convalescence, for instance, culminate in a rather underwhelming manner: "no severe or prolonged bodily illness followed this incident" (16; ch. 3). We might again notice a foreshadowing in that this episode prefigures Jane's later period of illness at the home of the Riverses, which is also depicted as an explicable if not exactly ordinary event, given the extremity of her hunger and exhaustion. So, too, does the graphically described, piteous state of little girls' hands and feet at Lowood, indicative of their material conditions, resolve somewhat naturalistically: "our ungloved hands became numbed and covered with chilblains," Jane's "feet inflamed," and the act of "thrusting the swelled, raw, and stiff toes into [her] shoes" is "torture" (51–2; ch. 7); but later, those same "wretched feet, flayed and swollen to lameness by the sharp air of January, began to heal and subside" (65; ch. 9).

What is suggestive about such scenes is that their dramatic force has to do less with the display of strange bodies, bodies under duress, than with the potential for engagement between individuals and contact among bodies. Importantly, no illness or pain or impairment is represented as fully singular or solitary, in large part because the travails of the body (including those of Bertha Mason Rochester) so often necessitate caretaking. Beth Torgerson has suggested that "Brontë's personal experience of illness as both caretaker and survivor enriches her use of illness as motif" (15); from a disability perspective, care has an ethical dimension that extends the orthodox feminist critique of caretaking as an unpaid form of labor for which women, nearly exclusively, are held responsible.[7] If the aftermath of Jane's night in the red-room seems in one sense vaguely anticlimactic, it is also marked by the "inexpressible relief" Jane feels in the presence of the apothecary Mr. Lloyd,

---

7. On this point, see Lloyd. On the ethics of caretaking, see Engster.

in addition to Bessie's "softly" tending to her need to sleep, eat, and drink (15–16; ch. 3). And if her obviously metonymic feet suffer cruel neglect at the Lowood school, at Thornfield they are solicitously looked after by Mrs. Fairfax: "If you have got your feet well warmed," she says, "I'll show you your bedroom" (85; ch. 11). It is as if each episode emphasizes the possibility of intersubjective regard to imply, when that possibility goes unrealized, that the problem resides not with corporeal excess or insufficiency but with an emotional, psychological incapacity that derives from the pressures of ideology and discourse.

Mrs. Reed again provides an instructive instance. On the night before Jane's departure from Gateshead, Mrs. Reed approaches Jane in bed to ask that she be remembered as Jane's "best friend," but Jane responds with silence, "turn[ing] from her to the wall" (35; ch. 5). Later, after Mrs. Reed's stroke, the scene is reversed: standing beside the bed, Jane "fasten[s]" her hand on her aunt's, but Mrs. Reed "[takes] her hand away" and "turn[s] her face" away as well (202; ch. 21). The chiastic repetition in these scenes seems to juxtapose wellness and disease, virtue and vice—the young girl's healthy, if unnurtured, body houses a pure soul; the older woman's impaired body, grown "stout" and "not strong," weakened by stroke and further diminished by an "apoplectic attack" brought on by the shock of John Reed's suicide, has been stricken for her sins (195–96; ch. 21).

There is, however, a more complex discontinuity at work, having to do with opposing motives or psychological intent exhibited as a more or less open interactional style. It is the obvious *gestural* tension between these scenes that matters, inviting us to gauge not better or worse bodies in relation to honest or dishonest selves but rather more or less capacity to approach boundaries, experience generosity, and receive expressions of care. The crucial difference is one of recognition rather than relative health. Mrs. Reed extends to Jane an inauthentic declaration of affection and in turn rebuffs a genuine willingness to forgive past betrayals; it is only Jane who can say, "I had once vowed that I would never call her aunt again; I thought it no sin to forget and break that vow now. My fingers had fastened on her hand [. . .] had she pressed mine kindly, I should [. . .] have experienced true pleasure" (202; ch. 21). Impairment and physical trauma do not make Mrs. Reed more or less spiteful and mean; on the contrary—and despite the rather dramatic piling up of her bodily predicaments—they seem simply to coincide with an *ongoing* nastiness in her character.

Perhaps the most obvious instances of the breakdown of recognition involve Bertha. When Rochester explains to Jane the sordid history of his connection to the Masons, he delivers a string of demeaning epithets that exaggerate his difference from that family as if he were violently expelling from himself any vestige of what they come to represent, which is being "mad," "lunatic," "a complete dumb idiot," "feeble," "common, low, narrow," "coarse and trite, perverse and imbecile," "violent and unreasonable," "absurd, contradictory," "pigmy" in intellect, and "giant" in propensity (and that is just one page [269; ch. 27]). This is no exciting "brush with otherness" that Benjamin describes as pertaining to the playful and "complex interaction" between selves responding to, translating, and recognizing each other, but rather a stark projection of "all that is bad and dreaded" onto the Other (*LSLO*, 87, 86). As is well understood, Rochester responds to the retroactive "degradation" of his desire for Bertha through radical repudiation, "conceal[ing] it" and its embodiment in the "goblin's cell" of his attic (272; ch. 27). To put this in terms of intersubjectivity, Rochester's inability to "*own*—assume responsibility for containing—" his own desire *and* destructiveness forces the mechanisms of splitting and subjection, and what Benjamin calls "the barbarism of incorporating the Other into the same" (*Shadow*, 99). Confining Bertha in the upper reaches of his own English manor house, Rochester allows himself the illusion of "the self-enclosed world of the subject," nursing his narcissistic wounds through guilt, shame, and the pleasures of confession (*Shadow*, 98).

The other, more prosaic "nurse" in this context, Grace Poole, fails Bertha in a less dramatic way but one that returns our attention to the importance of caretaking. Rochester calls Grace a "good keeper" despite the fault of her drinking (272; ch. 27), but later, when we learn along with Jane of the events that led to the Thornfield fire and Bertha's death, Grace emerges as care*less*, negligently lax. The innkeeper too describes Grace as "an able woman in her line, and very trustworthy" except for the "one fault—a fault common to a deal of them nurses and matrons—*she kept a private bottle of gin by her*"—but he goes on to assert that while such a habit may be "excusable" given a nurse's "hard life [. . .] still it was dangerous" (376; ch. 36). Since the proximate cause of Bertha's nocturnal excursions is that Grace Poole falls asleep after drinking, we might attribute at least some of the destruction that ensues to a neglectful watcher. But this is not to lay the "blame" for Bertha's death at Grace's doorstep. Grace Poole is merely the passive and occasional guardian of a "female grotesque" (to use Mary Russo's phrase) for whom Rochester, at least in one instance, plays a kind of barker, pulling aside the curtain to an astonished audience on this "strange wild animal [. . .] covered in clothing," a "clothed hyena" with "hind feet" (258; ch. 26). Such language exactly replicates the kind of advertising that compelled Victorian spectators to exhibitions of human oddities to recon-

firm their status as properly arrayed and bounded selves, if also to experience the (perhaps unconscious) thrill of proximity to their own mysterious
and unpredictable corporeality.[8] Rochester makes just this type of conflation obvious in his grindingly ironic juxtaposition of "*my wife*'" and "'this
young girl'" (258; ch. 26). In the horrified "retreat" of the gathered polite
company, anything like sympathetic "affiliation," to use Rebecca Stern's
word, collapses entirely.

If both Grace Poole and Rochester demonstrate the breakdown of
recognition in their relations with Bertha, is there anyone who does—or
could—succeed? Or does Brontë suggest that madness, unlike ailments more
conventionally understood to be of the body, precludes the very subjectivity upon which the notion of recognition depends? The argument that *Jane
Eyre* repeatedly interrupts stock associations between atypical bodies and
oddities of personality or sins of conduct may be complicated by the representation of Bertha to the degree that she is identified as morally suspect
from the start, her psychological condition presented as the exaggerated
consequence of her inordinate fleshly appetites, her refusal to curtail her
body's willful behavior. In feminist readings, Bertha becomes Jane's "truest
and darkest double" (Gilbert and Gubar, 360), the embodiment of Jane's
"anger, female sexuality, and frustration" (Torgerson, 61). More intriguingly, Rodas has pointed out the extensive similarities between Bertha and
Rochester, arguing that a "migration" of identity occurs between wife and
husband ("Brontë's *Jane Eyre*," 149). But if such analyses seek to retrieve
Bertha from the status of extreme Other by locating the putative evidence of
her madness in supposedly "healthy" characters, they may also risk a kind
of *scholarly* breakdown of recognition, depriving Bertha of separateness as a
character in her own right.

Importantly, in the "spectacle" scene invoked above, Jane does "recognize" Bertha. She tells us that when Bertha "parted her shaggy locks from
her visage, and gazed wildly at her visitors," she "recognised well that pur-
ple face—those bloated features" (258; ch. 26). Literally, she has seen this
face before, but her language also implies that she understands Bertha to
be a separate subject; Bertha's "features" are entirely her own, not metaphorical extensions of Jane. The failure of relational recognition might then
reveal that Jane is not always the good caretaker she proves herself else-

---

8. On the exhibition of anomalous bodies in both Victorian England and nineteenth-
and early twentieth-century America, cf. Tromp, Garland-Thomson's *Freakery*, Altick, Graham and Oehlschlaeger, Bogdan, and Fiedler. What Garland-Thomson calls "baroque staring" would also characterize the horrified but compelled looking at Bertha of the scene cited
above (*Staring*, 50–51 and passim).

where to be (Gilbert and Gubar have also likened her to the negligent Grace Poole [351]). For her part, Bertha, though violent in her reactions, is clearly quite cognizant of the events transpiring in the house below her. Would she be "capable" of the kind of recognition at issue here if others did not react to her by recoiling? This is not to ignore the extremity of her acts but to understand them in a certain context, where the problem is interactional rather than individual and pathological. In this, too, *Jane Eyre* might be said to intimate a basic tenet of disability scholarship concerning mental illness (argued perhaps most trenchantly by James Overboe), that designations of "madness" serve the perpetuation of narrowly defined conceptions of personhood.[9]

Against the failed intersubjective situations of Bertha's experience in Rochester's attic and Mrs. Reed's deathbed episode, as if to emphasize their inadequacies, the novel juxtaposes Jane's period of convalescence with the Riverses. Jane's collapse at the siblings' door marks an overdetermined threshold moment. In a self-imposed state of homelessness, weakened and "starving" like a "dog," Jane is once again unrecognizable to herself, not just strange but a "stranger" (288; ch. 28). Through the window at Moor House, she espies Diana and Mary—"ladies in every point" (292; ch. 28)— and overhears them studying German and conversing. Inside are education, gentility, and domestic organization; outside is a harsh world in which Jane is an "outcast" (290; ch. 28) without connection to name, place, or "friend" (287; ch. 28). Jane—her very existence as an embodied subject—hangs in the balance, in a most extreme state of peril, "trembling, sickening; [. . .] in the last degree ghastly, wild and weatherbeaten" (296; ch. 28).

What brings Jane back to "herself"? Her situation is importantly distinguished from Mrs. Reed's (or from her own prior experience at Lowood) again not so much by sickness as by environment of sickness and quality of care. Although the housekeeper Hannah initially reacts with suspicion, rebuffing the person she calls "a beggar-woman," St. John addresses her as a "young woman" and ushers her into his own home ahead of himself in a gesture of mannered politeness (296; ch. 28). Hannah "exclud[es]," St. John "admit[s]" her; Diana and Mary then go further, the one holding bread soaked in milk to Jane's "lips," the other removing Jane's bonnet and helping her to eat (296; ch. 28). With each successive action, physical distance between the siblings and the "stranger" narrows, until Diana's face is near enough that Jane can feel "her hurried breathing" and Mary's hand "lifted her head." The willingness to touch is crucial in that it breaches the

---

9. In addition to Overboe, see also Ingram; Wilson and Beresford; and Lewis.

radical separateness that maintains what the novel elsewhere presents as distinct identity categories: the privilege of wellness against the untouchables of disease and disability. Writing about touch in the context of disability, Janet Price and Margaret Shildrick argue that "touch *frustrates* hierarchy," because it "crosses boundaries rather than creates distance" ("Bodies Together," 69).[10] Touch can thus be read as an ethically inflected act of engagement that has the power to disrupt devaluing fantasies of autonomy, superiority, and normalcy. In this sense, Jane's recovery has as much to do with making contact with others, with the sisters' readiness to touch, converse, and care, as with the three days she spends "motionless" in a "torpid" sleep (298; ch. 29).

Slumped in the shadows after Hannah has "clapped" and "bolted" the door (295; ch. 28), Jane resigns herself to dying. But once she has "crossed the threshold of this home," "and once was brought face to face with its owners," she says, "I began once more to know myself" (297; ch. 28). Selfhood is defined here as requiring acceptance as a legitimate subject from a community of peers (precisely what is denied Bertha); when the siblings interact with Jane, rather than fearing or reviling her, Jane is restored to "[her]self," to recognition or self-knowledge. More radically, Jane is reborn at Moor House when she renames herself as Jane Elliott. It might seem that bodily trouble then becomes meaningful only insofar as it can be survived and transcended, that the extremity of hunger and fatigue Jane experiences matters (or can be endured) only because it brings her to this act of naming and determining herself, away from the overbearing effects of Rochester's attentions but within the confines of her proper class and domestic position. But Jane's entrance into Moor House has another significance, in that it puts each of the characters into contact with the *strange* as much as with the familiar. Despite but also because of the presence of the unknown, Jane and the Riverses achieve recognition, demonstrated by the trust and respect that allows them to forge relationships and that defines intersubjective touch.

READING THE "IRREGULAR"

While Jane lies in bed recuperating, she overhears St. John, Diana, and Mary discoursing about her physical appearance. In contrast to Mr. Brocklehurst, who once expressed surprise at the absence of "deformity" in one so clearly depraved as Jane Eyre (57; ch. 7), St. John remarks that Jane's

---

10. For more on this topic, see also Shildrick; Chinn.

"unusual physiognomy" is "certainly *not* indicative of vulgarity or degradation" (298; ch. 29; emphasis added). Whatever recourse the siblings have to phrenology in assessing Jane's character, illness is also a contributing factor in how they react to Jane's looks: They call her "emaciated, pallid," "fleshless and haggard," and one sibling remarks, "when in good health and animated, I can fancy her physiognomy would be agreeable" (298; ch. 29). At the same time, they each call attention to an underlying continuity in Jane's face that derives from the structure of her features rather than the transient effects of sickness. St. John says, for example, that "ill or well, [Jane] would always be plain"—though in his coolly rational way this does not entirely sound like an insult—and one of the sisters goes further: "She has a peculiar face [. . .] I rather like it" (298–99; ch. 29).

It seems provocative that illness is represented as negligible in its impact on a woman's attractiveness, and also that whatever assumptions about character the siblings make on the basis of Jane's "plain" and "peculiar" features, they nonetheless see something appealing there. Brontë may have held to the precepts of phrenology, but scenes like this also imply that her consideration of bodies is not so restrictively determinative, perhaps even locating "character" in some altogether other place—such as the threshold space of recognition between selves. It is part of the novel's subtly contestatory nature to suggest that what makes people who they "are" derives from *how* they are in their intersubjective relation with others. This might put some pressure on our understanding of the novel's references to physiognomy, to the degree that what so often becomes foregrounded is the interpretive moment more than cranial or facial structures themselves. To consider the source of at least some of *Jane Eyre*'s most explicit expressions of the practice, for example (such as the insufferable Lady Ingram's announcement that she is "a judge of physiognomy, and in [Jane's] [. . .] sees all the faults of her class" [155; ch. 17]), is to remember that bodies become meaningful in a discursive and ideological field sustained not by its truthfulness or accuracy but by a generally agreed-upon investment in its material benefits. The basic tenets of disability theory hold that the meaning of bodies is interpreted, not innate, and that bodily anomaly has currency only insofar as it is used to maintain the culturally powerful category of normalcy.

And yet the novel overall consistently problematizes the boundary between "outsider" bodies and "normate" bodies in part because so many bodies move in and out of states of health, injury, illness, damage, and because the categories of *normal* and *irregular* come under such scrutiny. Both Jane and Rochester, for example, are described in terms of their unbalanced features, but the novel complicates easy assignation of motive, moral character, or social worth based on those features. When Jane laments that "[she] felt it a misfortune that [she] was so little, so pale, and had features so irregular and so marked" (86; ch. 11), we might balance that self-judgment with her many fortunes in the story—or, to avoid the compensatory logic of such an equation, simply understand the statement as the hyperbole of a young woman who has been well schooled in the story of her insufficiencies. Rochester's features have an equally prominent role in the text. Jane reports that "he had a dark face, with stern features and a heavy brow" (99; ch. 12); she comments that his face "was dark, strong, and stern" (101; ch. 12), that he is not "graceful" (105; ch. 13), and twice Jane remarks on the fact that he is "broad-chested" (105; ch. 13) or of "considerable breadth of chest" (99; ch. 12). According to Jane, Rochester's eyes are "great, dark" (and she repeats this twice in rapid succession as well, 115; ch. 14). If nothing else, so much repetition tells us that Jane is paying very close physical attention to her employer, but there seems no clear or inevitable meaning attached to any of these characteristics.

While forthright Jane does tell Rochester she doesn't "think [him] hand-some"—in fact, she says she is "sure most people would have thought him an ugly man"—her descriptions of him emphasize mood or facial *expression* more than facial structure (115–16; ch. 14). For instance, "his eyes and gathered eyebrows looked ireful and thwarted just now" (99; ch. 12), his "full nostrils" indicate "choler," and his "mouth, chin, and jaw" are all "grim [. . .] very grim" (105; ch. 13). Those "great, dark eyes," too, are "not without a certain change in their depths sometimes" (115; ch. 14). The focus on body language in these moments reminds us that corporeality signi-fies in the subtlest of ways, and that interpretation not only happens all the time but manufactures complex states of mind out of minimal information. It also underscores the bodily conversation taking place between people; as Jane observes Rochester's expressions and attempts to understand what they mean, and he carefully observes Jane's attentions to him to determine her interest, their relationship evolves on a gestural and largely unarticu-lated level. Such moments call attention to the dynamics of psychological filtering—that is, we perceive what people look like by what we understand their emotional states to be or, maybe more urgently, by how emotional they make us feel. Subjects enter "the transitional space of communication" con-stantly, and always with the possibility for understanding another's mood, needs, personal history, grief, pain, and desire (Benjamin, *LSLO*, 169).

We might then compare the Rivers' physical assessments of Jane with Rochester's fanciful characterizations of her as otherworldly. In his descrip-tion of their first encounter on the road near Thornfield, Rochester asserts that Jane has "rather the look of another world." The sight of her makes him think "unaccountably of fairy tales," and he wonders "whether [she] had bewitched [his] horse" (107; ch. 13). Well into the novel, Rochester is still likening Jane to one of the "good genii" (133; ch. 15), "a dream or a shade" (215; ch. 22), an "almost unearthly thing" (224; ch. 23), a "pale, little elf" and "mustard-seed" (226; ch. 24), "a very angel" (228; ch. 24), his "cherished preserver" (133; ch. 15) and "ministrant spirit" (179; ch. 19), "'provoking puppet,' 'malicious elf,' 'sprite,' 'changeling'" and so on (241; ch. 24). Paul Pickrel contends that Rochester "delight[s]" in thus naming Jane "when he knows her better" (173), but these are hardly actualizing terms of deep familiarity or understanding; on the contrary, such epithets, affectionate and even admiring as they may seem, reduce Jane to an anomalous half-human, a magical, diminutive being who lacks substance. Indeed, Rochester's language explicitly invokes that of Jane's own description of the "spirit" figure she once saw in the mirror, the figure that reminded her of stories told by Bessie in which "tiny phantoms [. . .] com[e] out of lone, ferny dells in moors, and appea[r] before the eyes of belated travelers" (11; ch. 2). Confining Jane to the pages of those fairy tales, Rochester fails to recognize Jane in both a literal and psychical sense, revealing that his opinion of her is sometimes as faulty and dissociative as her own.

Recognition is by no means an inevitable or easily achieved state of engagement between people, and in *Jane Eyre*, even the most apparently "good" characters (such as Jane herself) sometimes fail to grant a legitimate subject position to others when bodily distress seems to amplify difference. Although the Rivers siblings, for example, in contrast to Rochester, seem to engage in frank appraisal of Jane's relative assets, identifying her through material clues such as clothing or accent rather than projecting their needs onto her, it could also be argued that they only fully accept Jane insofar as she seems—by those very material markers—to comply with the expectations of their social world. (As one of the sisters remarks, "She is not an uneducated person, I should think, by her manner of speaking; her accent was quite pure; and the clothes she took off, though splashed and wet, were little worn and fine" [298; ch. 29]). Unlike the Riverses, Rochester never engages with Jane in episodes of sickness that manifest her body's inconsistency and need for care, and he is guilty of reducing her to a spectral emanation in the sway of fantasy. Jane makes her own mistakes, falsely elevating Rochester to an "idol" (241; ch. 24). Yet these "irregular" characters do find each other across the threshold of their respective differences. It is "the process of recognition," as Benjamin writes, that "breaks up" the mechanism of projection and "modifies omnipotence" (*LSLO*, 86). "I never met your likeness," Rochester tells Jane, admiring rather than despising her uniqueness (229; ch. 24), and at no point does he attempt to tame the "strange" that she consistently represents.

ALTERNATIVE CONCLUSIONS

If Rochester does, however, also seem to revel in the power struggle of romantic gaming and to want to keep Jane tethered to him, "figuratively speaking," with a chain (238; ch. 24), what happens to address, to redress, the imbalance between its protagonists? Perhaps the obvious answer is, disability happens. As Gilbert and Gubar put it years ago, it is Rochester's blinding that levels the field: "when both were physically whole they could not [. . .] *see* each other because of the social disguises [. . .] blinding them, but now that those disguises have been shed, now that they are equals, they can (though one is blind) see and speak" (368). Such a formulation insists on disability as just the kind of "narrative prosthesis" that Mitchell and Snyder cite; without some diminishment in status, this "surface manifestation" (*Narrative Prosthesis*, 59) on his body, there is apparently no way to register the readjustment of Rochester's psychological position vis-à-vis Jane. Gilbert and Gubar construe embodiment in the most conservatively metaphorical way, with disability and scarring figured as loss of "wholeness," sight as the privileged mechanism of psychological understanding, and blindness (according to the blindness binary) as ignorance and insensitivity, intuition and insight. Disability is the threshold moment—nothing between Jane and Rochester can remain the same after its calamitous transformations—but compensation arrives ("*though* one is blind") in their rapprochement as "equals."

Yet Gilbert and Gubar go on to complain that while *Jane Eyre* seems to announce the possibility of a "democratically equal" marriage (354), by the end of the novel that "optimistic portrait of an egalitarian relationship" is effectively banished (369), its viability interrogated by the remote and seemingly asocial setting of Ferndean. This suggests not only that "such egalitarian marriages as theirs are rare, if not impossible" (369) but also that the very injuries they present as sufficiently mitigating Rochester's domineering ways also make him unfit for society; the broken man and his improperly independent wife must retreat to the woods. David Bolt has taken to task the "classic [feminist] exposition" of Jane's culminating empowerment for its complicity in denigrating disability (269); the ways in which Jane interacts with the blinded Rochester—gazing upon him, guiding him by the hand, later seeing "for" him—equate female authority with Jane's visual advantage. Furthermore, Bolt contends, in restoring sight to one of Rochester's eyes, "the conclusion of *Jane Eyre* [. . .] endorses the ocularcentric belief that a person cannot live happily ever after without sight" (285). The fulfillment of Jane's subjectivity, from this perspective, comes twice at Rochester's cost: first blinding him to grant her specular authority, then "sacrific[ing]" the blindman to restore visual dominance.

If the ending of *Jane Eyre* seems to fail its critics in these different ways, I would propose that continuities of plot also *disrupt* the ways in which disability seems either the necessary conduit toward feminist parity or a reentrenchment of ableism. Donaldson protests that "when madness is used as a metaphor for feminist rebellion, mental illness itself is erased" ("The Corpus of the Madwoman," 102), and, by a similar logic, when Rochester's injuries are used as metaphors for emasculation on one hand or magical healing on the other, disability is erased. If, however, we read those injuries in the context of recognition and the novel's sustained interest in challenging too quick assessments of subjectivity based on bodily traits, it becomes possible to understand the end of *Jane Eyre* as a continuation, rather than a reversal, of its protagonists' relationship.

Conventional readings of what happens to Rochester in the burning of Thornfield have a tendency to emphasize loss of sight over the loss of his hand, as well as the pathos of blindness as a signifier of his social and sexual weakening. As Martha Stoddard Holmes puts it, "the blinding of Rochester [. . .] is melodramatic" (22); disability, she argues, "is melodramatic machinery, a simple tool for cranking open feelings" (3). But it seems worth remembering that well before he becomes "[a] poor blind man, whom [she] will have to lead about by the hand," "[a] crippled man [. . .] whom [she] will have to wait on," bearing his "infirmities" and "deficiencies" (Brontë, 392; ch. 37), Rochester has repeatedly put before Jane the fact of his own "ugliness," his "deformities" (127; ch. 15). And though Bolt argues convincingly for the unequal dynamics inherent in Jane's staring at Rochester in his blindness, we might remember that Jane has been staring at Rochester all along, as evidenced by the boldly delivered *blazon* she delivers when she falls in love and tells us that "beauty is in the eye of the gazer" (153; ch. 17). To quote Janet Gezari, the novel "reconceiv[es] sight so that the very terms subject and object are false to the experience of Jane and Rochester" (68). Indeed, admitting that Rochester's "colorless, olive face, square, massive brow, broad and jetty eyebrows, deep eyes, strong features, firm, grim mouth—all energy, decision, will,—were not beautiful, according to rule," Jane singles out his "pith" and "power," his "interest" and "influence," as Rochester's most appealing characteristics (153; ch. 17). The "irregularity" of their looks is precisely what attracts each to the other, and the novel seems to work hard to establish disfigurement and disability not as a traumatic turning point that separates prefire Rochester from the enfeebled man for whom Jane's love is really a form of pity but rather a continuum of bodily types and aspects that have little to do—but also everything to do—with their love.[11] Such structural continuity works against the notion that disability marks a breach in the forward-motion of a life. On the contrary, these two discordant bodies come together throughout the novel.

Similarly, Jane neither heals Rochester nor saves him—not just in the magical or fantastical way in which he construes her effect on him but also the recuperative sense of narrative closure provided by marriage. To read the final pages of the novel this way is to insist on injury as a crossroads where debility will either sequester Rochester at Ferndean, a helpless and broken man, or require marriage as his only hope of regaining social and masculine position. But by the time Rochester is wounded and blinded by the fire, the novel has long established a pattern of "refusing," to quote Gezari again, "the logic of opposition" (68). Jane is indeed called forth to resume her place with Rochester, but of course, Rochester leans on Jane before his injuries, too ("'I've got a blow;—I've got a blow, Jane!' he staggered. [. . .] 'Jane, you offered me your shoulder once before; let me have it now'" [179; ch. 19]), just as her willingness to offer her care—at least to Rochester, Mrs. Reed, Adèle, or Helen Burns—never wavers. Does the novel foreground these troubled bodies to repair them within the boundaries of good family and class hierarchies, or does it show us what happens when subjects recognize each other as valuable and worthy of engagement, no matter what the contours or behaviors of their bodies? As Jane says of her interactions with Rochester in the first years of their marriage, *before* he has regained some sight in his one eye, "We talk [. . .] all day long: to talk to each other is but a more animated and an audible thinking. [. . .] [W]e are precisely suited in character—perfect concord is the result" (397; ch. 38).

Given that *Jane Eyre* entertains a progress narrative based on fantasies of "benevolent" people who can intercede on behalf of the weak, the poor, the downtrodden, the oppressed—as Lennard Davis puts it, "the desire for a cure is also the desire for a quick fix" (*Bending Over Backwards*, 99)—it seems interesting that the novel, so fascinated by the promise of recovery, would end on forms of physical disability and disfigurement that do

---

11. Torgerson writes that nineteenth-century medicine produced a "new understanding" that health and disease were not "polar opposites" but rather "occurred along a continuum" (13). On scars as forms of disfigurement, see Jeffreys.

not entirely "heal." A competing narrative throughout the text has to do with the power of a woman who *thinks* about what she wants (75; ch. 10). "Restlessness was in my nature," Jane tells us; "I believed in the existence of other and more vivid kinds of goodness" (95; ch. 12). It is in this realm of the *what-else* that *Jane Eyre* situates its engagement with forms of recognition and resists the seductive promise of cure. Many critics have reiterated this sense of *Jane Eyre* as a novel invested in changing patriarchal social structures, what Beth Torgerson calls "a little breathing room for [Brontë's] middle-class heroines" (133). But more than just Brontë's women are at stake; is there also more room for the anomalous body? When Jane says she "know[s] what it is to live entirely for *and with* what [she] love[s] best on earth" (396; ch. 38; emphasis added), she refers to a man she married when he had not regained sight in an eye, when he had lost the use of a hand—a man she recognized, in effect, both as disabled and regardless of disability. In this she reminds us of the possibility of alternative relationships and states of being, ones in which the oddities and excesses of the body simply take their place alongside other aspects of identity.

Chapter 8

VISIONS OF ROCHESTER

Screening Desire and Disability in
Jane Eyre

MARTHA STODDARD HOLMES

AS THE OTHER CHAPTERS demonstrate, *Jane Eyre,* particularly
in its resolution, is significantly concerned with disability. Jane's assumptions about disability as a source of dependency (for the disabled person)
and service (for his or her loved ones) are familiar and still conventional.
These assumptions, in turn, have been shared for decades by critics, whose
interpretive work regarding the role of disability in *Jane Eyre* continues
to gestate through an abundance of film and television adaptations (more
than twenty screen versions since 1910, with a new release in spring 2011).
Given the novel's emphasis on visuality and embodiment, and the thriving
relationship with its filmic offspring, the cultural impact of *Jane Eyre* and
the exploration of disability themes within its narrative must be considered with reference to visual as well as verbal versions. Indeed, an important minor thread in *Jane Eyre* and Brontë scholarship is film criticism.[1]
Despite the centrality of disability and embodiment to written and screen

1. Fansites are a strong part of this critical community, including numerous blogs that
catalog and comment on screen versions. Interposed between fan blogs and academic jour-
nals is the Brontë Society, a long-standing appreciation society that has—like many of the
appreciation societies—an increasingly scholarly element. It has published film criticism since
1944 in its journal. See Stoneman for the authoritative collection of explorations of Brontë
culture; see also Rubik and Mettinger-Schartmann.

versions, however, most film criticism does not consider disability as a key element in plot, characterization, or dialogue, much less within the cinematographic grammar of gender and power. As such, it tends to miss what is most interesting—and most progressive—about the film versions: that all grapple, consciously or otherwise, with deeply engraved social fears and values regarding disability and desire. In an effort to focus on this gap and initiate discourse around these subjects, this chapter undertakes readings of disability and embodiment in a number of iconic screen adaptations of *Jane Eyre*—the 1944 film directed by Robert Stevenson and starring Joan Fontaine and Orson Welles; the 1983 BBC miniseries directed by Julian Amyes and starring Zelah Clarke and Timothy Dalton; the 1996 film directed by Franco Zeffirelli and starring Charlotte Gainsbourg and William Hurt; the 1997 A&E miniseries directed by Robert Young and starring Samantha Morton and Ciáran Hinds; and the 2006 BBC miniseries directed by Susanna White and starring Ruth Wilson and Toby Stephens[2]—and investigates the most significant paradigms of disability and embodiment in the existing renditions on screen. It considers both the progressive possibilities that emerge and the enduring unease with which filmmakers and their audiences approach the representation of disability and bodily difference.

In academic contexts, where the main *Jane Eyre* text is usually literary, teachers regularly use screen interpretations of the novel to spark student engagement, illuminate key themes, and invite consideration of page-to-screen challenges and interpretive issues. However, since the enjoyment of nineteenth-century novels requires some effort and persistence on the part of a twenty-first century reader, many people outside the classroom may only "know" *Jane Eyre* through a screen version. *Jane Eyre* is an inviting text for the screen because of its embodied, highly visual narrative style and its recurrent thematic concern with bodies—how they look, how we look at them, and how they connect. The word *flesh* recurs some thirty-one times in the novel, and, to borrow Chivers and Markotić's term, *Jane Eyre* is from its earliest chapters focused on a spectrum of "problem bodies" with profound range, complexity, and interrelatedness. While Rochester memorably describes the "queer feeling" of "a string somewhere under my left

2. These versions are critically acclaimed and/or in active circulation through public libraries and video rental companies such as Netflix. While the 1970 British Lion television production directed by Delbert Mann and starring Susannah York and George C. Scott has generated substantial interest, it is no longer readily available for purchase or rental, at least in the United States, and thus not a focus of this chapter, which aims to be accessible to readers interested in viewing and possibly using film versions of the novel. While the 2011 Focus Features film directed by Cary Fukunaga and starring Mia Wasakowska and Michael Fassbender appeared too late for full discussion in this essay, I discuss it briefly in a later note.

ribs, tightly and inextricably knotted to a similar string situated in the corresponding quarter of [Jane's] little frame," theirs are hardly the only linked bodies in the novel (291; ch. 23).[3] The abused and "passionate" child-body of its plain protagonist; the "majestic [. . .] dark as a Spaniard" Blanche Ingram; and the Creoled, "mad," and animalized body of Bertha Mason seem no less interlinked than Rochester's "stern features and heavy brow" and the "Grecian profile" of St. John Rivers (134; ch. 12 and 508; ch. 37). As Elizabeth Donaldson has argued, the novel relies on "juxtapositions between normative and non-normative bodies, between the accidental and the congenital, between masculine rationality and feminine embodiment, and between melancholy and raving madness. Reading the body is a central practice in *Jane Eyre*" ("The Corpus of the Madwoman," 102). Julia Miele Rodas, similarly, has argued for the physiological likeness between Bertha and Rochester as well as between Bertha, Grace Poole, and Blanche Ingram ("Brontë's *Jane Eyre*").[4]

Given that Brontë's physiognomic emphasis in *Jane Eyre* includes recurrent views of the faces and bodies of all the significant characters, the novel provides substantial direction for its own translation from a verbal medium into the primarily visual one of film/television. Jane's narration is precisely descriptive, lending itself to stage directions, props, casting, and makeup. Its emphasis on looking (particularly Jane's looking at others) suggests camera orientations for point-of-view shots. Indeed, in its recurrent visuality and self-consciousness about the visual, the novel seems to invite representation in visual media despite being published some fifty years before the invention of cinema. The four scenes that construct disability illustrate both how films have taken careful direction from Brontë (and from earlier film versions) and also how they have diverged from the novel and from each other.

At the same time, *Jane Eyre* poses some fairly significant challenges for mainstream film and television, given that its continuing popularity hinges partly on its core plot of a *plain* heroine finding love and money. "Plain" Jane Eyre and "ugly" Edward Rochester are marketing problems in a cul-

---

3. The version of the primary text referred to in this chapter is Charlotte Brontë, *Jane Eyre* (London: Penguin, 2006).

4. A fuller analysis of film versions would attend to each film's casting choices for these interlinked bodies. For example, there is wide variation not only in the casting of Rochester and Jane, but (much more so) in the casting of Bertha, who in the Zeffirelli 1996 and White 2006 versions is clearly beautiful; in others, barely visible under a mass of hair; and in the always curious 1947 version, dressed like a genteel lady of the house, with her hair up, enquiring if she and Edward are going to be married again. The Bertha-Rochester body language is also worth analysis; in several versions, the notion of her jealousy of Jane is more developed than others, and in the 1997 version, he is tender to her, holding her and kissing her head after her outburst.

tural climate in which producers and viewers of popular film and television narratives (*Ugly Betty*, for example) typically denote "ugliness" by putting thick spectacles and orthodontic devices on otherwise conventionally attractive people, with the implication that as long as we can easily see it as located in discrete, removable components, "ugliness" is a transitory state that resides on the highly mutable visible surfaces of the social body. We are willing to suspend our disbelief in the character's ugliness because we don't truly have to suspend it at all. Rochester's multidimensional "ugliness," in contrast, presents a series of tough questions for cinema and television to address with casting, makeup, script, and direction.[5]

Even more significantly, the novel—and particularly its last few chapters—requires decisions about the visual representation of disability. Disablement is an important layer in Rochester's characterization, from Jane's initial encounter with him to the novel's close. Their first meeting engenders a temporary impairment, when Rochester's horse slips and throws him; Jane must aid her future employer, whose ankle is sprained, to remount, a prosthetic relationship that recurs as the novel draws to a close. After seeing the burnt ruins of Thornfield Hall, Jane learns that her former master has been made "stone-blind" and "a cripple" in a fire set by his "mad" wife Bertha and is called, once again, to support Rochester in his impaired condition (494; ch. 36). How to represent Rochester's disablement remains a fascinating question and opportunity for screen versions of the novel. Enactment of disability-inflected scenes is informed and complicated not only by the question of "faithfulness" to the written texts but also by various audience- and culture-based challenges. A mass-marketed production needs to provoke desire—both in Jane and Rochester, and in the audience as sutured to Jane and/or Rochester—sufficient to the plausibility of the ending in the context of popular expectations about a romance plot and its key personnel.

In negotiating these demands, most film representations of Rochester's disability focus on dependency, without considering other functions that disability, seen as a continuum and a set of variations on human distinction, might have for the narrative. Most film versions assume that disability means the end of sexuality, or else can only envision disabled sexuality within narrow limits. These expectations accord with a convention—dated

5. Physical appearance aside, for much of the novel he is rude, abrasive, cold, and simply unkind—disturbing, above all, not simply in his teasing of the besotted Jane but in his treatment of his "mad" wife Bertha. Even Jane, whose affinity for Rochester is at the start predicated on his "frown [and] roughness," must correct him and remind him of the cruelty of his "vindictive antipathy" for his wife, who cannot help her condition (134; ch. 12 and 347; ch. 27). Any of the dimensions of his disgust for Bertha, which intertwines sexism, racism, ableism, and colonialism, offers a cinematic production of *Jane Eyre* a hefty obstacle.

at least from the nineteenth century and the reification of disabled people as objects of charity—that disabled people are not sexual people.[6]

This is hardly Brontë's message. While the Jane of the novel ultimately becomes Rochester's "right hand" and "the apple of his eye," the couple first has a series of conversations about disability that lead to and enable the happy ending of marriage (519; ch. 38). Jane and Rochester's discussions about marriage and disability are much less conventional and have been much less thoroughly explored than the desexualized characterization of disability referenced above. In fact, the novel's distinctive enactment of desire *for* disability—not simply as that which mobilizes gendered power shifts or presents an opportunity for service but as a form of the *difference* that is part of the "sexual aesthetic"—is as innovative and important today as it was in 1847.[7] While the original text cannot be said to endorse a vision of the disabled Rochester as unsexed, the resilience of this interpretation—that sex and disability are mutually exclusive spheres—inflects *Jane Eyre* films and critical studies, and thus is ignored at the mainstream filmmaker's peril. In short, those film analyses of *Jane Eyre* that address disability extend and reinforce what the films themselves often tell us about common assumptions about the meaning and nature of disability; both film and film criticism tell us more about popular constructions of disability than they do about Brontë's use of disability in the novel.

Aficionados often see popular screen versions of *Jane Eyre* as providing "faithful" or "unfaithful" renditions of the novel. They may also be considered as endorsing or correcting the longstanding critical argument that Brontë uses disability symbolically as the only way to level Rochester's power and enable her vision of egalitarian marriage. My reading of these films is not invested in weighing in on those issues. Rather, I am fascinated by screen versions' repetition of conventions derived from popular beliefs about disability, from other screen versions, and, to some extent, from the novel. Scripts, acting, and direction reveal resilient ideas about disability, including anger and pity as obligatory gatekeepers to a happy ending

6. As Higashi argues, film versions often capitulate to the "narcotic" power of the romantic formula in which women are "encouraged to daydream about masterful lovers but not to analyze the realities of power in their relationships with men" (28). Paulson traces the connections between sight and sexuality in eighteenth-century French melodrama. Hahn argues both for a "subversive sensualism" associated with disability and for charity culture's desexualization of disabled adults (27). See Siebers's *Disability Theory* for a discussion of nondisabled people's resistance to disabled people's sexuality and the ways in which a disability-inflected, disability-authored sexual culture contributes to the positive transformation of bodies and sexuality more generally; see also McRuer and Mollow.

7. Rodas, e-mail message to the author, June 10, 2010. Thanks to Rodas for suggesting this useful term as a way to describe Jane and Rochester's relational dynamics.

between a blind man and a sighted woman, and the implication (by almost entirely erasing that part of the book) that desire for an amputated Rochester is queerly outside the limits of what filmmakers expect their audiences to imagine.

ROCHESTER ON HORSEBACK

The plethora of screen versions that have encountered the challenge of representing Rochester as concurrently "ugly," disabled, and desirable create an opportunity to reflect on the larger place of desire, difference, and embodiment in text and culture, through four key scenes that construct his disabled self, approaching bodily difference by a combination of the conventional, the innovative, and the divergent. Thus, in the pages to come, I examine the way film adaptations approach the following scenes: Jane's first meeting with Rochester when he falls from his horse; her first encounter with him in Thornfield Hall; her first sight of Thornfield—and then Rochester—after the fire that has damaged both; and finally, the scene that reestablishes Jane and Rochester's relationship as lovers. Against this fairly consistent ground, the films often enact choices noticeably at odds with the novel and/or with each other in ways that illuminate the cultural construction of disability.

Jane's first meeting with Rochester characterizes him in terms of his embodiment, both its athleticism and its vulnerability. The scene also establishes the physical nature of Jane's attraction to Rochester. She focuses first on his body (as he sits on a stile, in pain) and next on his face:

> His figure was enveloped in a riding cloak, fur collared and steel clasped; its details were not apparent, but I traced the general points of middle height and considerable breadth of chest. He had a dark face, with stern features and a heavy brow; his eyes and gathered eyebrows looked ireful and thwarted just now; he was past youth, but had not reached middle-age; perhaps he might be thirty-five. (134; ch. 12)

While distinctly distancing herself from any interest beyond "being useful, or at least officious," Jane authorizes her somewhat bold and familiar scrutiny with the statement that "[h]ad he been a handsome, heroic-looking young gentleman, I should not have dared to thus stand questioning him against his will, and offering my services unasked" (134; ch. 12). Here, the novel forges an important theme of Jane's sexuality; it is Rochester's "roughness" and misalignment with gendered ideals of beauty—his embodied "difference"—that generates the sense of ease and familiarity that spurs her attraction.

The scene, then, establishes an important instance of Jane and Rochester's sexual aesthetic, including an appreciation of their shared divergence from standard beauty and comportment. Antagonism, often based on their awareness of their class and power differences and their willingness to test the implied boundaries, is also established as a part of their dynamic. In this one scene, as Rochester transitions from high on horseback to low on the ground and his horse falls on top of him, a host of ideological implications are suggested by the fact that the powerful, muscular master is dependent upon the small servant for help.[8] Filmmakers have made much of this power shift and of the physical and class contrasts between two characters who are briefly connected by temporary disability. Stevenson's production creates a template for many later films with a scene that has the emotional muscularity of a Delacroix and, despite divergences, is relatively faithful to the novel.[9] In this version, director of photography George Barnes renders the suddenness of Rochester's arrival on horseback by working dramatically with camera angles (as will all later versions): high-angle shots make the horse and man loom even larger, while low-angle shots of Jane from the back make her a small silhouette in cloak and bonnet. After Rochester falls, the two characters' dramatic divergence in levels is erased. This scene includes a series of same-level close-ups suggesting parity between Jane and the man she does not know is her employer and toward whom, according to the novel, she feels "no fear [. . .] and but little shyness" (134; ch. 12).[10] Shot/reverse-shot editing, which lets us see each face from the other character's perspective, adds to this sense of mutuality.

Cinematography is often defined as writing with light and motion, and lighting and camera distance used together are crucial to the visual grammar of Jane and Rochester's relationship in all film versions. A distinctive feature of Stevenson's film is its use of lighting to present characters as emotionally open or impenetrable and to chart their power dynamics accordingly. This

8. Rodas, e-mail message to author, June 10, 2010. As Rodas has reminded me, there is some degree of fetishization of class and power differences, with Jane's insistence on calling Rochester "master" despite his explicit refusal to treat her as an inferior.

9. See Sconce for a fascinating history of the adaptation.

10. This stands in contrast to Welles's expressivist aesthetic in which compositional elements (i.e., *mise-en-scène*: characters, props, the set, lighting, and camera orientation) rather than close-ups articulate his or her situation and psychology. See Campbell for a discussion of Welles's instrumentality in the film despite not being the director of record. A subtler expressivism characterizes Fukunaga's version as well.

is particularly the case in the close-ups of Jane and Rochester's faces in this first encounter, where complementary lighting, with Rochester's face lit on the right side and Jane's on the left, makes the viewer's eye connect the two characters, building an affinity between them. Facial orientation and eye contact enhance this effect. A face filmed straight on performs openness and potential vulnerability or engagement, contributing to the illusion of eye contact—or its sense of possibility. Just as in an encounter with an actual person, a viewer or character's encounter with a film face is an event in which relationships are instantly established, even between strangers such as Jane and Rochester.

Later productions reiterate this moment and its literal and figurative levels of power. They also include something Stevenson's film does not—a shot of Rochester using Jane to limp to his horse—a device which further dramatizes both their difference in height (and class status) and their unexpected relationship, as well as foreshadowing his later disablement and her role as his prosthesis (ch. 38). Zeffirelli's *Jane Eyre* gives an even stronger dynamic of differences marked and later muted, by providing not only shot/reverse-shot sequences that view Rochester from a high angle and Jane from a low one (sometimes over his shoulder) but also shots incorporating both characters (i.e., a "two-shot"), making them equals in the same cinematic frame.

Levels are an important issue for the representation of dis/ability, particularly those disabilities whose distinctive qualities include situating a person above or below the mainstream level for standing or walking. While a concern for representing disability and desire is probably not the catalyst, an emphasis on low and high in the aesthetic of representing Rochester and Jane distinguishes all film versions and lends itself to the representation of not only class and gender but also disability. This same aesthetic becomes much more complex in cinematic renderings of the first formal meeting between the two characters.

ROCHESTER'S CHAIR

Jane's first formal introduction to Rochester occurs at the end of the same day as their surprise encounter. This encounter takes place within the physical and social constraints of Thornfield Hall, in the drawing room, where he lies "half-reclined on a couch," his "foot supported by the cushion" (141; ch. 8). Jane's description of Rochester is even more detailed than that in the horseback scene, expressly creating him as an object of her gaze. Starting

Chapter 8

with his face, her words (and eyes) move down her employer's body, leading the reader through a sustained moment of increasing intimacy:

> I knew my traveller with his broad and jetty eyebrows; his square forehead, made squarer by the horizontal sweep of his black hair. I recognised his decisive nose, more remarkable for character than beauty; his full nostrils, denoting, I thought, choler; his grim mouth, chin, and jaw—yes, all three were very grim, and no mistake. His shape, now divested of cloak, I perceived harmonised in squareness with his physiognomy: I suppose it was a good figure in the athletic sense of the term—broad-chested and thin-flanked, though neither tall nor graceful. (141; ch. 8)

Relentlessly evaluative and comparative, Jane completes a *blazon* of his appearance and judges Mr. Rochester's body "good," as she will later judge herself "bad" in comparison to Blanche Ingram.

Significantly, the novel's attention to visuality and looking works on both dramatic and metanarrative levels. Jane looks at Rochester, and Rochester notices her looking: "You examine me, Miss Eyre," said he: "do you think me handsome?" (154; ch. 14). Through their mutual looking (or staring) and a series of conversations in which Rochester interrogates Jane, the two characters reiterate the negotiation of gender, power, and embodiment that occurs in the horse scene, further developing what is still an ambiguous relationship.

Screen versions of *Jane Eyre,* as we might expect, retain an emphasis on the physical aspects of this negotiation. All seem to recognize that this meeting—indoors, amid class formalities and the visible signs of Rochester's power, and following closely on the heels of a meeting outdoors in circumstances that released them from all such constraints—is crucial to establishing Jane and Rochester's power dynamics and sexual attraction, which are overdetermined by the resonances of class, gender, and (in this case, temporary) disability. Successive screen productions inflect this dynamic differently, establishing the characters' conversational and body language through acting and *mise-en-scène* (i.e., the compositional elements of characters, props, set, lighting, and camera orientation). As an aesthetic of *Jane Eyre* films as well as a broader ideology of the body, these scenes offer fascinating messages about geographies of power and disability as negotiated through such elements as looking/staring and levels.

I call these scenes "chair scenes" because only Amyes's interpretation preserves Brontë's presentation of Rochester in a chaise longue at this meeting; the others situate Jane and Rochester in chairs opposite each other, convenient for the shot/reverse-shot sequences used (rather than the earlier two-shots binding them to one another) for their conversations. A highly charged dynamic, not only of talking but also looking, is thus created. The chair scenes illustrate the dynamics through which looking establishes relationships and hierarchies, a particularly loaded issue for films that represent blindness.[11] In Stevenson's production, acting, camera angles, and lighting make this looking unidirectional, a fact that has inspired debate among film critics.[12] The camera's function as an observer is evident in the cinematography. If Jane is not exactly *stared* at, the camera is certainly looking at her closely. The orientation of her face leaves a sense of the possibility of the viewer "catching her eye" as Rochester interrogates her or as she reacts to his harshness: we see her reactions. Further, as indicated through point-of-view shots and eyeline matches (i.e., shots edited together to connect one person's look with the object s/he regards), Stevenson's chair scene has Jane looking at Rochester (as she does in the novel).

Rochester, in contrast, is always looking to the side, away, or down; he directs questions at Jane or commands her, continually deflecting the viewer's attempts to understand his character. Chiaroscuro lighting, which leaves Jane's face fully lit and Rochester's dramatically shadowed, enhances his inaccessibility. In several screen versions, shots of Rochester place him in such deep profile within the back of the chair that neither Jane nor the audience has access to him. Acting and lighting thus reiterate Rochester as a man with many secrets, in opposition to Jane, a poor, plain, woman who lacks the ability to forestall the interrogative gaze of her employer.

Later film versions break Rochester's impenetrability to varying degrees. Lighting in the chair scenes still favors chiaroscuro,[13] with Jane frequently etherealized by backlighting. In terms of eye contact, however, Zeffirelli's and White's versions create particularly open Rochesters in Hurt's and Stephen's facial and eye orientations, using shot/countershot editing of character close-ups to produce a convincing sense of the dynamic interactions that build Jane and Rochester's attraction.

11. See Garland-Thomson for a useful discussion of the dynamics of eye contact (*Staring*, 40–41). Her scholarship on staring is particularly well attuned to film analysis, a discipline concerned with point of view, the gaze, and other aspects of visuality that inflect and are inflected by forms of embodied "difference," particularly gender difference. As I discuss later, Kleege and Cheu offer important discussions of eye contact, blindness, and "passing."

12. In brief, while Ellis and Kaplan argue that Jane's recurrent positioning as observer in the second part of the film makes her passive, Campbell and Soyoung Lee criticize this conclusion as reductive and insufficiently nuanced in terms of film elements such as *mise-en-scène*.

13. The use of chiaroscuro is especially noticeable in the Zeffirelli interpretation because of the contrast it forms to the egalitarian, day-lit scene that precedes it.

Screen versions of this scene are particularly fascinating for the consistency with which they approach the central prop of the chair, and the fact that the scene often goes against conventions of frame composition and power. Rochester is established as an authority by sitting in his chair with others moving around him, or directing Jane to move her chair near to him; but he also places Jane in his chair at several points, which, given his identification with it, produces a sense of intimacy. By repeatedly shooting Rochester in his chair, cinematographers and directors collaborate to create a visual message that Rochester's chair defines him, suggesting that he is overshadowed by it, literally and figuratively. The shots may also suggest, metonymically, a wheelchair, implying the antiquated but nevertheless familiar notion of the chair user as "wheelchair-bound" or "confined" to a wheelchair. In their respective portrayals of Rochester, for instance, Ciáran Hinds (Young's version) and Toby Stephens (White's production) are distinctively slumped into and contained by their chairs in ways that suggest—along with the oblique framing of Rochester in these chair shots—a sense of Byronic mystery blended with stereotyped "angry-cripple" alienation, a foreshadowing not only of Rochester's later disability but also of the potential for his attractive brusqueness to slip into an available narrative of disability and masculinity.

At the same time, there is never any suggestion that Rochester's being in a chair and at a lower level than Jane places him in a position of dependency, supplication, or vulnerability. While conventions of film interpretation indicate that the upper two thirds of the frame are the locus of power and that actions tend to originate on the left side of the frame and be received by the right side, these conventions of visual design are always inflected in any scene by dialogue, plotting, acting, lighting, and other elements of cinema that are inextricably part of *mise-en-scène*.[14] Rochester is by definition on a lower plane than Jane in this scene; thus, conventionally, he has less visual power within the frame. Other than having Jane kneel before him—which she does in the Stevenson version, to pour hot water into a basin for Rochester's foot after he snaps his fingers toward the kettle—there is no way to inscribe their power differential via levels alone. While slight camera angles in shot/reverse-shots do suggest Rochester's dominant position in some versions, most films work instead with body language/orientation/framing, lighting, and acting to present his interrogation of Jane. Regardless of the approach, Rochester is always presented as the more powerful figure in this

14. Just as Third Cinema theory has forced film scholars to reconsider the conventions of Western film in terms of its unexamined limits, one wishes for a Crip Cinema theory that would investigate ways of overturning assumptions about levels, perspective, etc.

scene, despite being seated and disabled. White's version emphasizes this by shooting at the level of Rochester's chair, so that, rather than looking down at him and sharing Jane's point of view, we look from his orientation up at her. His position in the chair determines the norm for the conversation, just as his questions dictate the topics for discussion. A key visual message, then, is that being at a lower level, as in a chair of any kind, does not inherently situate a body as powerless.

Rochester Disabled

While nineteenth-century novels can be notably ambiguous about some conditions of the body—not only pregnancy but also illness and disability— Brontë's description of Rochester after the fire that destroys Thornfield Hall is frank and direct: "one eye was knocked out, and one hand so crushed that Mr. Carter, the surgeon, had to amputate it directly" (494; ch. 36). Brontë is also very clear about each character's uncertainty as they approach the delicate negotiation of their new relationship. In this reunion scene, after observing Rochester unnoticed, Jane takes the place of a servant, replaying in miniature his cruelty to her during her governess days by not identifying herself to him immediately. The masquerade ends in Rochester's exclamation and a passionate embrace:

> He groped; I arrested his wandering hand, and prisoned it in both mine.
> [. . .] The muscular hand broke from my custody; my arm was seized, my shoulder, neck, waist—I was entwined and gathered to him. (500; ch. 37)[15]

When Jane kisses Rochester, the encounter becomes more complex: "I pressed my lips to his once brilliant and now rayless eyes—I swept his hair from his brow, and kissed that too. He suddenly seemed to arouse himself: the conviction of the reality of all this seized him" (501; ch. 37). Rochester becomes anxious about the nature of Jane's interest in him: "But as you are rich, Jane, you have now, no doubt, friends who will look after you, and not suffer you to devote yourself to a blind lameter like me?" (501; ch. 37).

15. See Bolt for an analysis of this moment's participation of "the motif of the groping blindman" and associations with lecherousness (272–73). The Young production improbably shifts Rochester's groping to the water glass. In several versions, Jane needs to guide the water to his lips despite the fact that he has clearly learned mobility techniques and would be unlikely to require so much assistance with an activity as daily as drinking from a glass.

For her part, Jane, even empowered by her gains in status, is also hesitant to assume that he wants her: "I suddenly remembered that I might have been all wrong, and was perhaps playing the fool unwittingly; and I began gently to withdraw myself from his arms" (502; ch. 37). While the pair does not completely settle their situation in this scene, they have found a level of comfort with each other's feelings that permits a frank and loving discussion of Rochester's changed body:

> "On this arm, I have neither hand nor nails," he said, drawing the mutilated limb from his breast, and showing it to me. "It is a mere stump—a ghastly sight! Don't you think so, Jane?"
>
> "It is a pity to see it; and a pity to see your eyes—and the scar of fire on your forehead: and the worst of it is, one is in danger of loving you too well for all this; and making too much of you."
>
> "I thought you would be revolted, Jane, when you saw my arm, and my cicatrised visage." (503; ch. 37)

In this startling scene of physical revelation, Brontë does little to develop the details of what the stump or scar look like; the reader is given no basis on which to evaluate whether s/he might find it a ghastly or revolting sight, and Jane's quick answer offers no suggestions of her reactions beyond the statement that "it is a pity" (which is not the same as saying that she pities him). Rochester's simply described action of "drawing the mutilated limb from his breast and showing it" is similarly undramatic, particularly in terms of the *melodramatic* conventions that in Brontë's time, and ours, tend to dominate cultural scripts of disability, particularly first revelations of disablement. As familiar as we may be with the ending of *Jane Eyre,* we may overlook—as many critics have—this progressive conversation about a changed body and about a relationship that is partly changed as well, but for the better.

Viewed symbolically, Rochester's disabilities have posed a continuing challenge for feminist critics. Helene Moglen sees his injuries as the necessary complement to Jane's independence, "the terrible condition of a relationship of equality" (142). Gilbert and Gubar argue for a symbolic interpretation beyond that of castration: "Apparently mutilated, he is paradoxically stronger [. . .]. [N]ow, being equals, he and Jane can afford to depend upon each other with no fear of one exploiting the other" (368–9). What is problematic about this emphasis is that it reads disability as purely symbolic, a critical gesture that simply tries to recuperate castration into the creation of metaphysical sight and strength. David Bolt's "The Blindman in the Classic: Feminisms, Ocularcentrism, and Charlotte Brontë's *Jane Eyre*" is a welcome exception to mainstream critical reading of Rochester's disabilities. But, arguing from a disability studies perspective, Bolt nevertheless believes that the resolution between Jane and Rochester reinforces blindness as deficiency and loss, as an emptiness that fills out the desires of the sighted Jane. One implication seems to be that the marriage that ensues is not about the body or sexuality; according to these interpretations, Jane and Rochester have found their egalitarian union away from society but also away from the embodiment that is central to the novel.[16]

At the same time, we can also read Rochester as resistant to Jane's encompassing narrative of his blindness: he shows her his stump, after all, and he tells her, "I want a wife" (512; ch. 37). He does not go gently into the good night of being a blind projection. In fact, Rodas suggests that we might read this moment as defiantly phallic: "What if [. . .] Rochester's disability is a beautiful thing within the Jane-Rochester sexual aesthetic, his stump manifestly, unapologetically erect, phallic, masculine?" (e-mail message to author, June 10, 2010). Rodas's reading suggests that we might consider this scene, and particularly the revelation of the stump, in terms of Robert McRuer's concept of "a critically queer and disabled" perspective, in which the gap between normative and queer sexualities—and normative and disabled bodies—is mobilized to reimagine and reshape "the limited forms of embodiment and desire proffered by the systems that would contain us all" (96). In other words, in this moment in the novel, Brontë powerfully enacts a disabled character refusing both normalization and marginalization: the "staree" (Garland-Thomson's term) wrests control of the scene of looking.

As with Rochester's fall from his horse and the various chair scenes, screen productions likewise continue to interpret and critique this reunion of the lovers in which one character is a blind amputee. Informed by the relentless emphasis on conventional beauty and a superficial and artificial sense of wholeness that characterizes the narratives of popular media, cultural ambivalence regarding disability is nowhere more evident than in the ways that filmmakers render the close of Brontë's novel. More changes seem to occur in screen interpretations of Jane's return to Rochester than in any other part of the novel. While these scenes, like the earlier ones, share touch-

16. Gilbert's later essay on "furious lovemaking" in *Jane Eyre* corrects that suggestion, noting Jane's return to the observations about his body that mark her first meeting with him and expressed desire to kiss not simply his brow but also his lips. "There can be no question, then, that what Jane calls the 'pleasure in my services' both she and Rochester experience in their utopian woodland is a pleasure in physical as well as spiritual intimacy, erotic as well as intellectual communion" (368).

points, there is substantially more variation in added dialogue (and added affect), as well as in the ways in which disability is represented as a physical, psychological, and social experience.

Jane's return to Rochester is fraught with increasingly mixed feelings as she apprehends the ruin of Thornfield Hall and the situation of her former master and fiancé. The return is also complex for the film audience, which has had many opportunities to become closely identified or *sutured* with Jane but not with Rochester. In Stevenson's rendition, by the time we enter the ruin (where this film relocates the reunion), we have looked at Jane and looked with Jane at Rochester, but we have been to a large extent prevented by the cinematography from ever *seeing into* him—having the illusion of access to his actual thoughts or feelings—because of Welles's acting, the *mise-en-scène* that takes the place of close-ups, and the chiaroscuro lighting that leaves him enigmatically in the dark and Jane in the light, vulnerable to view.

As with the chair scenes, certain filmic conventions have evolved for this moment of "seeing blindness," based loosely on the end of the novel.[17] Some versions develop this "seeing" gradually. Both Aymes and White render the first sight of Rochester outside Ferndean with some illuminating differences. Amyes's Rochester, for example, not only gropes his way out and back into the house but is also guided by a servant who holds him by the arm. White's Rochester, in contrast, has a cane he uses to navigate his own way outside and back into the house. This initial scene, in which Jane does not speak to Rochester, is followed by a second one in which she enters the room in the place of a servant, bringing him water. As we enter the room, sutured to Jane's point of view, we are guided by shot sequences to look at Rochester's blindness (and to look at Jane looking at blindness).

Young's version is particularly dramatic in its rendering of numerous close-ups of Rochester's face and in the special effects makeup that represents his blindness. Here the cinematic language of the earlier parts of the productions provides meaning through repetition with a difference: whereas in earlier scenes Rochester was guarded, three-quarter-turned, or in shadow, the post-disablement scenes offer up Rochester's face and body in full light to shots from Jane's point of view. Where before he looked at Jane but was inaccessible himself, the post-blinding shots make him vulnerable to our scrutiny and, following the conventions of cinematic representations of

17. The moment in which blindness or another disability is "seen" or materialized by another person (often the beloved) recurs in many narrative forms, as does the scene of vision's return in "cure" narratives. For an excellent study of eighteenth- and nineteenth-century scenes of returning vision in historical context, see Paulson.

blindness, unaware of our voyeuristic invasion. Some shots are even identical in framing to earlier ones. Jane's reaction shots establish her ability to look directly at him in a way that controls the gaze, unlike the earlier scenes in which she was in essence a face on display to his interrogation.

A return to disability studies theories of blindness and looking is helpful as we engage this scene. In particular, a recent essay by Johnson Cheu might be repurposed to examine cinema's use of blindness. Drawing on the work of Georgina Kleege, Rosemarie Garland-Thomson, and other disability studies scholars, Cheu's "Seeing Blindness on Screen" focuses on "the blind female gaze," exploring "blindness" and a distinctive "blind gaze" as an element filmmakers co-opt to shore up the power of the "normative" (male) gaze. Cheu points out that feminist film theory, though it has observed this feature, has not yet fully interrogated its meaning.[18] In this essay, Cheu indirectly reaffirms the possibility of reading Jane's reunion with Rochester as a scene in which she retrospectively establishes her own sense of equity in her relationship with him. Put another way, the scenario Cheu analyzes—that of sighted characters and moviegoers looking at the blind gaze of female characters—is significantly complicated by *Jane Eyre* and by this scene (see figure 1) of a sighted female character regarding a male character's "blind gaze."

Jane has repeatedly narrated her lack of object-status because she is plain, poor, and small; her descriptions of Rochester have objectified him, making her a surprisingly confident *looking* subject, if not one confident in her authority to desire a man who is her class superior. Later, however, she must acknowledge that she is, for him, an object of desire, as much as he is an object for her evaluation—a situation that enables her power of refusal. Finally, when she returns a rich woman and encounters Rochester after his disablement, we see Rochester as an object of interest, concern, and longing before he himself is aware of the gaze we share with Jane. Once alerted to her presence, Rochester again sees himself as an object for her evaluation, but with the additional concern of disability as a complication. Further, he is no longer a man with secrets he can—and believes he must—withhold from her. The cinematography of this scene reinforces Jane's new ownership of the look and the concurrent shift in power.

As before, levels are central to the figurative and literal dynamic between Jane and Rochester. The change in elevation (raising Jane up and bringing Rochester low) that so many critics observe in the novel is literal here. Jane

18. See Mulvey, DeLauretis, and Doane for key theoretical works on gender and the filmic gaze.

FIGURE 1. Jane's first view of Rochester blinded, with dog Pilot and cane, in the ruins of Thornfield Hall. Orson Welles stars in the 1944 film directed by Robert Stevenson. 20th Century Fox/The Kobal Collection/Art Resource.

enters a room in which Rochester is slumped in a chair, reminiscent of her first "official" meeting with him at Thornfield in which he is temporarily disabled. However, this is repetition with a difference: rather than a sprained ankle, he is blind and otherwise disabled (the "otherwise" indicated by a cane, a general appearance of fatigue, burn/cicatrix makeup, or, very rarely, signs of amputation). If in the earlier scene Rochester ignores Jane's entry because she is a governess and beneath his notice until he finds her interesting, in this one he doesn't notice her because he is incapable of noticing (the film would have us imagine that his blindness is an all-encompassing lack of awareness), and even when he is aware that someone is there, he does not know who it is until she speaks. Further, as Jane and Rochester interact, the literal changes in their levels break out of the repetitive framing; there are a number of shots (in several screen interpretations) that truncate Rochester to privilege the audience's view of Jane. Acting and directing exacerbate the message of disability as dependency in Young's version, while increasing the voyeuristic sense of staring at blindness; although the audience will later see Rochester grope Jane, in this scene Rochester gropes and fumbles for his water glass while the camera watches.

The visual economy of film thus reiterates Brontë's explicit visual empowerment of Jane, whose problematic aspects Bolt analyzes so effectively. In fact, the frequent repetition of earlier visual motifs, done with no apparent critical distance, reiterates what Bolt points out as one of the disappointing aspects of the novel, the message that "the misery of the blindman is integral to the happiness of not only the sighted woman, but also the sighted man whom Rochester becomes" (285).

Scripts for screen narratives of *Jane Eyre* suggest that misery alone is insufficient, and that twentieth- and twenty-first century interpretations of the novel must carry the freight of contemporary fixations about disabled masculinity: they must engage angrily with the assumption of pity. In Stevenson's very compressed version of the ending of Brontë's novel, Jane sees Rochester walking in the ruined part of Thornfield with the dog Pilot and a cane. Where Pilot, earlier in the plot, works as an extension of Rochester's masculinity and class power, here the dog is repurposed as a different kind of prosthesis. The dog and cane read as two assistive devices that overdetermine, as visual metonyms, the message of his disablement, without transcribing Brontë's descriptions of Rochester's amputation and blindness. Welles performs blindness with one eye opened to reveal more white than the other, and with the "zombielike stare" Kleege notes as a convention of cinematic representations of blindness (45). Jane works no deception in this production; Rochester simply detects Jane's presence and shouts at her; she identifies herself; he touches her; and they resolve their situation in a brief conversation and an embrace. But as brief as the scene is, it has time for this conversation:

> "Jane—all you can feel now is mere pity. I don't want your pity."
> "Edward."
> "You can't spend your life with a mere wreckage of a man. You're young and fresh. You ought to get married."
> "Don't send me away. Please don't send me away!"
> "Do you think I want to let you go?"

A passionate clinch closes the scene, followed by a summary ending and the closing credits. Compression is the principle guiding the production, but curiously, in compressing the much longer scenes in the novel, screenwriters tend to use "pity" as shorthand for the much more complicated emotional dynamic offered by Brontë.

Moreover, Stevenson's early cinematic adaptation is not especially dated in its popular representation of blind masculinity. Nearly forty years later, Amyes's production, "faithful" in other ways, includes an angry Rochester who retorts that as a rich woman, Jane has "friends enough who will not suffer you to devote yourself to a lame blind wreck. This is pity, not love. Leave me!" Young's interpretation makes a very similar move within a much more elaborate development of Jane and Rochester's reunion. The words *companion* and *nurse* trigger the following, a clear departure from Brontë's text: "I don't want a companion! Neither do I want a nurse." He continues, "I might have known—so you have come back to take pity on a poor blind man. Is that it? Who told you?" Similarly, where Brontë includes a discussion of Rochester's "hideousness" as a moment in which he feels out Jane's attitude towards him and she responds with a humor that indicates she is unwilling to simply soothe his anxiety, the Young production's script generates an angrily bitter Rochester who snarls, "Take a good look. It was a narrow escape. You could have been married to this hideous blind wreck," and responds to Jane's assurances of love with, "How can you love me like this? Do not speak these words out of pity." Several screen interpretations of the meeting between Jane and Rochester, then, find it necessary to supplement the novel with scripts that depict him as resolutely angry and focused on pity and shame.

The Zeffirelli and White versions stand out for actively working to render the closing scenes in ways that invite viewers to think beyond these received cultural assumptions that disability is the occasion for anger and pity but not sexuality. Zeffirelli's version exemplifies the power of *mise-en-scène* to convey relationships far more effectively than added dialogue (particularly when the dialogue delivers a complex interaction in reductive terms). The resolution is compressed, like most things in this production: The two reencounter each other; Jane avows that she will never leave Rochester; they kiss; he laments his "ruined" state; she denies it; and they embrace again. The next scene provides an excerpt from the novel's epilogue. Jane and Rochester's development of a new configuration for their relationship, however, is something lighting and camera work communicate in significant and effective ways. She finds him in a room with low vaulted ceilings where shafts of sunlight from arched, churchlike windows counteract the room's central darkness and cryptlike tone. Chiaroscuro externalizes Rochester's emotional liminality, but the sunlight combined with the low ceilings presents the space more as attic than crypt, suggesting that he is now contained by Thornfield, as Bertha was before. A series of two-shots position the pair together but alternate whose face is at eye-level (whether sitting or standing) and, indeed, who sits or kneels or stands. Zeffirelli follows the convention of Rochester standing up as he voices concerns about Jane's plan to be his companion and nurse (the word *nurse* usually generates the movement), but his rise to his feet does not seem to signal anger about pity but rather a sadness for his changed self that is quickly dispelled by Jane's rebuttals about vigor. The scene closes with a tableau of them embracing under the curve of the vaulted ceiling. If other aspects of the film have been accused of muting Brontë's gender-egalitarian vision, its cinematography of bodies and relationships conveys a strong message of equal potential for self-determination, regardless of gender or dis/ability.

The visual eloquence of the scene is undisturbed by Whitemore and Zeffirelli's script. When Jane avows that she will never leave Rochester again, he says, "So you will stay with me. How?" This is neither reproach nor suspicion, but a crucial question that both need to answer. The quickness with which it is resolved may not be fully plausible, but it is much less troubling than the compulsion to add in pity and anger.

White's version handles the reunion in a much more extended form, separating Jane's first view of ruined Thornfield from her encounter with Rochester, as the novel does, and giving her an opportunity to learn of the fire (but not Rochester's disabilities) before seeking him out at Ferndean. It thus honors the novel's extended reestablishment of Jane and Rochester's relationship and the issue of "how" they will relate with their changed circumstances. While it shares with other films some visual conventions of blindness as incapacity, this version is striking for its overturning of the message that disabled people are not sexual subjects.

We enter the room in which Rochester is engulfed, through chiaroscuro, in darkness, his white shirt and the white bandages that wrap one hand standing out from his figure slumped in a chair. Jane actually pours the drink into his mouth; as in Young's version, White dramatizes blindness as groping not simply for Jane's body but for everything—despite Rochester's effective use of the cane in the outdoor shot. Following this moment, however, there are no angry outbursts or discussions of pity. Jane and Rochester embrace; he weeps, and then "feels her up"—but rather than leave this single anchor to the "groping" language of the novel, Sandy Welch's screenplay normalizes the groping by following it with other moments of sexual mutuality in the film's closing scenes, mirroring those before the failed wedding. Jane not only sits in his lap (an action she takes, and takes time to justify, in the novel) but lies on top of him on a riverbank. While the propriety of the nineteenth-century novel, already strained by Brontë, would draw the line at such representations, their inclusion in film interpretations creates a powerful statement that is arguably in the novel as well: Rochester blinded and amputated is no less sexual a being than he was before the fire, and Jane is no less desiring of him. The film ends with a horizontal two-shot and a horizontal pan that moves across their intertwining feet (cinematic shorthand for sexual intercourse) as Jane lies on top of Rochester.

A distinctive feature of screen versions is how they work with Brontë's very clearly articulated directions about Rochester's amputation. In almost every version, Rochester's blindness and the scarring on his face are suggested somehow through props and special-effects makeup. While Orson Welles seems simply to widen one eye, Ciáran Hinds wears an opaque contact lens; Stephens seems simply to have burn makeup, and the burn makeup worn by Timothy Dalton's and William Hurt's Rochesters suggests that the left eyelid in each instance has fused over the eye socket to the left cheek. In almost every version, however, both of Rochester's hands are completely or virtually intact. In Young's production, Hinds's left hand has some burn makeup; in White's interpretation, Stephens's left hand is bandaged; but only in Amyes's version is Rochester actually given a visible amputation, albeit virtually indistinguishable from the cuff of his shirt.

In this context, it is striking not so much that some versions ignore major plot elements—after all, adaptation is usually a craft of compression—but that some of the most "faithful" versions have moments in which they completely depart from the novel, suggesting that while Brontë had no difficulty imagining Jane desiring Rochester just as much (or more) with an amputation, twentieth- and twenty-first century film is less convinced of the marketability of such a narrative. This is particularly interesting in terms of White's BBC interpretation, which otherwise may provide the most normalizing approach to disability and desire by making Jane and Rochester's relationship at the end as sexualized as it is in the middle. All the same, whether it's because an amputation is a deal-breaker and blindness isn't—or because an amputation presents more involved "cure" sequences than regained sight—White's sexual Rochester is still only a blinded Rochester.

Taken in the aggregate, popular film versions of *Jane Eyre* consistently articulate—as does Brontë's novel—desire in the context of blindness. At the same time, however, anger and pity are almost always presented as obligatory gatekeepers to the happy ending, which is not the case in Brontë's novel. Further, films rarely visually represent Rochester's amputation, suggesting that a blind Rochester can be desiring and desirable, but that a blind amputee as desirable is more than filmmakers currently expect of their audiences. Whether it is the queerness of the amputation—itself a potentially hyperphallic symbol—that makes it alarming, or the extra layer of perceived "dependence" it may imply, a handless Rochester remains absent from *Jane Eyre* films.[19]

These concerns notwithstanding, film has much to contribute to our visually oriented concept of interpersonal relations, where eye contact dominates. In the scenes of Jane's reunion with Rochester, proxemics and shot length are almost as important as eye contact to establish point of view and, furthermore, to suggest that point of view is not restricted to being able to view things with the eyes. In Zeffirelli's *Jane Eyre,* for example, the camera lingers at the level of the seated, blinded Rochester, establishing his orientation to the world as the norm. The work done by the earlier "chair scenes," which counter conventions of *mise-en-scène* and power, persists in these more explicitly disability-focused scenes and prevent us from assuming that the seated person is automatically diminished and dependent. Jane is out of the frame when they embrace but is not "looked up to" as some distant and longed-for ideal. Indeed, Rochester does not look up at Jane at all but rather is present and close to the viewer, with intimacy created not simply through faciality but also through embodiment. While some productions (Young's, in particular) pause on the standing embrace between the two, lingering on Jane's face and reactions as central to the shot, in Zeffirelli's film, Rochester

---

19. The dearth of film stills that show Rochester visibly disabled is significant. While film versions rarely picture his disabilities in any detail, the archives of publicity stills seem to enact a further erasure of meaningful renderings of disability from the public and popular narrative of *Jane Eyre.*

and Jane alternate being present in the frame as a body and being present as a face. Soyoung Lee's description of the scene is apt:

> The depiction of Rochester and Jane's emerging [*sic*] into each other is not effected through a seamless fusion, but a montage of images, differently framed and from different angles, signifying their multiple positions and [the] complex dynamics which are involved in their negotiating of the[m] selves in marriage. (302)

This visual medium, then, actually argues for the value of tactility, instructing sighted audiences that you don't have to see to have a presence or a perspective, or to have your point of view central to an important human moment.[20]

Key feminist readings of *Jane Eyre* films criticize productions which remove Jane's opportunities for individuation by softening the domineering

20. This visual focus on embodiment and tactility distinguishes the Jane-Rochester reunion embrace in Cary Fukanaga's 2011 film as well. Fukunaga's *Jane Eyre*, perhaps more than any other popular screen version, shows us how film and poetry function similarly. Its muted palette and meticulously detailed sets evoke a nearly visceral progression of moods that respect the blend of depression and passion that distinguishes much of Bronte's fiction. The socially insightful *mise-en-scène* (recurrent point-of-view shots that show Jane's ambiguous position of governess enmeshed in, but not truly part of, the upper-class society she serves) combined with painterly lighting that recalls the Baroque paintings of Georges de laTour (and, in that mode, Cocteau's *La Belle et La Bête*) generate this distinctive tone. With emotional landscape its priority, it makes sense that Fukunaga takes the necessary compression of the novel to an extreme: a combination of compression and discontinuity—in which various connectives are stripped away—make the film function much as a poem does, moving from resonant image to resonant image without explanation. For example, instead of a gradual approach to the ruins of Thornfield Hall—a device other versions use as a transition to Rochester's disablement—Fukunaga heightens the impact of Jane's first view. In this film, Rochester's disability is signaled by his immobility (an echo of the chair scene) and a close-up on his face that reveals alteration and lack of focus in his eyes, probably a combination of special effects contact lenses and acting. In addition, his hair is particularly long and shaggy; as my colleague Ann Fox commented, "he looks like a war veteran." In fact, Rochester echoes, for those of us old enough to remember this important contribution to disability consciousness and culture, Jon Voight in *Coming Home.* The hair is also a nod to Jane's observations in the novel about his "thick and uncut locks" and need for rehumanizing: "your hair reminds me of eagles' feathers; whether your nails are grown like birds' claws or not, I have not yet noticed" (ch. 37). While in the novel, however, Jane's comment provides the opening for Rochester to reveal his amputation, the 2011 film, like most of the others, leaves both of his hands intact. What is particularly lost in the Fukunaga film's resolution—and perhaps most distinctive about it—is any negotiation between Rochester and Jane about the meaning of his changed bodily state for their relationship. It is even briefer in its resolution than the Orson Welles version. One might argue that in Fukunaga's vision of Rochester and Jane's relationship, the conversation about disability and marriage—will Jane be a nurse or a wife?—is vestigial, an unnecessary and outdated obstacle to the superseding "moment of being" of their union. This viewer, however, missed it.

aspects of Rochester that spur her development, and/or by actually cutting the scenes in which Jane individuates in her time away from Thornfield.[21] These readings also evaluate the rendering of disability as a key element in Brontë's argument about female individuation and egalitarian marriage, building on literary criticism that looks at Rochester's disabilities as judgments—if not punishments—Brontë enacts (along with Jane's inheritance) to resolve Jane and Rochester's power disparities. For many critics, disability as total dependency sums up its function in the novel. Patsy Stoneman's summary of several feminist critics' objections to a perceived "dilution of Jane's rebellious spirit" (Ellis and Kaplan, 192) in most film versions reaffirms that critics see Rochester's disability as inversely related to Jane's independence: "Rochester is not sufficiently injured to need Jane's assistance [. . .]. In the fire, Rochester is not scarred and does not lose a hand, *which means that the promise of restored sight brings him back to his original strength*" (23; emphasis added). Sumiko Higashi's essay on the way film versions of *Jane Eyre* capitulate to the market forces of the Hollywood romance argues that the representation of disability in *Jane Eyre* films fails to render convincingly what she sees as the novel's message, that Rochester is "totally dependent" on Jane (22). Higashi appears to criticize Welles's Rochester for being either not disabled enough or too sexual to be disabled; for example, "he claims her with a passionate kiss placed squarely on the mouth. Rather good aim for a blind man" (23). Similarly, Soyoung Lee's nuanced discussion of three film versions of *Jane Eyre* and their use of cinematic techniques to portray gendered power dynamics, nevertheless criticizes Stevenson's film because it represents the disabled Rochester as high-functioning and sexual: "The ruins are an obvious symbolism of Rochester's state, however, his posture is still as vigorous as before: his right hand is intact and although blind, he does not falter a bit," "his masculinity [is] intact" (287–88). What is striking about most such criticism is not only that it tends to fault films that reduce Rochester's disablement but also that the theory emerging from this stance requires us to understand disability as an icon of dependency and asexuality.

Rochester's undiminished and *unchastened* disablement in Stevenson's film is a primary criticism of Kate Ellis and E. Ann Kaplan's much-cited feminist analysis. Orson Welles's nondisabled Rochester "always dominates whatever scene he is in," and the camera repeatedly situates Jane as an observer of Rochester, a position they posit as being passive (196). Specifically, Ellis and Kaplan criticize the ending's failure to demonstrate

---

21. See Ellis and Kaplan; Higashi.

that Rochester has received his comeuppance through disablement: "Welles limps through the ruins but is hardly the mellowed, chastened Rochester (could Welles ever appear chastened?) of Brontë's closing chapters. Their coming together simply represents the typical lovers' reunion, with male and female traditionally placed" (198). In other words, Rochester is neither dependent nor diminished enough to resolve the imbalance between him and Jane, though disability was apparently supposed to enact these changes.

In short, those film analyses of *Jane Eyre* that address disability extend and reinforce what the films themselves often tell us about common assumptions regarding disability. These constructions of disability are focused entirely on dependency, without consideration of other functions, and they seem to assume, along with Helene Moglen, that disability means the end of sexuality: "Jane's development [can] be maintained only at the cost of Rochester's romantic self-image. [. . .] It is not a lover he requires, but a mother [. . .]. And it is this function which Jane will gratefully assume" (142–43).[22]

Along with these shortcomings, film critics' interpretations of Rochester's disabilities tend to focus on a limited vocabulary of film effects, and thus to read reductively. Indeed, most film criticism, regardless of subject, does not consider disability as a key element in plot, characterization, dialogue, *mise-en-scène,* or other important elements of cinematic meaning. As such, critics are prone to elide what is most worth discussing in film versions of *Jane Eyre:* the way each thinks through longstanding cultural narratives of disability and sexuality. Communicating in a primarily visual medium, these films ultimately invite us to reconsider desire, as well as human presence and identity, within a broader aesthetic than that defined by conventional faces, ordinary vision, and upright posture.

---

22. Moglen, like many other critics, looks at the ending of *Jane Eyre* as parallel to the role Brontë assumed in relation to her father, Patrick Brontë, who had cataracts.

Abraham, Karl. "Manifestations of the Female Castration Complex." In *Selected Articles of Karl Abraham,* 338–69. London: Maresfield Library, 1988.

Altick, Richard D. *The Shows of London.* Cambridge: Belknap Press, 1978.

American Psychiatric Association. *Diagnostic and Statistical Manual of Mental Disorders: DSM-IV-TR.* 4th ed., text revision 2000. Washington, DC: American Psychiatric Association, 2000.

———. *Diagnostic and Statistical Manual of Mental Disorders: DSM-5 Development.* 2010. Web. 14 Sept. 2010.

Armstrong, Nancy. *Desire and Domestic Fiction: A Political History of the Novel.* New York: Oxford University Press, 1987.

Asperger, Hans. "'Autistic Psychopathy' in Childhood." In *Autism and Asperger Syndrome,* edited by Uta Frith, 37–92. New York: Cambridge University Press, 1991.

Avalos, Hector. "Redemptionism, Rejectionism, and Historicism as Emerging Approaches in Disability Studies." *Perspectives in Religious Studies* 34.1 (2007): 91–100.

———, Sarah J. Melcher, and Jeremy Schipper, eds. *This Abled Body: Rethinking Disabilities in Biblical Studies.* Atlanta: Society of Biblical Literature, 2007.

Barton, John, and John Muddiman, eds. *The Oxford Bible Commentary.* Oxford: Oxford University Press, 2001.

Beaty, Jerome. *Misreading Jane Eyre: A Postformalist Paradigm.* Columbus: The Ohio State University Press, 1996.

Bellis, Peter. "In the Window-Seat: Vision and Power in *Jane Eyre.*" *English Literary History* 54.3 (1987): 639–52.

Benjamin, Jessica. *Like Subjects, Love Objects: Essays on Recognition and Sexual Difference.* New Haven, CT: Yale University Press, 1995.

————. *Shadow of the Other: Intersubjectivity and Gender in Psychoanalysis.* New York: Routledge, 1998.

Bettelheim, Bruno. *The Empty Fortress: Infantile Autism and the Birth of the Self.* New York: Free Press, 1967.

Bogdan, Robert. *Freak Show: Presenting Human Oddities for Amusement and Profit.* Chicago: University of Chicago Press, 1988.

————. "The Social Construction of Freaks." In *Freakery: Cultural Spectacles of the Extraordinary Body,* edited by Rosemarie Garland-Thomson, 23–37. New York: New York University Press, 1996.

Bolt, David. "The Blindman in the Classic: Feminisms, Ocularcentrism, and Charlotte Brontë's *Jane Eyre.*" *Textual Practice* 22.2 (2008): 269–89.

Bordo, Susan. *The Male Body: A New Look at Men in Public and in Private.* New York: Farrar, Straus and Giroux, 1999.

Bozovic, Miran, ed. *The Panopticon Writings.* London: Verso, 1995.

Breitenberg, Mark. *Anxious Masculinity in Early Modern England.* Cambridge: Cambridge University Press, 1996.

Brontë, Charlotte. *Jane Eyre.* 1847. Edited by Margaret Smith. Oxford: Oxford University Press, 1975.

————. *Jane Eyre.* 1847. New York: Bantam, 1981.

————. *Jane Eyre.* 1847. 2nd ed. Edited by Richard J. Dunn. New York and London: Norton, 1987.

————. *Jane Eyre.* 1847. London: Penguin Popular Classics, 1994.

————. *Jane Eyre.* 1847. Oxford: Oxford University Press, 2000.

————. *Jane Eyre.* 1847. Mineola: Dover Publications, 2002.

————. *Jane Eyre.* 1847. London: Penguin, 2006.

————. "To W. S. Williams, 4 January 1848." In *The Letters of Charlotte Brontë with a Selection of Letters by Family and Friends,* edited by Margaret Smith, 3–6. Vol. 2. Oxford: Clarendon Press, 2000.

————. *Villette.* 1853. Edited by Mark Lilly. New York: Penguin, 1985.

Burke, Lucy. "Introduction: Thinking about Cognitive Impairment." *Journal of Literary & Cultural Disability Studies* 2.1 (2008): i–iv. Web. 3 Aug. 2009.

Butler, Judith. *Bodies That Matter: On the Discursive Limits of "Sex."* New York: Routledge, 1993.

Caminero-Santangelo, Marta. *The Madwoman Can't Speak: Or, Why Insanity is Not Subversive.* Ithaca, NY: Cornell University Press, 1998.

Campbell, Gardner. "The Presence of Orson Welles in Robert Stevenson's *Jane Eyre* (1944)." *Literature-Film Quarterly* 31.1 (2003): 2–9.

Chard, M. Joan. "'Apple of Discord': Centrality of the Eden Myth in Charlotte Brontë's Novels." *Brontë Society Transactions* 19.5 (1988): 197–205.

Chase, Richard. "The Brontës, Or Myth Domesticated." 1948. In *Jane Eyre: An Authoritative Text, Backgrounds, Criticism,* edited by Richard J. Dunn, 462–71. New York: Norton, 1971.

Chen, Chih-Ping. "'Am I a monster?': Jane Eyre Among the Shadows of Freaks." *Studies in the Novel* 34.4 (2002): 367–84.

Chesler, Phillis. *Women and Madness.* Garden City, NJ: Doubleday, 1972.

Cheu, Johnson. "Seeing Blindness on Screen." *Journal of Popular Culture* 42.3 (2009): 480–96.

Chinn, Sarah E. "Audre Lorde and the Power of Touch." *GLQ* 9.1–2 (2003): 181–204.

Chivers, Sally, and Nicole Markotić, eds. *The Problem Body: Projecting Disability on Film*. Columbus: The Ohio State University Press, 2010.

Chow, Rey. "When Whiteness Feminizes: Some Consequences of a Supplementary Logic." *Differences: A Journal of Feminist Cultural Studies* 11.3 (1999): 137–68.

Connell, R. W. *Masculinites*. Berkeley: University of California Press, 2005.

Corker, Mairian, and Tom Shakespeare. *Disability/Postmodernity: Embodying Disability Theory*. London and New York: Continuum, 2002.

Couser, G. Thomas. "Beyond the Clinic: Oliver Sacks and the Ethics of Neuroanthropology." In *Vulnerable Subjects: Ethics and Life Writing*, 74–122. Ithaca, NY: Cornell University Press, 2004.

———. *Recovering Bodies: Illness, Disability, and Life Writing*. Madison: University of Wisconsin Press, 1997.

Cushing, Pamela, and Tanya Lewis. "Negotiating Mutuality and Agency in Caregiving Relationships with Women with Intellectual Disabilities." *Hypatia* 17.3 (2002): 173–93.

David and Lisa. DVD. Directed by Frank Perry. Produced by Paul M. Heller. United States: Continental Distributing, 1962.

David and Lisa. DVD. Directed by Lloyd Kramer. Produced by Oprah Winfrey. Chicago: Harpo Productions, 1998.

Davies, John D. *Phrenology, Fad and Science: A 19th-Century Crusade*. New Haven, CT: Yale University Press, 1955.

Davies, P. R. "Daniel." In *The Oxford Bible Commentary*, edited by John Barton and John Muddiman, 563–71. Oxford: Oxford University Press, 2001.

Davis, Lennard J. *Bending Over Backwards: Disability, Dismodernism, and Other Difficult Positions*. New York: New York University Press, 2002.

———. "Constructing Normalcy: The Bell Curve, the Novel, and the Invention of the Disabled Body in the Nineteenth Century." In *The Disability Studies Reader*, edited by Lennard J. Davis, 9–28. New York: Routledge, 1997.

———. *Enforcing Normalcy: Disability, Deafness, and the Body*. London: Verso, 1995.

de Beauvoir, Simone. *The Second Sex*. New York: Vintage, 1974.

de Lauretis, Teresa. *Alice Doesn't: Feminism, Semiotics, Cinema*. Bloomington: Indiana University Press, 1984.

Deleuze, Gilles, and Félix Guattari. *Anti-Oedipus: Capitalism and Schizophrenia*. Translated by Robert Hurley, Mark Seem, and Helen R. Lane. New York: Viking Press, 1977.

Derrida, Jacques. "Deconstruction and the Other." In *Dialogues with Contemporary Continental Thinkers: The Phenomenological Heritage*, edited by Richard Kearney. Manchester: Manchester University Press, 1984.

———. *Memoirs of the Blind: The Self-Portrait and Other Ruins*. Chicago and London: University of Chicago Press, 1993.

———. *Of Grammatology*. Baltimore: Johns Hopkins University Press, 1977.

Devereaux, Mary. "Oppressive Texts, Resisting Readers and the Gendered Spectator: The New Aesthetics." *Journal of Art and Art Criticism* 48.4 (1990): 337–47.

Doane, Mary Ann. *The Desire to Desire: The Woman's Film of the 1940s*. Bloomington: Indiana University Press, 1987.

Dodds, Allan. *Rehabilitating Blind and Visually Impaired People: A Psychological Approach.* London: Chapman and Hall, 1993.

Donaldson, Elizabeth J. "The Corpus of the Madwoman: Toward a Feminist Disability Studies Theory of Embodiment and Mental Illness." *National Women's Studies Association Journal* 14.3 (2002): 99–119.

———. "The Psychiatric Gaze: Deviance and Disability in Film." Special issue, "The Discourse of Disability," *Atenea* 25.1 (2005): 31–48.

Dooley, Lucile. "Psychoanalysis of Charlotte Brontë as a Type of the Woman of Genius." *American Journal of Pscyhology* 31 (1920): 221–272.

Dunn, Richard J., ed. *Jane Eyre: An Authoritative Text, Backgrounds, Criticism.* New York: Norton, 1971.

———, ed. *Jane Eyre* by Charlotte Brontë. 2nd ed. New York: Norton, 1987.

Durkheim, Emile. *Suicide: A Study in Sociology.* Edited by George Simpson. London: Routledge and Kegan Paul, 1970.

Dwyer, Ellen. *Homes for the Mad: Life inside Two Nineteenth-Century Asylums.* New Brunswick, NJ: Rutgers University Press, 1987.

Eagleton, Terry. "Jane Eyre's Power Struggles." In *Myths of Power: A Marxist Study of the Brontës.* Totowa: Barnes and Noble, 1975. Reprinted in Dunn, *Jane Eyre: An Authoritative Text, Backgrounds, Criticism.* 491–96.

———. *Myths of Power: A Marxist Study of the Brontës.* London: Macmillan, 1988.

Ehrenreich, Barbara, and Deirdre English. *Complaints and Disorders: The Sexual Politics of Sickness.* Old Westbury, NY: Feminist Press, 1973.

Eiesland, Nancy L. *The Disabled God: Towards a Liberatory Theology of Disability.* Nashville, TN: Abingdon, 1994.

Ellis, Kate, and E. Ann Kaplan. "Feminism in Brontë's Novel and Its Film Versions." In *Nineteenth-Century Women at the Movies: Adapting Classic Women's Fiction to Film,* edited by Barbara Tepa Lupack, 192–206. Bowling Green, OH: Bowling Green State University Press, 1999.

Engster, Daniel. "Rethinking Care Theory: The Practice of Caring and the Obligation to Care." *Hypatia* 20.3 (2005): 50–74.

Etcoff, Nancy. *Survival of the Prettiest: The Science of Beauty.* London: Little, Brown, 1999.

Felman, Shoshana. "Women and Madness: The Critical Phallacy." In *Feminisms: An Anthology of Literary Theory and Criticism,* edited by Robyn R. Warhol and Diane Price Herndl, 7–20. New Brunswick, NJ: Rutgers University Press, 1997.

Fiedler, Leslie. *Freaks: Myths and Images of the Secret Self.* New York: Simon and Schuster, 1978.

Fink, Bruce. *The Lacanian Subject: Between Language and Jouissance.* Chichester: Princeton University Press, 1995.

Flint, Kate. "Disability and Difference." In *The Cambridge Companion to Wilkie Collins,* edited by Jenny Bourne Taylor, 153–67. Cambridge: Cambridge University Press, 2006.

———. *The Victorians and the Visual Imagination.* Cambridge: Cambridge University Press, 2000.

"Form, n.15.a." *The Oxford English Dictionary.* 2nd ed. 1989. *OED Online.* Oxford University Press. Web. 15 Sept. 2009.

Works Cited

Foucault, Michel. *Discipline and Punish: The Birth of the Prison.* London: Penguin, 1977.

———. *Madness and Civilization: A History of Insanity in the Age of Reason.* 1965. Translated by Richard Howard. New York: Random House, 1988.

Frawley, Maria. *Invalidism and Identity in Nineteenth-Century Britain.* Chicago: University of Chicago Press, 2004.

Freeman, Janet. "Speech and Silence in *Jane Eyre.*" *SEL* 24 (1984): 683–700.

Freud, Sigmund. "Mourning and Melancholia." (1917). In *On Metapsychology,* edited by Angela Richards, 251–68. London: Penguin, 1991.

Gardiner, Judith Kegan. "Introduction." In *Masculinity Studies and Feminist Theory: New Directions,* edited by Judith Kegan Gardiner, 1–30. New York: Columbia University Press, 2002.

Garland-Thomson, Rosemarie. *Extraordinary Bodies: Figuring Physical Disability in American Culture and Literature.* New York: Columbia University Press, 1997.

———. "Feminist Theory, the Body, and the Disabled Figure." In *The Disability Studies Reader,* edited by Lennard J. Davis, 279–92. New York: Routledge, 1997.

———. Introduction. In *Freakery: Cultural Spectacles of the Extraordinary Body,* edited by Rosemarie Garland-Thomson, 1–19. New York: New York University Press, 1996.

———. *Staring: How We Look.* Oxford: Oxford University Press, 2009.

———, ed. *Freakery: Cultural Spectacles of the Extraordinary Body.* New York: New York University Press, 1996.

Gerschick, Thomas J. "Sisyphus in a Wheelchair: Physical Disabilities and Masculinity." 1998. In *Sociology: Exploring the Architecture of Everyday Life,* edited by David M. Newman and Jodi O'Brien, 165–78. Thousand Oaks, CA: Pine Forge Press, 2006.

———. "Toward a Theory of Disability and Gender." *Signs* 25.4 (2000): 1263–68. *JSTOR.* Web. 31 July 2005.

Gerschick, Thomas J., and Adam Stephen Miller. "Coming to Terms: Masculinity and Physical Disability." In *Men's Lives,* edited by Michael S. Kimmel and Michael A. Messner, 262–75. Boston: Allyn and Bacon, 1995.

Gezari, Janet. *Charlotte Bronte and Defensive Conduct: The Author and the Body at Risk.* Philadelphia: University of Pennsylvania Press, 1992.

Gilbert, Sandra M. "Jane Eyre and the Secrets of Furious Lovemaking." *Novel: A Forum on Fiction* 31.3 (1998): 351–73.

———, and Susan Gubar. *The Madwoman in the Attic: Women Writers and the Nineteenth-Century Literary Imagination.* 1979. 2nd ed. New Haven, CT: Yale University Press, 2000.

Gilman, Sander. *Seeing the Insane.* New York: Wiley, 1982.

Girl, Interrupted. DVD. Directed by James Mangold. Produced by Cathy Konrad and Douglass Wick. Culver City, CA: Columbia Pictures, 1999.

Goffman, Erving. *Asylums: Essays on the Social Situation of Asylum Patients and Other Inmates.* Garden City, NJ: Anchor Books, 1961.

Gordon, Emily Fox. *Mockingbird Years: A Life in and out of Therapy.* New York: Basic Books, 2000.

Gothika. DVD. Directed by Mathieu Kassovitz and Thom Oliphant. Produced by Susan Downey. Burbank, CA: Dark Castle Entertainment, 2003.

Works Cited

180

Graham, Peter W., and Fritz Oehlschlaeger. *Articulating the Elephant Man: Joseph Merrick and His Interpreters*. Baltimore: Johns Hopkins University Press, 1992.

Grandin, Temple. *Thinking in Pictures and Other Reports from My Life with Autism*. Foreword by Oliver Sacks. New York: Vintage, 1995.

Grandin, Temple, and Margaret M. Scariano. *Emergence: Labeled Autistic, A True Story*. New York: Warner, 1986.

Griffin, Gail. "Once More to the Attic: Bertha Rochester and the Pattern of Redemption in *Jane Eyre*." In *Nineteenth-Century Women Writers of the English Speaking World*, edited by Rhoda Nathan, 89–97. New York: Greenwood Press, 1986.

Grob, Gerald. *Mental Illness and American Society, 1875–1940*. Princeton, NJ: Princeton University Press, 1983.

Grudin, Peter. "Jane and the Other Mrs. Rochester: Excess and Restraint in *Jane Eyre*." *Novel: A Forum on Fiction* 10. 2 (1977): 145–57.

Guttentag, Marcia, Susan Salasin, and Deborah Belle. *The Mental Health of Women*. New York: Academic Press, 1980.

Haddon, Mark. *The Curious Incident of the Dog in the Night-Time*. New York: Doubleday, 2003.

Hahn, Harlan. "Can Disability Be Beautiful?" *Social Policy* 18.3 (1988): 26–32.

Halberstam, Judith. "The Good, the Bad, and the Ugly: Men, Women, and Masculinity." In *Masculinity Studies and Feminist Theory: New Directions*, edited by Judith Kegan Gardiner, 344–67. New York: Columbia University Press, 2002.

Haraway, Donna. "The Biopolitics of Postmodern Bodies: Determinations of Self in Immune System Discourse." In *Feminist Theory and the Body: A Reader*, edited by Janet Price and Margrit Shildrick, 203–14. New York: Routledge, 1999.

———. *Modest_Witness@Second_Millennium. FemaleMan©_Meets_OncoMouse™: Feminism and Technoscience*. New York: Routledge, 1997.

Hartley, Lucy. *Physiognomy and the Meaning of Expression in Nineteenth-Century Culture*. Cambridge, MA: Cambridge University Press, 2001.

Heilman, Robert B. "Charlotte Brontë's 'New' Gothic." In *From Jane Austen to Joseph Conrad*, edited by Robert Rathburn and Martin Steinman, Jr., 118–32. Minneapolis: University of Minnesota Press, 1958. Reprinted in Dunn, *Jane Eyre: An Authoritative Text, Backgrounds, Criticism*. 458–62.

Higashi, Sumiko. "'Jane Eyre': Charlotte Brontë vs. The Hollywood Myth of Romance." *Journal of Popular Film* 6.1 (1977): 13–31.

Holbrook Jackson, George. *The 1890s: A Review of Art and Ideas at the Close of the Nineteenth Century*. Hassocks: Harvester Press, 1976.

Holmes, Martha Stoddard. *Fictions of Affliction: Physical Disability in Victorian Culture*. Ann Arbor: University of Michigan Press, 2004.

Horne, Simon. "'Those Who Are Blind See': Some New Testament Uses of Impairment, Inability, and Paradox." In *Human Disability and the Service of God: Reassessing Religious Practice*, edited by Nancy Eiesland and Don Saliers, 88–101. Nashville, TN: Abingdon, 1997.

Howell, Elizabeth, and Marjorie Bayes, eds. *Women and Mental Health*. New York: Basic Books, 1981.

Huet, Marie-Hélène. *Monstrous Imagination*. Cambridge, MA: Harvard University Press, 1993.

Hughes, Bill, and Kevin Paterson. "The Social Model of Disability and the Disappearing Body: Towards a Sociology of Impairment." *Disability & Society* 12.3 (1997): 325–40.

Ingram, Allan. Introduction. *Patterns of Madness in the Eighteenth Century*. Liverpool: Liverpool University Press, 1998.

Ingram, Richard. "Reports from the Psych Wars." In *Unfitting Stories: Narrative Approaches to Disease, Disability, and Trauma*, edited by Valerie Raoul, Connie Canam, Angela D. Henderson, and Carla Paterson, 237–45. Waterloo, ON: Wilfred Laurier University Press, 2007.

Iwakuma, Miho. "The Body as Embodiment: An Investigation of the Body by Merleau-Ponty." In *Disability/Postmodernity: Embodying Disability Theory*, edited by Mairian Corker and Tom Shakespeare, 76–87. London: Continuum, 2002.

Jane Eyre. DVD. Directed by Julian Amyes. Screenplay by Alexander Baron. Directors of Photography David Doogood, John Kenway, and Keith Salmon. Performed by Timothy Dalton and Zelah Clarke. 1983. Burbank: BBC Warner, 2005.

Jane Eyre. DVD. Directed by Robert Stevenson. Screenplay by John Houseman, Aldous Huxley, and Robert Stevenson. Director of Photography George Barnes. Performed by Orson Welles and Joan Fontaine. 1944. Century City: 20th Century Fox Home Entertainment, 2006.

Jane Eyre. DVD. Directed by Susanna White. Screenplay by Sandy Welch. Director of Photography Mike Eley. Performed by Toby Stephens and Ruth Wilson . London: BBC, 2006. Boston: WGBH Boston, 2006.

Jane Eyre. VHS. Directed by Robert Young. Screenplay by Richard Hawley, Kay Mellor, and Peter Wright. Director of Photography John McGlashan. Performed by Ciáran Hinds and Samantha Morton. 1997. New York: A&E Home Video, 1999.

Jane Eyre. DVD. Directed by Franco Zeffirelli. Screenplay by Hugh Whitemore and Franco Zeffirelli. Director of Photography David Watkin. Performed by William Hurt and Charlotte Gainsbourg. New York: Miramax, 1996. New York: Miramax, 2003.

"*Jane Eyre: An Autobiography*. By Currer Bell." *Christian Remembrancer* 15 (1848): 396. Reprinted in Dunn, *Jane Eyre: An Authoritative Text, Backgrounds, Criticism*. 438–40.

Jeffreys, Mark. "The Visible Cripple (Scars and Other Disfiguring Displays Included)." In *Disability Studies: Enabling the Humanities*, edited by Sharon L. Snyder, Brenda Jo Brueggemann, and Rosemarie Garland-Thomson, 31–39. New York: Modern Language Association, 2002.

Jenkins, Keith Allen. "The Influence of Anxiety: *Bricolage* Brontë Style." PhD diss., Rice University, 1993.

Jones, Kathleen. *Mental Health and Social Policy, 1845–1959*. London: Routledge & Kegan Paul, 1960.

Jordan, Rita, and Stuart Powell. "Encouraging Flexibility in Adults with Autism." In *Adults with Autism: A Guide to Theory and Practice*, edited by Hugh Morgan, 74–88. Cambridge: Cambridge University Press, 1996.

Joshua, Essaka. "'Almost my hope of Heaven': Idolatry and Messianic Symbolism in Charlotte Brontë's *Jane Eyre*." *Philological Quarterly* 81.1 (2002): 81–107.

Kanner, Leo. "Autistic Disturbances of Affective Contact." *Nervous Child* 2 (1943): 217–50. Reprinted in Anne M. Donnellan, ed. *Classic Readings in Autism*, 11–52. New York: Teachers College Press, 1985.

Kaplan, Cora. "Afterword: Liberalism, Feminism, and Defect." In *"Defects": Engendering the Modern Body,* edited by Helen Deutsch and Felicity Nussbaum, 301–18. Ann Arbor: University of Michigan Press, 2000.

———. *Victoriana—Histories, Fictions, Criticism.* New York: Columbia University Press, 2007.

Kelly, Christine. "Making 'Care' Accessible: Personal Assistance for Disabled People and the Politics of Language." *Critical Social Policy* 31.4 (2011): 1–21. Web. 14 July 2011.

Kendrick, Robert. "Edward Rochester and the Margins of Masculinity in *Jane Eyre* and *Wide Sargasso Sea.*" *Papers on Language and Literature* 30.3 (1 June 1994): 235–56. *Academic Search Premier.* Web. 5 Dec. 2009.

Kesey, Ken. *One Flew Over the Cuckoo's Nest.* New York: Signet Books, 1962.

Kipling, Rudyard. *The Light That Failed.* (1891). London: Penguin, 1988.

Kirtley, Donald D. *The Psychology of Blindness.* Chicago: Nelson-Hall, 1975.

Kittay, Eva Feder. *Love's Labor: Essays on Women, Equality, and Dependency.* New York: Routledge, 1999.

Kleege, Georgina. *Sight Unseen.* New Haven, CT, and London: Yale University Press, 1999.

LaCom, Cindy. "'It Is More than Lame': Female Disability, Sexuality, and the Maternal in the Nineteenth-Century Novel." In *The Body and Physical Difference,* edited by David T. Mitchell and Sharon L. Snyder, 189–201.

Laing, R. D. *The Divided Self: A Study of Sanity and Madness.* London: Tavistock, 1960.

Landow, George P. *Victorian Types, Victorian Shadows.* London: Routledge and Kegan Paul, 1980.

Lavatar, John Caspar. *Essays on Physiognomy.* Translated by Henry Hunter. London: John Murray, 1789.

Lee, Hermione. "Emblems and Enigmas in *Jane Eyre.*" *English: The Journal of the English Association* 30.138 (1981): 233–55.

Lee, Soyoung. "Jane's Progress in Three Film Adaptations of *Jane Eyre.*" *Feminist Studies in English Literature* 10 (2002): 277–307.

Lerner, Laurence. "Bertha and the Critics." *Nineteenth-Century Literature* 44.3 (1989): 273–300.

Lewes, George Henry. Review of *Jane Eyre. Fraser's Magazine* (Dec. 1847): 690–94. Reprinted in Dunn, *Jane Eyre: An Authoritative Text, Backgrounds, Criticism.* 436–37.

Lewis, Bradley. "A Mad Fight: Psychiatry and Disability Activism." In *The Disability Studies Reader,* 3rd ed., edited by Lennard J. Davis, 160–76. New York: Routledge, 2010.

Linton, Simi. *Claiming Disability: Knowledge and Identity.* New York: New York University Press, 1998.

Lloyd, Margaret. "The Politics of Disability and Feminism: Discord or Synthesis?" *Sociology* 35.3 (2001): 715–28.

Longmore, Paul K. *Why I Burned My Book and Other Essays on Disability.* Philadelphia: Temple University Press, 2003.

———, and Lauri Umansky, eds. *The New Disability History: American Perspectives.* New York: New York University Press, 2001.

Losano, Antonia. "Reading Women/Reading Pictures: Textual and Visual Reading in Charlotte Brontë's Fiction and Nineteenth-Century Painting." In *Reading Women:*

Literary Figures and Cultural Icons from the Victorian Age to the Present, edited by Janet Badia and Jennifer Phegley, 27–52. Toronto: University of Toronto Press, 2005.

Marcus, Sharon. "Profession of the Author: Abstraction, Advertising and *Jane Eyre.*" *PMLA* 110.2 (1995): 206–19.

Margalioth, Daniel. "Passion and Duty: A Study of Charlotte Brontë's *Jane Eyre.*" *Hebrew University Studies in Literature* 7 (1979): 182–213.

Martin, Robert Bernard. *The Accents of Persuasion: Charlotte Brontë's Novels.* New York: Norton, 1966.

McCandless, Peter. "Dangerous to Themselves and Others: the Victorian Debate over the Prevention of Wrongful Confinement." *Journal of British Studies* 23.1 (1983): 84–104.

McDonagh, Patrick. *Idiocy: A Cultural History.* Liverpool: Liverpool University Press, 2008.

McElaney, Hugh. "Alcott's Freaking of Boyhood: The Perplex of Gender and Disability in *Under the Lilacs.*" *Children's Literature* 34.1 (2006): 139–60. *Project Muse.* Web. 11 Aug. 2008.

McIlvenny, Paul. "The Disabled Male Body 'Writes/Draws Back': Graphic Fictions of Masculinity and the Body in the Autobiographical Comic *The Spiral Cage.*" In *Revealing Male Bodies,* edited by Nancy Tuana et al., 100–125. Bloomington: Indiana University Press, 2002.

McRuer, Robert. "Compulsory Able-Bodiedness and Queer/Disabled Existence." In *Disability Studies: Enabling the Humanities,* edited by Sharon L. Snyder, Brenda Jo Brueggemann, and Rosemarie Garland-Thomson, 88–99. New York: Modern Language Association, 2002.

———, and Anna Mollow, eds. *Sex and Disability.* Durham, NC: Duke University Press, 2012.

Memmi, Albert. *Dependence: A Sketch for a Portrait of the Dependent.* Boston: Beacon Press, 1984.

Metzl, Jonathan M. *The Protest Psychosis: How Schizophrenia Became a Black Disease.* Boston: Beacon Press, 2009.

———. *Prozac on the Couch: Prescribing Gender in the Era of Wonder Drugs.* Durham, NC: Duke University Press, 2003.

Michie, Helena. "Under Victorian Skins: The Bodies Beneath." In *A Companion to Victorian Literature and Culture,* 407–24. Malden: Blackwell, 1999.

Milton, John. *Samson Agonistes. The Poetical Works of John Milton.* Edited by Helen Darbishire. London: Oxford University Press, 1958.

Mitchell, David T., and Sharon L. Snyder. "'Jesus Thrown Everything Off Balance': Disability and Redemption in Biblical Literature." In *This Abled Body: Rethinking Disabilities in Biblical Studies,* edited by Hector Avalos, Sarah J. Melcher, and Jeremy Schipper, 173–83. Atlanta: Society of Biblical Literature, 2007.

———. *Narrative Prosthesis: Disability and the Dependencies of Discourse.* Ann Arbor: University of Michigan Press, 2000.

———, eds. *The Body and Physical Difference: Discourses of Disability in the Humanities.* Ann Arbor: University of Michigan Press, 1997.

Mitchell, Stephen. *Hope & Dread in Psychoanalysis.* New York: Basic Books, 1995.

Moglen, Helene. *Charlotte Brontë: The Self Conceived.* Madison: University of Wisconsin Press, 1984.

Moi, Toril. *Sexual/Textual Politics: Feminist Literary Theory.* London: Methuen, 1985.

Mollow, Anna. "'When *Black* Women Start Going on Prozac . . .': The Politics of Race, Gender, and Emotional Distress in Meri Nana-Ama Danquah's *Willow Weep for Me.*" In *The Disability Studies Reader,* 2nd ed., edited by Lennard J. Davis, 283–99. New York: Routledge, 2006.

Moss, Candida R. *The Other Christs: Imitating Jesus in Ancient Christian Ideologies of Martyrdom.* Oxford: Oxford University Press, 2010.

Morison, Alexander. *The Physiognomy of Mental Disease.* London: Longman, 1840.

Mulvey, Laura. *Visual and Other Pleasures.* Bloomington: Indiana University Press, 1989.

———. "Visual Pleasure and Narrative Cinema." *Screen* 16.3 (1975): 6–18.

Murray, Stuart. "Autism and the Contemporary Sentimental: Fiction and the Narrative Fascination of the Present." *Literature and Medicine* 25.1 (2006): 24–45.

Nestor, Pauline. *Charlotte Brontë's Jane Eyre.* London: Harvester/Wheatsheaf, 1992.

Nicki, Andrea. "The Abused Mind: Feminist Theory, Psychiatric Disability, and Trauma." *Hypatia* 16.4 (2001): 80–104.

Nussbaum, Martha C. *Frontiers of Justice: Disability, Nationality, Species Membership.* Cambridge, MA: Harvard University Press, 2006.

———. "'Secret Sewers of Vice': Disgust, Bodies and the Law." In *The Passions of the Law,* edited by Susan A. Bandes, 19–62. New York: New York University Press, 2001.

Oliver, Michael. *Understanding Disability: From Theory to Practice.* London: Macmillan, 1996.

Olyan, Saul M. *Disability in the Hebrew Bible: Interpreting Mental and Physical Differences.* Cambridge: Cambridge University Press, 2008.

One Flew Over the Cuckoo's Nest. DVD. Directed by Milos Forman. Produced by Michael Douglas. Burbank, CA: Warner Studios, 1975.

Otiento, Pauline A. "Biblical and Theological Perspectives on Disability: Implications on the Rights of Persons with Disability in Kenya." *Disability Studies Quarterly* 29.4 (2009): 1–16.

Overboe, James. "Ableist Limits on Self-narration: The Concept of Post-personhood." In *Unfitting Stories: Narrative Approaches to Disease, Disability, and Trauma,* edited by Valerie Raoul, Connie Canam, Angela D. Henderson, and Carla Paterson, 275–82. Waterloo, ON: Wilfred Laurier University Press, 2007.

Paterson, Kevin, and Bill Hughes. "The Social Model of Disability and the Disappearing Body: Towards a Sociology of Impairment." *Disability and Society* 12.3 (1997): 325–40.

Paulson, William R. *Enlightenment, Romanticism, and the Blind in France.* Princeton, NJ: Princeton University Press, 1987.

Peterson, Carla L. *The Determined Reader: Gender and Culture in the Novel from Napoleon to Victoria.* Piscataway, NJ: Rutgers University Press, 1986.

Pfister, Joel. "Glamorizing the Psychological: The Politics of the Performances of Modern Psychological Identities." In *Inventing the Psychological: Toward a Cultural History of Emotional Life in America,* edited by Joel Pfister and Nancy Schnog, 167–213. New Haven, CT: Yale University Press, 1997.

Pickrel, Paul. "*Jane Eyre*: The Apocalypse of the Body." *English Literary History* 53.1 (1986): 165–82.

Pratt, Mary Louise. *Imperial Eyes: Travel Writing and Transculturation*. New York and London: Routledge: 1992.

Prendergast, Catherine. "On the Rhetorics of Mental Disability." In *Towards a Rhetoric of Everyday Life: New Directions in Research on Writing Text and Discourse*, edited by Martin Nystrand and John Duffy, 189–206. Madison: University of Wisconsin Press, 2003.

Price, Janet, and Margrit Shildrick. "Bodies Together: Touch, Ethics and Disability." In *Disability/Postmodernity: Embodying Disability Theory*, edited by Mairian Corker and Tom Shakespeare, 62–75. London: Continuum, 2002.

Prince-Hughes, Dawn. *Songs of the Gorilla Nation: My Journey Through Autism*. New York: Three Rivers, 2004.

Purinton, Margean. "Byron's Disability and the Techno-Gothic Grotesque in *The Deformed Transformed*." *European Romantic Review* 12.3 (2001): 301–20.

Quayson, Ato. *Aesthetic Nervousness: Disability and the Crisis of Representation*. New York: Columbia University Press, 2007.

Rée, Jonathan. *I See A Voice: A Philosophical History of Language, Deafness and the Senses*. London: HarperCollins, 1999.

Rhys, Jean. *Wide Sargasso Sea*. New York: Norton, 1966.

Rich, Adrienne. "Jane Eyre: The Temptations of a Motherless Woman." In *Jane Eyre* by Charlotte Brontë, 2nd ed., edited by Richard J. Dunn, 462–75. New York: Norton, 1987.

Rigby, Elizabeth. "*Vanity Fair* and *Jane Eyre*." *Quarterly Review* 84 (1848): 153–85. Reprinted in Dunn, *Jane Eyre: An Authoritative Text, Backgrounds, Criticism*. 440–43.

Robinson, Wendy. *Gentle Giant: The Inspiring Story of an Autistic Child*. Shaftesbury, Dorset: Element Books, 1999.

Rodas, Julia Miele. "Brontë's *Jane Eyre*." *The Explicator* 61.3 (2003): 149–51.

———. E-mail message to author. 10 June 2010.

———. "Mainstreaming Disability Studies?" *Victorian Literature and Culture* 34.1 (2006): 371–86.

———. "'On the Spectrum': Rereading Contact and Affect in *Jane Eyre*." *Nineteenth-Century Gender Studies* 4.2 (2008): n. p. Web. 3 Aug. 2009.

Rothman, David. *The Discovery of the Asylum: Social Order and Disorder in the New Republic*. Boston: Little, Brown, 1971.

Roy, Parama. "Unaccommodated Woman and the Poetics of Property in *Jane Eyre*." *SEL: Studies in English Literature* 29.4 (1989): 713–27.

Rubik, Margarete, and Elke Mettinger-Schartmann, eds. *A Breath of Fresh Eyre: Intertextual and Intermedial Reworkings of* Jane Eyre. Amsterdam and New York: Rodopi, 2006.

Rubin, Gayle. "The Traffic in Women: Notes on the Political Economy of Sex." In *Toward an Anthropology of Women*, edited by Rayna Reiter, 157–210. New York: Monthly Review Press, 1975.

Rubin, Theodore I. *Lisa and David*. New York: Macmillan, 1961.

Russo, Mary. *The Female Grotesque: Risk, Excess, and Modernity*. New York: Routledge, 1994.

Rutter, Michael. Commentary on Kanner's "Autistic Disturbances of Affective Contact." In *Classic Readings in Autism,* edited by Anne M. Donnellan, 50–52. New York: Teachers College Press, 1985.

Rycroft, Charles. *A Critical Dictionary of Psychoanalysis.* London: Penguin, 1972.

Sacks, Oliver. "An Anthropologist on Mars." In *An Anthropologist on Mars.* New York: Vintage Books, 1995.

———. "The Autist Artist." In *The Man Who Mistook His Wife for a Hat and Other Clinical Tales.* New York: HarperPerennial, 1990.

———. "Face-Blind: Why Are Some of Us Terrible at Recognizing Faces?" *New Yorker* (30 Aug. 2010): 36–43.

———. "The Twins." In *The Man Who Mistook His Wife for a Hat and Other Clinical Tales.* New York: HarperPerennial, 1990.

Schaff, Barbara. "The Strange After-Lives of *Jane Eyre.*" In *A Breath of Fresh Eyre: Intertextual and Intermedial Reworkings of Jane Eyre,* edited by Margarete Rubik and Elke Mettinger-Schartmann, 25–36. Amsterdam: Rodopi, 2007.

Sconce, Jeffrey. "Narrative Authority and Social Narrativity: The Cinematic Reconstitution of Brontë's *Jane Eyre.*" In *The Studio System,* edited by Janet Staiger, 140–62. New Brunswick, NJ: Rutgers University Press, 1995.

Scull, Andrew T. *Museums of Madness: The Social Organization of Insanity in Nineteenth-Century England.* New York: St. Martin's Press, 1979.

Seidel, Kathleen, ed. *neurodiversity.com.* 2004–6. Web. 14 Sept. 2010.

Shakespeare, Tom. "Review of Oliver Sacks' *An Anthropologist on Mars.*" *Disability and Society* 11.1 (1996): 137–39.

———, ed. *The Disability Reader: Social Science Perspectives.* London: Cassell, 1998.

Shannon, Edgar F., Jr. "The Present Tense in Jane Eyre." *Nineteenth Century Fiction* 10.2 (1955): 141–45.

Shapiro, Joseph P. *No Pity: People with Disabilities Forging a New Civil Rights Movement.* New York: Random House, 1993.

Shelley, Mary. *Frankenstein; or, the Modern Prometheus.* 2nd ed. Edited by Johanna M. Smith. New York and Boston: Bedford/St. Martin's, 2000.

Shildrick, Margrit. *Embodying the Monster: Encounters with the Vulnerable Self.* London: Sage, 2002.

———, and Janet Price. "Breaking the Boundaries of the Broken Body." In *Feminist Theory and the Body,* edited by Janet Price and Margrit Shildrick, 432–44. New York: Routledge, 1999.

Shirai, Yoshiaki. "Ferndean: Charlotte Brontë in the Age of Pteridomania." *Brontë Studies* 28 (2003): 123–30.

Shortt, S. E. D. *Victorian Lunacy: Richard M. Bucke and the Practice of Late Nineteenth-Century Psychiatry.* New York: Cambridge University Press, 1986.

Showalter, Elaine. *The Female Malady: Women, Madness, and English Culture, 1830–1980.* New York: Pantheon, 1985.

Shumway, Suzanne Rosenthal. "The Chronotope of the Asylum: *Jane Eyre,* Feminism, and Bakhtinian Theory." In *A Dialogue of Voices: Feminist Literary Theory and Bakhtin,* edited by Karen Hohn and Helen Wussow, 152–70. Minneapolis: University of Minnesota Press, 1994.

Shuttleworth, Russell P. "Disabled Masculinity: Expanding the Masculine Repertoire."

In *Gendering Disability,* edited by Bonnie G. Smith and Beth Hutchison, 166–78. New Brunswick, NJ: Rutgers University Press, 2004.

Shuttleworth, Sally. *Charlotte Brontë and Victorian Psychology.* Cambridge: Cambridge University Press, 1996.

Siebers, Tobin. "Disability in Theory: From Social Constructionism to the New Realism of the Body." *American Literary History* 13.4 (2001): 737–54.

———. *Disability Theory.* Ann Arbor: University of Michigan Press, 2008.

Silberman, Steve. "The Geek Syndrome." *WIRED* 9.12 (2001). Web. 14 Sept. 2010.

Sontag, Susan. *Illness as Metaphor.* New York: Farrar, Straus and Giroux, 1977.

Spender, Dale. *For the Record: The Meaning and Making of Feminist Knowledge.* London: Women's Press, 1985.

Spivak, Gayatri Chakravorty. *In Other Worlds: Essays in Cultural Politics.* New York and London: Methuen, 1987.

———. "Three Women's Texts and a Critique of Imperialism." *Critical Inquiry* 12.1 (1985): 243–61.

Squier, Susan. "Meditation, Disability, and Identity." *Literature and Medicine* 23.1 (2004): 23–45.

Stallybrass, Peter, and Allon White. *The Politics and Poetics of Transgression.* London: Methuen, 1986.

Stern, Madeleine, comp. *A Phrenological Dictionary of Nineteenth-Century Americans.* Westport, CT: Greenwood Press, 1982.

Stern, Rebecca. "Our Bear Women, Ourselves: Affiliating with Julia Pastrana." In *Victorian Freaks: The Social Context of Freakery in Britain,* edited by Marlene Tromp, 200–33. Columbus: The Ohio State University Press, 2008.

Stiker, Henri-Jacques. *A History of Disability.* Translated by William Sayers. Ann Arbor: University of Michigan Press, 1999.

Stoneman, Patsy. *Brontë Transformations: The Cultural Dissemination of Jane Eyre and Wuthering Heights.* New York: Prentice Hall/Harvester Wheatsheaf, 1996.

Szasz, Thomas R. *The Myth of Mental Illness: Foundations of a Theory of Personal Conduct.* New York: Harper & Row, 1974.

Tammet, Daniel. *Born on a Blue Day: Inside the Extraordinary Mind of an Autistic Savant, A Memoir.* New York: Free Press, 2006.

Theweleit, Klaus. *Male Fantasies. Vol. I. Women, Floods, Bodies, History.* Translated by Stephen Conway. Minneapolis: University of Minnesota Press, 1987.

Thomas, Calvin. "Reenfleshing the Bright Boys; or, How Male Bodies Matter to Feminist Theory." In *Masculinity Studies and Feminist Theory: New Directions,* edited by Judith Kegan Gardiner, 60–89. New York: Columbia University Press, 2002.

Thormählen, Marianne. *The Brontës and Religion.* Cambridge: Cambridge University Press, 1999.

Thoreau, Henry David. "Civil Disobedience." In *The Portable Thoreau,* edited by Carl Boone, 109–37. New York: Penguin, 1982.

Tkacz, Catherine Brown. "The Bible in *Jane Eyre.*" *Christianity and Literature* 44.1 (1994): 3–27.

Tobe, Keiko. *With the Light: Raising an Autistic Child.* Translated by Satsuki Yamashita. Originally published in Japanese as *Hikari To Tomoni.* New York: Yen Press, 2007.

Works Cited

Tomes, Nancy. *The Art of Asylum-Keeping: Thomas Story Kirkbride and the Origins of American Psychiatry.* Philadelphia: University of Pennsylvania Press, 1994.

———. "Feminist Histories of Psychiatry." In *Discovering the History of Psychiatry,* edited by Mark S. Micale and Roy Porter, 348–83. New York: Oxford University Press, 1994.

———. "Historical Perspectives on Women and Mental Illness." In *Women, Health, and Medicine in America: A Historical Handbook,* edited by Rima Apple, 143–71. New York: Garland, 1990.

Torgerson, Beth. *Reading the Brontë Body: Disease, Desire, and the Constraints of Culture.* New York: Palgrave Macmillan, 2005.

Tromp, Marlene, ed. *Victorian Freaks: The Social Context of Freakery in Britain.* Columbus: The Ohio State University Press, 2008.

Vargish, Thomas. *The Providential Aesthetic in Victorian Fiction.* Charlottesville: University of Virginia Press, 1985.

Whitman, Walt. *Leaves of Grass.* 2nd ed. New York: Fowler & Wells, 1856.

Williams, Donna. *Nobody Nowhere: The Extraordinary Autobiography of an Autistic.* New York: Perennial, 2002.

———. *Somebody Somewhere: Breaking Free from the World of Autism.* New York: Three Rivers, 1994.

Wilson, Anne, and Peter Beresford. "Madness, Distress and Postmodernity: Putting the Record Straight." In *Disability/Postmodernity: Embodying Disability Theory,* edited by Mairian Corker and Tom Shakespeare, 143–58. London: Continuum, 2002.

Wilson, James C., and Cynthia Lewiecki-Wilson. "Disability, Rhetoric, and the Body." In *Embodied Rhetorics: Disability in Language and Culture,* edited by James C. Wilson and Cynthia Lewiecki-Wilson, 1–24. Carbondale: Southern Illinois University Press, 2001.

Wilson, Philip K. "Eighteenth-Century 'Monsters' and Nineteenth-Century 'Freaks': Reading the Maternally Marked Child." *Literature and Medicine* 21.1 (2002): 1–25.

Wiltshire, Stephen. *Cities.* London: Dent, 1989.

———. *Drawings.* London: Dent, 1987.

———. *Floating Cities: Venice, Amsterdam, Leningrad—and Moscow.* London: Joseph, 1991.

———. *Stephen Wiltshire's American Dream.* London: Joseph, 1993.

Winnifrith, Tom, and Edward Chitham. *Charlotte and Emily Brontë: Literary Lives.* Basingstoke: Macmillan, 1989.

Woolf, Virginia. "'Jane Eyre' and 'Wuthering Heights.'" In *The Common Reader.* First Series. New York: Harcourt, Brace, 1925.

Wright, David. *Mental Disability in Victorian England: The Earlswood Asylum, 1847–1901.* Oxford: Oxford University Press, 2001.

Wylie, Judith. "Incarnate Crimes: Masculine Gendering and the Double in *Jane Eyre.*" *Victorians Institute Journal* 27 (1999): 55–69.

York, R. A. *Strangers and Secrets: Communication in the Nineteenth-Century Novel.* London and Toronto: Associated University Presses, 1994.

DAVID BOLT is Director of the Centre for Culture & Disability Studies in the Graduate School, Faculty of Education, Liverpool Hope University, where he is also Lecturer in Disability Studies. He is editor of *Journal of Literary & Cultural Disability Studies* and an editorial advisor for *Disability & Society* and *Journal of Visual Impairment and Blindness*. He is founder of the International Network of Literary & Cultural Disability Scholars. He has numerous publications to his name, including journal articles, chapters, special issues, and creative writing, and is currently working on a monograph titled *The Metanarrative of Blindness*.

LENNARD J. DAVIS is Professor in the English Department in the School of Arts and Sciences at the University of Illinois at Chicago. In addition, he is Professor of Disability and Human Development in the School of Applied Health Sciences and Professor of Medical Education in the College of Medicine. He is also director of Project Biocultures. His books include *Enforcing Normalcy: Disability, Deafness, and the Body* (1995); *The Disability Studies Reader* (1997); *Bending over Backwards: Disability, Dismodernism, and Other Difficult Positions* (2002); and *Obsession: A History* (2008).

ELIZABETH J. DONALDSON is Associate Professor of English at New York Institute of Technology, where she teaches courses in American literature, writing, and medical humanities. She has published essays on mental illness in film, antipsychiatry in Lauren Slater's memoirs, physiognomy and madness in *Jane Eyre*, teaching Melville online, and the poetry of Amy Lowell, among other subjects. Her current research project focuses on representations of schizophrenia and psychosis in film and popular media.

D. CHRISTOPHER GABBARD is Associate Professor of English at the University of North Florida. He earned his M.A. at San Francisco State University and his Ph.D. from Stanford University. His articles have appeared in *PMLA, Eighteenth-Century Studies, SEL, ELN,* and *Restoration.* Currently he is at work on *Idiocy and Wit: Reading Intellectual Dis/Ability in the Enlightenment,* a study of mental ability in texts by John Locke, Daniel Defoe, Alexander Pope, Jonathan Swift, John Cleland, Lawrence Sterne, and Frances Burney. He serves on the editorial board of *Journal of Literary & Cultural Disability Studies.*

MARTHA STODDARD HOLMES is Professor and Chair of Literature and Writing Studies at California State University, San Marcos, where she teaches Victorian Literature, Children's Literature, and Body Studies. Author of *Fictions of Affliction: Physical Disability in Victorian Culture* (2004) and coeditor of *The Teacher's Body: Embodiment, Authority, and Identity in the Academy* (2003), she has published extensively on the cultural history of the body from the Victorian era to the present, from representations of disability to the public culture of cancer.

ESSAKA JOSHUA is Teaching Professor in the Department of English and Director of the College Seminar at the University of Notre Dame. Her B.A. is from Oxford University, and her Ph.D. from the University of Birmingham. She is the author of *The Romantics and the May Day Tradition* (2007) and *Pygmalion and Galatea: The History of a Narrative in English Literature* (2001). She has published widely on Romantic and Victorian literature and is currently working on a monograph on physical disability in Romantic-era literature.

SUSANNAH B. MINTZ is Associate Professor and Associate Chair of the Department of English at Skidmore College in Saratoga Springs, NY. She is the author of *Threshold Poetics: Milton and Intersubjectivity* (2003); *Unruly Bodies: Life Writing by Women with Disabilities* (2007); and numerous articles and chapters on disability in literature, autobiography, early modern poetry, psychoanalytic theory, and lyrical essay. She is currently at work on a book studying the representations of pain in literature.

JULIA MIELE RODAS is Associate Professor of English at Bronx Community College of the City University of New York (CUNY) and is also on the faculty of the master's program in Disability Studies at the CUNY School of Professional Studies. Her writing has appeared in *Victorian Literature & Culture, Dickens Studies Annual, Encyclopedia of American Disability History* (Facts on File, 2009), *Victorian Review, Disability Studies Quarterly, The Explicator,* and *Journal of Literary & Cultural Disability Studies.* She is currently working on a book—*A Manner of Speaking*—that theorizes the role of autistic rhetoric and aesthetic in literature.

MARGARET ROSE TORRELL is Coordinator of Writing Programs and Associate Professor of English at the State University of New York College at Old Westbury, where she teaches courses in Disability Studies, women's literature, English literature, and composition. Her work in disability studies focuses on the portrayal of disabled masculinity and community in women-authored texts. She has also authored book chapters on critical pedagogy and other issues in education.

Index

ableism, xi, xii, 5, 6, 72, 77, 79, 88, 90, 99, 104–5, 109, 130, 147, 153n5
alterity, 33, 34–36, 37, 39, 48, 80, 105
Altick, Richard, 98, 140n8
animalism, 3, 26, 26n18, 35–36, 39, 55, 63, 73, 74n2, 76, 78, 98, 99, 100, 102, 103, 105, 124–25, 127, 139, 152
antipsychiatry, 5, 12, 30
Aristotle, 36, 74
Armstrong, Nancy, 53, 68
asexuality, 34, 87, 173
Asperger, Hans, 5, 57–58, 60n4
asylum, 2, 4, 12, 14, 22, 22n15, 25, 98, 99–100, 101, 101n5. *See also* Bethlem Royal Hospital
autism, xii, 4, 5–6, 9, 52, 56, 57–61, 58n3, 60n4, 62–64, 62n8, 66–70, 67n10, 94, 106
Avalos, Hector, 112, 112n1

Bakhtin, Mikhail, 95
Barton, John, and John Muddiman, 124

beauty, 16–17, 34, 35, 36–37, 39, 50, 68, 83, 121–22, 135, 147, 156, 158, 163
Bellis, Peter, 118–19
Bethlem Royal Hospital (Bedlam), 4, 22–23, 24, 98. *See also* asylum; Cibber
Bettelheim, Bruno, 57
Bible: Daniel, 26, 124–26; John, 116–17, 120–21, 123, 127; Judges, 121–23; Luke, 115, 116; Mark, 117; Matthew, 116, 117–18, 128; Numbers, 121; Revelations, 126
bildungsroman, 7, 92–93, 103, 109
blindness, x–xi, 2, 5, 7, 8–9, 23, 23n16, 25–26, 33, 34, 39–42, 45–46, 48–49, 78, 79, 80, 114, 118–24, 118n7, 119n8, 125–27, 146, 147, 159, 159n11, 163, 164–65, 164n17, 167, 170–71
Bogdan, Robert, 96n3, 97, 140n8
Bolt, David, x, 5, 9, 77, 79–80, 87, 89, 91, 119, 121n10, 123, 146, 147, 161n15, 162–63, 167
Brocklehurst, Mr., 7, 76, 77–78, 79, 90, 107, 109, 116–17, 135, 142